Professional Negotiation
in Public Education

# Professional Negotiation in Public Education

**T. M. Stinnett · Jack H. Kleinmann · Martha L. Ware**

NATIONAL EDUCATION ASSOCIATION

*The Macmillan Company, New York*
*Collier-Macmillan Limited, London*

# Preface

SINCE ABOUT 1960, there have been concerted drives to gain for public school teachers the right to collective action in negotiating with school boards regarding salaries, conditions of work, and other matters. One of the drives has been fostered by the American Federation of Teachers for acceptance and adoption of collective bargaining in the labor context, as developed in private industry. The other has been under the aegis of the National Education Association, in collaboration with its affiliated state education associations, for acceptance and adoption of *professional negotiation,* a new process designed to serve the unique needs of the teaching profession in the public service.

Since professional negotiation has been adopted in several hundred school districts and is under study in most states and in thousands of local associations affiliated with NEA, and since the movement is gaining great momentum, the need for comprehensive work on the process has become apparent. Although much has been written in the field, most of the writing has appeared only in professional journals and in unpublished addresses. This volume, therefore, was prepared to provide basic information on all aspects of the professional negotiation process.

The authors have sought to adhere primarily to a discussion of professional negotiation per se. Such material as has been included on collective bargaining is simply for the purpose of comparison and is not meant to be considered as a comprehensive treatment. Many volumes are available on collective bargaining, and the authors, by including herein only superficial material on that process, were motivated by that fact and not by any intent to slight its importance.

The NEA Office of Professional Development and Welfare has the assigned responsibility for developing guidelines to stimulate the study of professional negotiation, for providing publications about the process, and for working toward wide acceptance of professional negotiation procedures; the authors have been closely involved in these responsibilities. The NEA Urban Services Division has the responsibility for implementing professional negotiation agreements.

Naturally, the authors have had access to the publications, records, and experiences of all NEA units having direct or indirect concerns for the development of professional negotiation, and they acknowledge indebtedness to these units and their individual staff members during the preparation of this volume. Naturally, too, the authors have sought to reflect accurately the official NEA policies as they understood them. However, at many points, the views expressed are strictly their own. The contents of this volume, therefore, are the responsibility of the authors and not the National Education Association.

T. M. S.
J. H. K.
M. L. W.

*Washington, D.C.*

# Contents

# Chapter 1. Origin and Development of Professional Negotiation

THE UPSURGE in recent years of demands by teachers to participate in policy-making has brought into the public schools a new cluster of procedures. This upsurge has created the need for new concepts of employer-employee relationships. It seems likely, as a result, that boards of education and teacher organizations in the larger school sytems will increasingly require the services of specialized personnel for the purpose of carrying on policy negotiations.

These developments constitute another evolutionary step in the democratizing of school administration. School administration, mostly self-propelled, has evolved steadily in this direction, at least throughout this century. The cult of efficiency, with heavy overtones of industrial management techniques, which permeated concepts of good school administration in the early years of this century, has slowly given way to more enlightened personnel policies. This trend has been away from almost exclusive reliance upon the efficiency of supervisory staffs to produce results to greater emphasis upon individual competence and staff involvement. It would appear, too, that the trend is away from the hierarchical concept of school administration.

This upsurge has, of course, created a new vocabulary in employer-employee relationships. Such terms as collective bargaining, professional negotiation, strikes, sanctions, or alternative terms of collective negotiation, cooperative determination, have become common in recent years, particularly since 1960. There is an evident trend to merge the nomenclature of professional negotiation and collective bargaining into collective negotiation.

1

As has been pointed out, school administration has steadily grown toward the democratic concept. Teachers have suddenly demanded formalization of the process of employer-employee relationships into officially adopted written procedures. This demand was given great impetus by the collective bargaining election in New York City in 1961, and the resulting contract between the board of education and the United Federation of Teachers. Prior to these events, enlightened personnel policies had been developed and adopted by boards of education in many school districts throughout the nation. But the missing ingredients were (1) the guarantee of teacher participation in the formulation of policy; (2) the formalization of procedures for such participation by official adoption of the board, with a spelling out of the ground rules governing employer-employee relationships; and (3) the providing of an appeals procedure in case of an impasse between the board and the teachers.

## What Is Professional Negotiation?

Professional negotiation has been defined as a set of procedures, written and officially adopted by the local staff organization and the school board, which provides an orderly method for the school board and staff organization to negotiate on matters of mutual concern, to reach agreement on these matters, and to establish educational channels for mediation and appeal in the event of an impasse.

Professional negotiation means much more than the simple right to be heard; most staff organizations have had this right, or privilege, for many years. It means, specifically, that boards of education must be prepared to engage in give-and-take negotiations over policy matters with staff organizations. For example:

The staff organization presents proposals on many different matters affecting its own welfare and the quality of the educational program, such proposals made at meetings called specifically for the purpose of negotiation, and supported by argument, evidence, and data. The staff proposals are followed by an exchange of specific counterproposals from the board and by counter-counterproposals from the staff organization. Through this process of give and take areas of agreement are defined, areas of disagreement are narrowed and finally eliminated, and the staff organization and board reach final, bilateral agreement on policy. Or, alternatively, despite many meetings and good faith and earnest efforts to reconcile differences, areas of disagreement remain, and the parties may come to an impasse with neither side willing to make an additional concession, at which time the good offices of an impartial, educationally oriented mediator or fact-finder are brought into play.

The basic justification for professional negotiation is the added power generated by participation as equals. With a clear and meaningful share in the formulation of policy, teachers (or any workers) are impelled toward higher levels of productivity. They are stimulated by the urge to make their own policies work. They are propelled by the sense of being personally involved in a creative enterprise. The deadly monotony of performing routine tasks, made so by unilateral planning, is transformed into an exciting, jointly planned venture.

## Factors in Teacher Demands for Participation

The demand of teachers for recognition and participation has generally been put in the framework of the emergence of teacher restiveness or teacher aggressiveness; and sometimes it has been characterized as the emergence of teacher militancy. Call it what one will, this whole ferment is a concomitant of deeper and more subtle influences.

The impacts of the dramatically sudden demands of teachers for recognition and participation in the formulation of school policies caught school boards and superintendents—and for that matter their respective organizations, to some extent—unprepared to accept so drastic a change. They were puzzled over the causes; and many still are perplexed at the development. The first reaction was doubtless one of suspicion of increased radical elements in teaching. The next reaction was probably that the new wave of teacher aggressiveness was a spillover from the militancy of the teachers' unions. And the third reaction, it may be surmised, was that the restiveness was a temporary phenomenon that would pass in time, and that the customary attitudes in school staff relationships would be resumed. Overlooked in these reactions, these assumptions, was a complex cluster of social, economic, and political factors far-reaching in their implications.

### What Are the Causal Factors?

There are no easy answers to this question; and it is virtually impossible to identify all the factors. Some major ones follow.

1. The mounting impatience of teachers with what they consider to be economic injustice is a factor of considerable significance. The point of view here is that teacher salaries have historically lagged behind the returns to other comparable groups, and often behind the pay of unskilled workers. Teachers dislike the resistance of the public to reasonable adjustments in their pay in an affluent society which they have had a significant part in creating. As a quite general practice, soothing phrases about the importance of teachers has been proffered them in lieu of increased economic rewards. It is obvious that teachers have increasingly taken the position that they will no longer rely solely upon boards and legislatures for adequate remuneration, but will themselves become vigorously involved in the search for economic justice.

2. As an integral part of their own search for economic justice, teachers have grown increasingly bitter at the neglect of schools by our affluent society. They have been disturbed about inadequate support of the total school program. This was the root of the revolt in Utah, not salaries alone. They behold powerful national groups plugging for ever-growing federal appropriations for military hardware and to put a man on the moon, but consistently fighting grants for the schools. They observe that we continue to build up our nuclear power while we let the power of too many human beings go down the drain at home due to too few educational opportunities or retraining opportunities. They know that forty per cent of the young men in teaching, indeed about three fourths of the married ones, have to hold one, two, three, and even four extra jobs to support their families. Only in the first session of the 89th Congress, in 1965, was a giant start made by the federal government toward helping to meet the accumulated educational needs of the nation. In the meantime, teachers had grown bitter over obsolete school

buildings, inadequate facilities and supplies, overloaded classrooms, and the general deterioration in the quality of education offered children. Again, teachers came to the conclusion that they dared not continue the passive attitude of relying solely upon official bodies to correct these conditions; but that they must join in a vigorous effort to effect needed changes.

3. Another deeply significant psychological factor involved in the hunger for recognition by teachers is the matter of bigness— the bigness of cities and of school districts, with the resultant loss of identity of the teachers. This involves both the staggering rapidity of the urbanization of the United States, and the steadily enlarging size of school districts. In 1930, for example, there were about 130,000 school districts; now only about 27,000 actually operate schools. With this growth in size, communication becomes more difficult; and unless the temptation to develop a bureaucratic administrative structure is carefully resisted, there is unwittingly the pitfall of complex administrative machinery and unintentionally a kind of paternalism. It has been said that "in the small community, the teacher is everything; in the great city he is nothing." This has a devastating effect upon the spirit of any human being, especially upon the articulate, perceptive teacher. He resents the loss of identity. As a result, he often tends in overt ways to gain some kind of solid recognition. If he doesn't get such recognition in well planned ways, he will seek it in rebellious ways, or ways that appear to be rebellious in the light of past mores.

4. Any list of causal factors should also include the impact of a rapid emergence of a new status for public employees in general. Greatly increased levels of preparation and of the nature of services are demanded. These levels apply with peculiar emphasis to teachers.

5. The demand for recognition and participation in policy formation by teachers is a product of the times. The emergence of new nations as a result of the twilight of colonialism as a political philosophy—and of paternalism as its companion piece—is a part of the commitment of peoples throughout the world to a new status and dignity. Individuals, too, are caught up in this commitment, and so are teachers.

6. The dramatic push of American Negroes for human and civil

rights, for elevation to first class citizenship has had great impact everywhere, especially upon the people of the United States. It is not farfetched to assume that there has been a psychological effect on teachers. Teachers, too, have often viewed themselves as oppressed; they have viewed their treatment by society as being far less than commensurate with the importance of their contribution to the general welfare. Apparently, the activism of the civil rights movement and the effectiveness of that activism have had a significant impact upon the behavior patterns of teachers who have aspired to improve their status.

The foregoing are only some of the major factors behind the demands for professional negotiation. What teachers hunger for most, above salaries and welfare matters—as important as these are—is recognition and dignity. And the answer to this hunger is to be found in enlightened personnel policies which, in fact, reflect society's recognition of teachers as competent professionals, who, if competent to teach our children, are competent to have a real, not token, part in the planning of the educational program for those children.

## Beginning of the Professional Negotiation Concept

The belief is quite widely held that the struggles between the New York City Board of Education and the United Federation of Teachers (1960–62) constituted the origin of the demands of teachers for participation in policy-making. This is not the case. The beginnings antedate the New York City turmoil by some years. It is doubtless true that the New York City developments dramatized teachers' demands and gave impetus to their aspirations.

It is also quite widely believed that the entrance of the professional associations into the field of collective negotiation was the resolution adopted by the NEA Representative Assembly in 1962 (see Appendix A). This is also erroneous. It is true that this resolution did mark the official entry of the NEA in this process.

In the evolution of the democratic concept in school administration, the Educational Policies Commission spelled out, in 1938, a philosophy for involvement of the total school staff in developing the school program:

*The Entire Staff of the School System Should Take Part in the Formulation of the Educational Program.* In all that is proposed with respect to the administration of schools, there is implicit an acknowledgment of the contribution to be made by the educational profession. To indicate the place of leadership in all good administration is not to deny the large part to be played in the development of policy by all professional workers. Our schools are organized for the purpose of educating children, young people, and adults for participation in a democratic society. Any significant realization of this purpose will require independent thinking, a large degree of cooperative endeavor, and broad sympathy and understanding on the part of all who are enrolled in educational institutions. Certainly these virtues may not be expected to abound among those who are taught unless they are found also in the experience of teachers. Surely in no area may teachers more certainly exercise understanding than in their daily professional work. It is sound procedure to provide for the active participation of teachers in the development of administrative policy.

Apparently the first collective negotiation agreement of an independent association was the Norwalk, Connecticut group contract, an agreement between the board of education and the Norwalk Teachers Association in 1946. This contract resulted from a bitter teachers' strike. At that time, NTA was not affiliated with any state or national organization. The Association affiliated with the Connecticut Education Association and the NEA in 1957.[1] In 1951, the Connecticut Supreme Court of Errors held that teachers were entitled to organize and that boards of education could negotiate with them. The court ruled out the right of public employees, including teachers, to strike.

In 1957, the Norwalk teachers negotiated an agreement that provided an appeals procedure in the form of mediation by the State Commissioner of Education. This is believed to be the first agreement, under what is now termed professional negotiation, providing appeal provisions.

In the years between 1946 and 1962, many agreements were

---

[1] See James P. Steffensen, *Teachers Negotiate with Their School Boards,* Washington, D. C.: U. S. Government Printing Office, 1964, pp. 15–17.

entered into by boards and school staffs, which were, in effect, what are now termed professional negotiation agreements. Most of these were in Connecticut, some designated by the title "cooperative determination" agreements. Virtually all these early agreements, including those in Connecticut, except the Norwalk contract, were informal in nature but were officially adopted by the boards and recorded in their minutes.

In 1951, as a direct result of the court's ruling on the Norwalk strike and teachers' rights to organize, the Connecticut Commissioner of Education appointed a committee to draft a proposal regarding working relationships between boards of education and teachers organizations. The committee consisted of representatives of the Connecticut Education Association, the Connecticut Federation of Teachers, the Connecticut Association of School Boards, the Connecticut Association of Public School Superintendents, and the Connecticut State Department of Education. The first report of this committee was issued in 1952. After several revisions, and approval in principle by the CEA, the school boards association and the association of superintendents, the report was approved by the State Board of Education in 1957. This document was subsequently revised in the light of experience and adopted by the State Board in 1962 as Bulletin 85—1962 revision (see Chapter 4). By 1965, a total of 68 school districts in Connecticut had adopted agreements under the principles enunciated in this Bulletin.

By 1960 the rising demands for teacher participation, nationwide, in the shaping of school policies had reached such proportions that a resolution was introduced in the NEA Representative Assembly (Los Angeles Convention) proposing the formalization of the negotiation process. As early as 1957, the National Association of State Secretaries of State Teachers Associations devoted its national meeting to the need for negotiation agreements.

Doubtless, pressures of legislation enacted in some states, legislation sponsored by organized labor, to bring public employees under labor-law processes and machinery and renewed activities of the American Federation of Teachers contributed to these concerns. It is apparent, however, that there was a larger consideration —the burgeoning aspirations of teachers for a greater degree of self-determinism.

But the idea had not matured in the minds of the delegates to the 1960 NEA Convention. Starting with a modest proposal, the ensuing debate demonstrated a great diversity of points of view. The resolution read (this was Resolution 7 presented to that convention, originally prepared by the NEA Defense Commission):

*Representative Negotiation.* The National Education Association recognizes that representative negotiation by teachers with their governing boards concerning conditions of employment is compatible with the ethics and dignity of the teaching profession.

Such negotiations should be conducted by teachers' associations whose primary purposes are to promote the cause of education in the United States and to elevate the character and advance the interests of the profession of teaching without special commitment to any paricular segment of the community.

The procedures of negotiation should be consistent with the teachers' obligation to maintain the uninterrupted operation of the public schools.[2]

Obviously, this mild resolution was intended to project a desire of teachers for more meaningful participation in policy making. Yet it attempted to allay apprehensions that a radical movement was operative by adhering to the stated purposes of the National Education Association, as set forth in its Congressional Charter of 1906. Finally, the resolution sought to adhere to the widely accepted mores of the teaching profession by indicating opposition to affiliation with other employee groups and to interruption of teaching services. Of course, the affiliation statement was generally applicable, but it is clear that the particular implication was an opposition to affiliation with organized labor (and thus, to teachers' unions) and to teachers' strikes.

Discussion of this semingly innocuous resolution on the floor of the Representative Assembly indicated the division of sentiment among the delegates. Some wanted the resolution watered down, while many wanted it strengthened. Efforts were made to amend the motion to provide for an appeals or mediation procedure in cases of impasse between school staffs and boards of education.

---

[2] For detailed discussion on motion see *Addresses and Proceedings* (98th Annual Meeting of the National Education Association, Los Angeles), Washington: National Education Association, Vol. 98, 1960, pp. 153 et seq.

In the discussion of this proposal, it was brought out that in two or three states, such appeals machinery had already been imposed through state laws sponsored by organized labor. The proposal was to provide for mediators appointed by the profession and to consist of members of the profession. This was to get such appeals out of the jurisdiction of state labor departments and provide for settlement of issues through professional channels. Efforts were also made to change the resolution from representative "negotiation" to representative "conference" with school boards.

The attempts (in 1960) to reconcile the divergent points of view toward the resolution failed. Consequently, the Representative Assembly voted to refer Resolution 7 to the NEA Board of Directors for further study. Pursuant to this action, the president of the NEA appointed a committee to draft a resolution to be submitted to the Board of Directors in October. The report of this committee (still adhering to the term "representative negotiation") submitted a proposed resolution to the Board at its October 1960 meeting. The Board voted to adopt the statement submitted by the committee only as a working document, subject to review and action at its March 1961 meeting. In the meantime, the Board invited comments and suggestions from interested individuals, associations, parents, and school board members.

It is significant that the proposed resolution submitted to the Board the following March had a change in title—from "Representative Negotiation" to "Teacher-Board of Education Relationships." There were at least two reasons for this change: (1) there was apprehension that the former title implied a radical change in employer-employee relationships; (2) there was apprehension that "negotiation" would be confused with or equated with "collective bargaining" in the labor context.

Although the Board adopted the report of the Committee, two dissenting actions were appended. The first directed that the proposed resolution be referred to the Resolutions Committee and that its contents be publicized widely prior to the NEA Atlantic City Convention, in July 1961. The second directed that NEA conduct a comprehensive study of the need for and the implications of legislation requiring school boards to meet with representatives of the teaching profession.[3] This proposed resolution came before the Atlantic City Convention (June 30, 1961) as Resolution 17, and was approved. Resolution 17 thus became the first officially adopted policy of NEA on professional negotiation, although this term was avoided.

At Denver in July 1962, the NEA Representative Assembly adopted Resolution 18, an amendment to Resolution 17. In this version, the title of Professional Negotiation was first used. Moreover, two fundamental changes were made in the first resolution. The first was a paragraph renouncing the use of labor machinery as follows:

> Under no circumstances should the resolution of differences between professional associations and boards of education be sought through channels set up for handling industrial disputes. The teacher's situation is completely unlike that of an industrial employee. A board of education is not a private employer, and a teacher is not a private employee. Both are public servants. Both are committed to serve the common, indivisible interest of all persons and groups in the community in the best possible education for their children. Teachers and boards of education can perform their indispensable functions only if they act in terms of identity of purpose in carrying out this commitment. Industrial-disputes conciliation machinery, which assumes a conflict of interest and a diversity of purpose between persons and groups, is not appropriate to professional negotiation.

And the second was an outright demand for legal provisions to assure the rights of professional negotiation for teachers.

> The National Education Association calls upon its members and upon boards of education to seek state legislation and local board action which clearly and formally establishes these rights for the teaching profession.[4]

The demand for an appeals procedure through educational channels was repeated.

The dissent in the Representative Assembly over the paragraph

---

[3] *Addresses and Proceedings* (99th Annual Meeting of NEA, Atlantic City), Washington: National Education Association, Vol. 99, 1961, pp. 270–71.

[4] *Addresses and Proceedings* (100th Annual Meeting of NEA, Denver), Washington, D. C.: National Education Association, Vol. 100, 1962, pp. 174–183.

renouncing use of labor machinery arose from the feeling that this was a negative statement and that it had no place in an otherwise affirmative document. There was also extensive feeling that the paragraph was susceptible to the interpretation that NEA was expressing an antilabor bias. So strong was this feeling that a separate resolution was adopted expressing sympathetic support for the labor movement. This negative paragraph was removed from the resolution at the NEA Convention in Seattle in 1964.

The demands for legal enactments to guarantee teachers' rights to negotiate were opposed by some upon the grounds that such a measure would impinge upon the legal authority of school boards.

## The Meaning of the Denver Resolution

Resolution 18, adopted by the NEA Representative Assembly at Denver in July 1962, was a much more aggressive one than that adopted at Atlantic City the previous year. This resolution marked the official entry of NEA into the area of professional negotiation. The subsequent reactions of the American Association of School Administrators (AASA) and the National School Boards Association (NSBA) indicated their belief that NEA had, in effect, embraced the same tactics as the teachers unions; and, despite different phraseology, NEA had adopted the labor processes under different names.

Board members were especially disturbed at the demand for legalizing negotiation rights and for an appeals machinery. The latter demand, in the opinions of board members, was a confirmation that the intent of the package was to usurp a major portion of their legal authority to make all policy decisions regarding the operation of local schools.

The attitudes of board members were further hardened by the adoption of the resolution on sanctions. To board members, this action seemed to provide a companion piece for professional negotiation, a powerful weapon to enforce teachers' demands. In this framework, many board members could see no reasonable distinction between the strike and sanctions.

In its meeting (following the NEA Denver Convention), in April 1963, NSBA adopted the following resolution, categorically rejecting the processes of the professional associations and the teachers unions:

The efforts of teacher unions to obtain collective bargaining rights and the activities and programs of professional teacher organizations calling for professional negotiations and sanctions will have significant effect upon the operation of our public schools in the years ahead. The National School Boards Association is opposed to sanctions, boycotts, strikes or mandated mediation against school districts and does not consider them to be proper remedies for use in problem situations. The authority of the board of education is established by law and this authority may not be delegated to others.

The National School Boards Association, therefore, reaffirms and endorses its policy on teacher relations. In order that the course of action necessary to implement this policy may be planned deliberately and purposely, NSBA urges each local board to review its policies, procedures, and activities and to give careful consideration to incorporating the following items if they are not included.

(a) Procedures which will actively involve school boards, the administrative staff and teachers in discussing total budget needs with particular emphasis on the determination of salaries and the handling of grievances.

(b) Written policies concerning the above procedures that are widely disseminated, and presented in such a way that they are clearly understood by all parties concerned—the teacher, administrative staff, the board of education and the general public.

(c) Policies whereby the superintendent, as administrative officer of the board, can function as a channel and interpreter of teacher concerns to the board and of board responsibilities and concerns to the teacher. Direct hearings with the board should be arranged through the superintendent if this proves inadequate.

In addition, local boards should support their state school boards associations in opposing legislation which condones sanctions, boycotts, strikes, or mandated mediation against school districts. In the event such legislation or judicial decision exists, state school boards associations are urged to seek appropriate legal means to repeal or overrule them.[5]

---

[5] *Resolutions Adopted by the 1963 NSBA Delegate Assembly* (Denver, April 27–30, 1963), Information Service Bulletin, Vol. 1, No. 8, Chicago: National School Boards Association, 1963 (mimeographed).

In fairness, it should be noted that the full text of this resolution of NSBA reaffirmed its long-standing position regarding the right of teachers to "discuss" with the board details of salaries, working conditions, and other matters of mutual concern. The NSBA simply rejected the principle of negotiating these matters with teachers and, of course, the sanctions concept.

The AASA, while not reacting so bluntly as the NSBA, quite naturally had some serious reservations about both the professional negotiation and professional sanctions resolutions of NEA. It had reservations about the implied threats of these processes to the legal authority of the board and to the role of the superintendent. The AASA position, however, went much further than the NSBA resolution, giving tacit approval to a fact-finding procedure in cases of impasse.

The following excerpt from an AASA publication, issued after the professional negotiation and sanctions resolutions were adopted, while enunciating much of the philosophy expressed in the professional negotiation resolution, nevertheless expresses, also, some apprehensions.

We believe that both the board and the professional staff—teachers, principals, and other adminstrators—should, at a time that is free from tension and controversy, develop together a plan to be used in case of persistent disagreement. In those few, highly unusual instances where major controversy threatens to disrupt the schools, an appeal to an unbiased body should be available to either the board or the teachers, or both. The function of this third party should be limited to fact finding and to advisory assistance. Its identity might vary from state to state, but it should always be an agency which has responsibility for some segment of public education in the state. Included among such organizations might be a state board of education, a state department of education, a state university, or a state public college. It should be made clear that such a study would be conducted without disruption of the schools. A report should be made to both the board of education and the staff. Alternatives to such an appeal procedure which have been tried include:

- Strikes, demogogic appeals, threats, withheld services, and sanctions or threatened sanctions by teachers;
- Withholding of contracts, blacklisting, failure of promotion, and other punitive action by school boards; and

- Yielding to undue influence of vested interests on the part of both school boards and teachers.

We believe that such arbitrary action by either staff or school board is not likely to lead to lasting and satisfying resolution of disagreements.[6]

The full meaning of the NEA Professional Negotiation Resolution adopted at Denver in 1962 is difficult to assess. This inaugurated an evolving process, the full import of which is not yet fully discernible. It seems apparent, however, that the resolution launched an irrepressible movement to formalize procedures for teacher-school board relationships, and to legalize these procedures, either through state law or school board sanction. This is another way of saying that the drive to accord teachers real participation in policy formation was launched by this resolution. And it seems reasonable to assume that this drive is still in the developmental stage; that it will gather greater momentum. Evidence on this point consists of several hundred professional negotiation agreements and laws in several states authorizing the process.

### Professional Negotiation and Collective Bargaining Contrasted

This volume is devoted to the concept of professional negotiation, an approach to collective negotiation advocated by professional education associations. Inevitably, however, comparisons of the concept of professional negotiation with collective bargaining in private employment are made. Thus a brief discussion on this point is necessary.

In any discussion of the similarities and differences between professional negotiation and collective bargaining, it is easy to slip into a discussion of the organizations which advocate each. That subject, although perhaps important in how either process operates, is not the one to be considered here. Discussion here focuses upon the processes themselves.

A list of similarities set down beside a list of differences would

6 *Roles, Responsibilities, Relationships of the School Board, Superintendent, and Staff,* Washington, D. C.: American Association of School Administrators, 1963, p. 14.

be the longer. If length is the deciding factor, then it must be said that professional negotiation is quite similar to, and perhaps only semantically different from, collective bargaining. But if the *kinds* of differences involved are crucial to large numbers of the teaching profession, then that is what is important, though there are only two or three crucial differences. Similarities and differences aside, it should be noted that teachers' associations and teachers' unions will undoubtedly continue to endeavor to represent teachers under whichever process is the rule or law in their jurisdiction.

The primary differences might be gathered under two related headings with "subdifferences" stemming in whole or in part from the two. The two differences are: (1) Professional negotiation procedures can result in the removal of teachers and school boards from the operation of labor laws and labor precedent, whereas collective bargaining procedures, adapted from the private sector, will not. (2) For the purposes of mediation and appeal, procedures will go through educational channels under professional negotiation and through labor channels under collective bargaining.

The "subdifferences" which flow from the two major differences are primarily two. First, the local certificated employees make unit determinations under professional negotiation so that certain levels of employees are not automatically excluded as "supervisory" and thus could be appropriately included. Second, precedents set will be education oriented under professional negotiation procedures. This is not as likely to be true if appeals and mediation are handled by labor agencies, which, of course, have only labor-oriented precedent on which to draw. The hand of precedent is a heavy one. For example, in Wisconsin, teachers have been operating under the public employees collective bargaining statute since 1962. That statute makes no reference to unit determination, except to say that in representation questions the Wisconsin Employment Relations Board, the state agency which handles labor relations questions, is to determine the appropriate unit. At this writing, the WERB has excluded supervisory certificated school personnel from each of the bargaining unit determinations it has made. This, of course, is quite in line with much private collective bargaining precedent. The WERB has followed this precedent (not required by the statute) rather than recognizing organizational practice in many Wisconsin communities in which professional associations have long been comprised of teachers and supervisory personnel. It is emphasized that this requirement is stipulated for contract bargaining purposes only; all-inclusive organizations are still in existence in Wisconsin for other purposes. Even so, the WERB ruling is used as an example of decisions based solely upon labor precedent, bearing no relationship whatever to the wishes of the parties concerned

## Types of Professional Negotiation Agreements

That professional negotiation is a new, and still somewhat groping, process is indicated by the fact that three kinds of agreements were initially acceptable to the public school teaching profession. This diversity, one would have to admit, was simply a bow to ingrained customs in teacher-board relationships. It was a transitional concession to such customs, in the belief that patient effort would achieve full negotiation rights for teachers.

The first edition of *Guidelines for Professional Negotiation,*[7] issued by NEA, was an admittedly somewhat naive document, at least by comparison with collective bargaining guidelines in private industry, developed over years of experience. The second edition clearly reflects a more realistic approach to professional negotiation.[8]

The first edition of the *Guidelines* suggested three types or levels of professional negotiation agreements.

Level I is simply a recognition type agreement. It recognizes teaching as a profession and a local education association as the representative of the professional staff. It expresses the intent of the board to hear proposals of the recognized association. This is simply an agreement on the parts of the board and the administrator to discuss matters with the teachers (which they generally do anyway). It is not a commitment to negotiate issues.

A Level II agreement includes the features of Level I and, in

---

[7] *Guidelines for Professional Negotiation,* Washington, D. C.: Office of Professional Development and Welfare, National Education Association, 1963, 45 pp.

[8] *Guidelines for Professional Negotiation,* Rev. ed., 1965, 54 pp.

addition, contains an outline of the procedures to be followed in the negotiation process. Sometimes, too, the Level II agreement spells out the areas of teacher concerns considered negotiable.

A Level III agreement contains the ingredients of Levels I and II plus a written appeals procedure providing for impartial, third-party mediation or fact-finding in the event of impasse or persistent disagreement. The impasse procedure, although in educational channels, is one which school boards and administrators object to most of all as impinging upon the legal authority of the board. However, Level III is the type of agreement which the teaching profession must seek exclusively. Illustrative of this point is the fact that the second edition of *Guidelines for Professional Negotiation* includes a discussion only of the Level III type.

Professional negotiation must mean something more than the right to be heard. Most teachers associations have had this right for years. The right only to be heard might be simply an annual supplicatory pilgrimage to the board of education, resulting only in warm expressions of gratitude and goodwill by both parties. This routine could consist of a polite presentation by the teachers, blank stares from the board, a polite "thank you." Then follows an interminable wait by the teachers; and finally reading of the board's action in the local newspaper or via the superintendent's bulletin with any connection between teachers' requests and board action strictly coincidental. This, of course, is not professional negotiation.

## Progress in Professional Negotiation

As of September 20, 1965, some 388 professional negotiation agreements, in 35 states, had been filed with NEA (see Appendix D). Of these 388 agreements, 158 (41 per cent) are of the Level III type; 125 (32 per cent) are of the Level II type; and 105 (27 per cent) are of the Level I type. There are probably additional hundreds of professional negotiation agreements, copies of which have not yet been filed with NEA; perhaps a total of as many as 1,000. It is known that approximately 500 written agreements, resulting from designation, stipulation, or elections, were adopted between September and December of 1965.

In addition, a statewide set of suggested policies has been adopted by the Kansas School Boards Association and the Kansas State Teachers Association. And statewide procedures have been agreed upon (Bulletin 85) in Connecticut, involving the State Board of Education, the State Association of School Boards, the State Society of Superintendents and the Connecticut Education Association. In all, nine states have adopted joint guidelines (See Chapter 4).

Legislation is another important method of securing negotiation agreements between staff organizations and boards of education. At the beginning of 1965 three collective bargaining laws applying to all public employees, including teachers, were in existence: Alaska (1959), New Hampshire (1955), and Wisconsin (1962).

Eight laws were passed in 1965. California, Connecticut, Florida, New Jersey,[9] Oregon, and Washington enacted negotiation statutes pertaining specifically to public school employees, and the states of Massachusetts and Michigan enacted collective bargaining statutes applying to all public employees, including school employees (see Appendixes E and F for the texts of these statutes).

In summary, professional negotiation is based on a written set of orderly procedures, officially adopted by the school board and the recognized local association, for formulation of policies under which the professional staff works. The process is designed to be a cooperative one, although at points there will inevitably be conflicts. With adequate appeals procedures, however, impasses can be resolved.

---

[9] This legislation was vetoed by the governor of New Jersey.

# *Chapter 2.* Legal Status and Implications

PROFESSIONAL NEGOTIATION is affected by the law governing public education and public employment. This body of law must be considered and understood, for it will affect the negotiation procedures established and the negotiation process.

## Legal Setting of the Schools

Public education is a function of the state. The state provides for public education in its constitution and statutes. It can alter public education by amending its constitution and statutes. Public elementary and secondary schools are governed by agencies variously called school boards, boards of trustees, school committees, boards of education, or school directors. By whatever name, these governing boards act as agents of the state, though the individual members who serve on them are appointed or elected at the local level.

The territorial units governed by school boards are school districts created by state legislatures to operate public schools. Sometimes school districts are coterminous with existing municipalities; sometimes there are several districts in one large city; sometimes the county unit is used so that the school district is coterminous with county boundaries. Whatever the territorial arrangement, and this can and does vary within states as well as from state to state, the school board's responsibility is to govern the schools and not to perform any other governmental function. Conversely, the function of governing the schools has not been given by the legislatures

20

to any other governmental unit, even though some school districts must seek budget approval or funds from some other unit. (There are, of course, some schools that are connected with correctional institutions, as well as federally governed schools such as the Indian and Overseas Dependents Schools.) In every state, without exception, and however organized, the legislatures established or authorized to be established legal entities to provide public education. Much local autonomy is provided the school districts, but where a state policy is required it is set at the state level by a state education agency established to perform educational functions which might be necessary at the state level. So at the state level in many states, as well as at the local level, the legislatures have established agencies whose sole function is to deal with public education.

Negotiation procedures which take into account the schools' legal setting will more likely be successful, both in the practical and legal sense, than those which ignore this setting. Professional negotiation is designed to do this: to fit into the existing patterns of law applicable to public education. Obviously, variations are many among the states and within some states. Nevertheless, professional negotiation is designed to complement existing educational patterns.

## Legal Setting of Public Employment

Professional negotiation and other negotiation procedures are affected by other legal precedent, in addition to the law governing public education (that is the body of law and precedent which has arisen around public employees in general, and professional school employees in particular). From a legal standpoint, it is difficult to separate public *school* employees from public employees generally. Of the small number of cases and statutes on the relationship of public employers to public employees, few specifically concern public school employees. This is changing, however, as the teaching profession becomes increasingly active in efforts to govern itself through professional practices acts and to have a voice in policy making through negotiations. Nevertheless, it is necessary to consider the legal setting in which public employees as a whole find themselves and then to note the similarities or differences which may exist with regard to public school employees.

It is also necessary to distinguish between professional employees (for example, classroom teachers, supervisors, research workers, and administrators) and noneducational employees of schools (for example, custodians and engineers). The employment problems of the noneducational employees in the public schools are more akin to the problems of other custodians and engineers, whether employed publicly or privately, than they are to the problems of professional school employees. If this is a valid distinction, the noneducational school employees are more likely to fall in the group of general public employees when distinctions are made between professional school employees and public employees generally in this chapter.

## Membership in Employee Organizations

There is little doubt today that certificated school employees have the right to organize and to join employee organizations, including professional associations and unions. This right has been questioned in the past, however, and therefore has been established in some states by statute.

The right to join and participate in employee organizations is based on the Constitution of the United States. The First Amendment forbids Congress to make any law abridging "the right of the people peaceably to assemble, and to petition the government for a redress of grievances." The Fourteenth Amendment to the Constitution forbids any state to "make or enforce any law which shall abridge the privileges or immunities of citizens of the United States; nor shall any State . . . deny to any person within its jurisdiction the equal protection of the laws." The Fourteenth Amendment has been declared to place on the states the same restrictions as are placed on the Congress in the first 10 amendments. These are the Constitutional provisions which give public employees, as citizens, the right to assemble peaceably and to petition the government. To deny this Constitutional right afforded citizens in general, would be to deny the equal protection of the laws. School boards are agencies of the state and have no right to do what is forbidden to the state.

This right of public employees and professional school employees to form and join employee organizations has been reinforced by statute in several states. This statutory expression of the right to join has come in several forms. For example:

- "Public employees have the right to join, or not to join employee organizations." Statements resembling such a "right-to-work" provision are in statutes in effect in Arizona, California, Connecticut, Hawaii, Kansas, Minnesota, Texas, and Utah.[1]

- "Public employees have the right to form and join employee organizations and unions," or, "public employers are prohibited from deterring employees from joining." Variations of such statements, sometimes including the right to "present grievances," or "present proposals," to employers are found in statutes in Florida, Massachusetts, Michigan, New Jersey, North Dakota, Oregon, Rhode Island, Virginia, Washington, and Wisconsin.[2]

- The right to join employee organizations is protected or implied in several other states in statutory language which, for example, permits recognition of or negotiation with employee organizations or unions and allows public employers to deduct dues payable to such

---

[1] In California, Connecticut, Hawaii, and Minnesota, the laws are applicable to public employees and not to private employees: *West's California Education Code Annotated*, secs. 13080-13088 (specifically applicable to school employees); *West's California Government Code Annotated*, secs. 3500-3509 (specifically applicable to public employees, except school employees); *Connecticut General Statutes Annotated*, Title 10, sec. 10-153a (specifically applicable to professional school employees); *Minnesota Statutes Annotated*, Chapter 179, secs. 179.52–179.56. In Arizona, Kansas, Texas, and Utah, the laws are "right-to-work" laws applicable to private employment which also specifically include public employees: *Arizona Constitution*, Article 25; *Arizona Revised Statutes Annotated*, Title 23, secs. 23-1301–1370; *Kansas Constitution*, Article 15, sec. 12; *Vernon's Texas Civil Statutes*, Article 5154c; *Utah Code Annotated 1953*, Title 34, secs. 34-16-1–34-16-18. In Hawaii, such provisions are applicable only to civil service employees; professional school employees are not mentioned: *Revised Laws of Hawaii 1955*, Chapter 3, sec. 3-80.

[2] *Florida Statutes Annotated*, Chapter 230, sec. 230.23, and Chapter 839, sec 839.221; *Massachusetts General Laws Annotated*, Chapter 149, secs. 149:178D–149:178N; *Michigan Public Act 379*, 1965; *New Jersey Constitution*, Article I, sec. 19; *North Dakota Century Code*, Chapter 34-11, sec. 34-11-01; *Oregon Revised Statutes*, Chapter 243, secs. 243.720–243.730; *General Laws of Rhode Island 1956*, Title 36, secs. 36 11-1–36-11-5; *Virginia Laws of 1946*, Joint Senate Resolution, #12 (public employees may form organizations *not* affiliated with labor organizations); *Laws of Washington 1965*, Chapter 143; *West's Wisconsin Statutes Annotated*, Chapter 111, secs. 111.70(1)–111.70(2) (school employees specifically included).

organizations. This type of statutory approval of employee organizations exists in Alaska, Illinois, New Hampshire, New York, and Puerto Rico.[3]

- Public employee membership in public employee organizations has been held permissible in a few states by state attorneys general or state courts. Rulings of this type, in absence of statutes either authorizing or prohibiting such membership, have occurred in Idaho, Iowa, Kentucky, Michigan, Missouri, New Mexico, Oklahoma, Pennsylvania, and West Virginia.[4]

[3] *Alaska Statutes,* Title 23, secs. 23.40.010 and 23.40.030 (defines "labor organization" as an organization to bargain or deal with a public employer and authorizes public employers, including school boards, to enter into contracts with such organizations); *Smith-Hurd Illinois Annotated Statutes,* Chapter 102, secs. 35.1–35.2 (authorizes public employers, including school districts, to withhold dues payable to professional organizations and unions and to be reimbursed by such organizations for doing so); *New Hampshire Revised Statutes Annotated 1955,* Chapter 31, sec. 31:3 (towns may recognize unions and enter into collective bargaining agreements with them); *New York Education Law,* sec. 237; *New York Labor Law,* sec. 217; *New York General Municipal Law,* sec. 93-b (teachers' organizations may declare themselves to be professional associations and public employers are authorized to deduct dues payable to employee organizations or associations); *Laws of Puerto Rico Annotated,* Title 3, sec. 702 (public employees may authorize dues deductions for one employee organization).

[4] *Idaho A.G.O.,* No. 64-7, May 1, 1964: There is nothing in the statutes to prohibit union affiliation by public employees and public employers to bargain with union representatives. *Iowa A.G.O.,* August 16, 1961: State employees may organize labor unions. *Kentucky A.G.O.,* No. 32,305, September 25, 1952: Public employees may join any organization with a lawful purpose. *Michigan A.G.O.,* No. 4306, March 18, 1964, issued prior to the 1965 law specifically authorizing public employee membership in employee organizations: A board of education may recognize an association, selected by a majority of teachers, as exclusive negotiation representative. *Magenheim* v. *Board of Education of District of Riverview Gardens,* 347 S.W. (2d) 409 (Missouri 1961): A board of education has the right to adopt a salary schedule clause requiring membership in certain professional associations in order for a teacher to obtain the benefits of the schedule. *New Mexico A.G.O.,* No. 63-52, May 10, 1963: A public employer may consult with, negotiate with, and listen to an employee union, but cannot enter into a collective bargaining agreement. *Oklahoma A.G.O.,* issued March 31, 1961: No statutory prohibition against the organization of state employees by labor unions. *Broadwater* v. *Otto,* 88 A. (2d) 878 (Pennsylvania 1952): Public employees are not prohibited from forming unions. *West Virginia A.G.O.,* issued June 29, 1962: Public employers may recognize a union, professional teaching association, or nonteaching association representing employees.

It is clear that in those 31 states and Puerto Rico, public employees, usually including public school employees, have the right to form and join employee organizations whether designated professional associations or unions. In these states the right is based upon state statute which expressly or implicitly grants the right; or, in absence of statute, upon attorneys' general opinions or court decision. In the other states the right, though it is likely to exist, is not mentioned specifically in the statutes or by the courts.

LIMITATIONS ON THE RIGHT TO JOIN. There have been and still are in some states, limitations placed upon the rights of public employees to form organizations for their mutual benefit and to affiliate with others of similar interests.

For example, at least 20 states have so-called "right-to-work" provisions in statutes or constitutions. These laws prohibit various labor-management agreements that require membership in a labor union as a condition of attaining or retaining employment. They prohibit closed and union shops, and are in addition to those statutes mentioned above, which provide specifically that public employees may or may not join employee organizations. In the view of organized labor, "right-to-work" laws are considered a "limitation" on the right to join unions and employee organizations in private employment. However, in *public* employment such laws have been used in several instances to protect the right of a public employee to join an employee organization or union, as have those laws just discussed, laws applicable only to public employees.

The repeal, if it should occur, of section 14b of the Taft-Hartley Act,[5] under which states are permitted to enact "right-to-work" laws prohibiting union shops, would have far-reaching effects on private employment. Since the federal government by repeal would preempt the field, the state "right-to-work" laws, so far as private employment which affects interstate commerce is concerned, would be nullified. However, the states would retain the right to pass or retain such laws if they did not affect interstate commerce. Since public employees, including teachers, are exempt from the federal labor laws in question, the repeal of 14b would have no effect on the "right-to-work" provisions applicable to them. Whether the

[5] *United States Code,* Title 29, sec. 164(b).

changes which undoubtedly would take place in the private sector would influence the states regarding these laws applicable to public employees remains to be seen.

The following discussion of the "right-to-work" laws includes a discussion of those applicable to private employees, although such laws would no longer be applicable to private employment, which affects interstate commerce, if section 14b of the Taft-Hartley Act is repealed. The "right-to-work" laws, except those of Arizona, Kansas, Texas, and Utah, cited earlier, were not intended to apply to public employment. However, in at least two states, Arkansas and South Dakota, the laws have been made applicable to public employees by judicial decisions.[6]

The remaining 14 "right-to-work" laws neither mention public employees nor have been judicially interpreted to include them.[7]

Among public employees, policemen, and firemen and, to a lesser extent, teachers, are the types of employees most often prevented from joining labor organizations.

Several state laws and city ordinances prohibiting policemen

---

6 *Arkansas Constitutional Amendment*, No. 34; *Arkansas Statutes 1947 Annotated*, Title 81, secs. 81-201–81-204. This "right-to-work" law does not mention public employees but the court invalidated a statute denying policemen membership in a labor union. *Potts* v. *Hay*, 318 S.W. (2d) 826 (Arkansas 1958); *South Dakota Constitution*, Article VI, sec. 2; *South Dakota Code, 1960 Supp.*, Chapter 17.10, secs. 17.1101 and 17.9914. This "right-to-work" law does not mention public employees but was held by the court to invalidate a municipal resolution denying policemen membership in a labor union. *Levasseur* v. *Wheeldon*, 112 N.W. (2d) 894 (South Dakota 1962).

7 *Code of Alabama 1940*, Title 26, secs. 375(1)–395; *Florida Constitution*, Declaration of Rights 12; *Code of Georgia Annotated*, Title 54, sec. 54-901; *Iowa Code Annotated*, Chapter 736A, secs. 736A.1–736A.8; *West's Louisiana Statutes Annotated*, Title 23, secs. 23:881–23:889; *Mississippi Constitution*, Article 7, sec. 198-A; *Mississippi Code 1942 Annotated*, Title 25, sec. 6984.5; *Constitution of Nebraska*, Article XV, secs. 13, 14, 15; *Revised Statutes of Nebraska 1943, Reissue of 1960*, Chapter 48, secs. 48-217–48-219; *Nevada Revised Statutes*, Title 53, secs. 613.230–613.300 and 613.130; *General Statutes of North Carolina*, Chapter 95, secs. 95-78–95-84 and sec. 95-100; *North Dakota Century Code*, Chapter 34-09, secs. 34-09-01 and 34-01-14; *Code of Laws of South Carolina 1962*, Title 40, secs. 40-46–40-46.8; *Tennessee Code Annotated*, Title 50, secs. 50-208–50-212; *Code of Virginia 1950*, Title 40, secs. 40-68–40-74.5; *Wyoming Statutes*, Title 27, secs. 27-245.1–27-245.8.

involved professional school employees. The Montana court struck down a compulsory membership provision in an agreement and the Missouri court upheld one in a salary schedule. In 1959, the Montana Supreme Court held that a clause which provided for a union shop for teachers was invalid.[16] The clause was part of a contract negotiated by a teachers' union with a local board of education. This was the first case on this point involving public school teachers. The contract clause provided that if tenure teachers did not become members of the union, they could not benefit from salary increases negotiated by the union. The provision stated:

(a) All members now employed by the Board, who are not now members of the Union, must become members of the Union on or before the 4th day of September, 1956, and shall maintain their membership in the Union in good standing as defined by the constitution and by-laws of the Union during the term of their employment.

(b) All teachers now employed by the Board, who are now members of the Union, shall maintain their membership in the Union in good standing as defined by the constitution and by-laws of the Union and by-laws of the Union during the term of their employment.

(c) All new teachers or former teachers employed by the Board shall become members of the Union within thirty (30) days after date of their employment and shall maintain their membership in good standing as defined in the constitution and by-laws of the Union during the term of their employment.

The provisions of this Union Security Clause shall be adopted as a Board Rule and shall be a condition of all contracts issued to any teacher covered by this agreement.

Any teacher who fails to sign a contract which includes the provisions of this Union Security Clause and who fails to comply with the provisions of this Union Security Clause shall be discharged on the written request of the Union, except that any such teacher who now has tenure under the laws of the State of Montana shall not be discharged but shall receive none of the benefits nor salary increases negotiated by the Union and shall be employed, without contract, from year to year on the same terms and conditions as such teacher was employed at during the year 1955–56.

[16] *Benson* v. *School District No. 1 of Silver Bow County,* 344 P. (2d) 117 (Montana 1959).

This provision in the contract was held null and void as to tenure teachers. In its opinion, the court stated the traditional judicial view on this point:

It is not competent for the school trustees to require union membership as a condition to receiving the increased salary. So far as this case is concerned it is sufficient to say that the Legislature has not given the school board authority to make the discrimination sought to be imposed here.

\* \* \*

For the purposes of this case it is sufficient to say that the School Trustees have no authority or power to discriminate between the teachers employed by it as to the amount of salary paid to each because of their membership or lack of membership in a labor union. The School Trustees have no authority to invade that field. As well might it be argued that the Board of School Trustees might provide that the increased salary shall not be allowed to those who do not affiliate with a certain lodge, service club, church or political party.

In the other case involving teachers, the Missouri court came to a different conclusion in 1961.[17] A teacher who had not been reemployed for the 1959–60 school year sued the board of education, requesting the court to order his reinstatement or award him damages. He also requested the court to declare that a provision in the 1955 and 1958 salary schedules be declared unreasonable, void, and beyond the authority of the board to adopt. The court refused to uphold either of the teacher's requests. On the employment question (details on this point are omitted here), the court held that the teacher had only an annual contract and that, therefore, nonreemployment could be effected upon proper notice.

The salary schedule provision which the teacher sought to have declared null and void stated:

Each person on this salary schedule shall join the professional organizations which include the community Teachers' Association, the National Education Association, The Missouri State Teachers' Association, and the St. Louis Suburban Teachers' Association. Failure to

---

17 *Magenheim* v. *Board of Education of the District of Riverview Gardens,* 347 S. W. (2d) 409 (Missouri 1961); motion for rehearing or for transfer to Supreme Court of Missouri denied July 11, 1961.

join such organizations precludes the benefits derived through the salary schedule and places such person outside the salary schedule.

The school board had the legal right to adopt the provision under the broad statutory authority granted to school boards to manage the school affairs and "to make all needful rules and regulations for the organization, grading and government in the school districts," the court held. It also ruled that the teacher, having accepted the salary according to the schedules during his employment in the school district, could not recover the amount of the dues he paid to the local education organizations.

The Missouri court did not ignore the Montana decision. It distinguished the cases by distinguishing the organizations involved. It stated on this point:

Union membership per se has no connection with teaching competence. Plaintiff Magenheim was not *required* to meet the conditions stated in Paragraphs 15 and 18 of the Salary Schedules. Teachers employed by the defendant District who do not choose to meet the conditions stated for compensation under the Salary Schedules will have an individually negotiated compensation.

An obvious distinction of the cases is that in the Montana case the teachers were on tenure, while in the Missouri case the teacher was not. But the Missouri court did not mention this point at all. As it indicated in the above quotation, the court thought Magenheim could negotiate separately for his salary, and differentiated between professional organizations and unions. On the latter point, the court discussed membership in professional organizations:

In the teaching profession, as in all professions, membership in professional organizations tends to increase and improve the interest, knowledge, experience and overall professional competence. Membership in professional organizations is no guaranty of professional excellence, but active participation in such organizations, attendance at meetings where leaders give the members the benefit of their experience and where mutual problems and experiences and practices are discussed, are reasonably related to the development of higher professional attainments and qualifications. Such membership affords an opportunity for self-improvement and self-development on the part of the individual member. It is the duty of every school board to obtain the services of the best qualified teachers, and it is not only within their power but it is their duty to adopt rules or regulations to elevate the standards of teachers and the educational standards within their district.

It should be noted that in neither Montana nor Missouri was there a statute which specifically authorized or prohibited such clauses in teachers' contracts.

Which decision will courts faced with similar cases in the future likely follow? Predictions of future trends in judicial views are not only dangerous but may serve little purpose. It may be more helpful to consider some of the points which may be before the courts in future cases. For example, the Montana view is undoubtedly the traditional view: compulsory membership in employee organizations—the union shop—has no place in public employment in the absence of specific statutory authorization. Undoubtedly, persuasive argument will be needed in a future case to convince a court to deviate from this view.

Yet, deviate is precisely what the Missouri court did. The deviation would not be so compelling if the court had distinguished the Montana case on the basis of the tenure status of the Montana teachers and the Missouri teacher's lack of it. For tenure teachers have more employment rights and protections than nontenure teachers. *But it did not do so.* Instead, it chose to distinguish on the basis of the type of organization involved. A court in a similar future case may have to decide whether the tenure issue will be an important one. And, undoubtedly, it will have before it the Missouri court's language on the function and meaning of professional organizations if the case could possibly turn on the issue of the type of organization in which membership is required.

### The Right to Strike

The power concomitant to collective bargaining exercised by private employees is the strike. The right of the private employee to strike is upheld by courts and protected by statutes. The opposite is true in public employment. There are statutes in 15 states[18] pro-

---

[18] *Connecticut Public Act* 298, 1965, applicable specifically to teachers; *Florida Statutes Annotated,* Chapter 839, sec. 839.221, applicable to public employees; *Code of Georgia Annotated,* Title 89, secs. 89-1301–89-1304,

hibiting various types of public employees, often including teachers, from striking. Federal employees are also prohibited from striking by law.[19] There are no statutes which provide that teachers may strike. Even in the absence of statutory prohibition, the traditional judicial view is that public employees do not have the right to strike. For example:

- Discharge of public employees for strike activity upheld[20]
- Public employee unions, their officers, and public employees enjoined from striking, ordering strikes, or participating in strikes against a governmental unit[21]
- Union enjoined from striking to coerce a governmental unit to engage in collective bargaining[22]
- Public employees held to have no right to strike[23]

applicable to state employees, probably not to teachers; *Revised Laws of Hawaii 1955,* Chapter 3, sec. 3-80 and Chapter 5, secs. 5-7–5-10, applicable to public employees; *Massachusetts General Laws Annotated,* Chapter 149, sec. 178M, applicable specifically to school employees; *Michigan Statutes Annotated,* Title 17, sec. 17.455(1)–17.455(2), applicable specifically to school employees; *Minnesota Statutes Annotated,* Chapter 179, secs. 179.52–179.57, applicable to public employees; *Revised Statutes of Nebraska 1943, Reissue of 1960,* Chapter 48, secs. 48-801–48-823, applicable to public employees; *New York Civil Service Law,* sec. 108, applicable specifically to school employees; *Page's Ohio Revised Code Annotated,* Title 41, Chapter 4117, secs. 4117.01–4117.05, applicable specifically to school employees; *Oregon Revised Statutes,* Chapter 243, sec. 243.760, applicable to public employees; *Purden's Pennsylvania Statutes Annotated,* Title 43, secs. 215.1–215.5, applicable to public employees; *Vernon's Texas Civil Statutes,* Article 5154c, applicable to public employees; *Code of Virginia 1950,* Title 40, secs. 40-65–40-67, applicable to public employees; *West's Wisconsin Statutes Annotated,* Chapter 111, sec. 111.70(4) (L), applicable specifically to school employees.

19 *United States Code,* Title 5, secs. 118p–118r.
20 *Goodfellow et al. v. Civil Service Commission,* 20 N.W. (2d) 170 (Michigan 1945).
21 *City of Los Angeles et al. v. Los Angeles Bldg. & Contr. Trades Council,* 210 P. (2d) 305 (California 1949); *Westchester County v. Westchester County Federation of Labor,* 115 N.Y.S. (2d) 144 (New York 1952); *Cleveland v. Division 268 of Amalgamated Association of Street & Electric Railway & Motor Coach Employees of America,* 90 N.E. (2d) 711 (Ohio 1949).
22 *Dade County v. Amalgamated Association of Street Electric Railway & Motor Coach Employees of America,* 157 So. (2d) 176 (Florida 1963).
23 *McAleer v. Jersey City Incinerator Authority,* 190 A. (2d) 891 (New Jersey App. Div. 1963); *Broadwater v. Otto,* 88 A. (2d) 878 (Pennsylvania 1952).

- State employees held to have no right to strike.[24]

Several judicial decisions on strikes by public employees have concerned school employees specifically. For example:

- A union of custodial employees was enjoined from striking to compel a school board to recognize and sign an agreement with the union.[25]
- Teachers have no right to strike.[26]
- A teachers association was enjoined from striking.[27]
- Teachers' absence, en masse, from duty for an unlimited time is prohibited under the antistrike law, and the law is constitutional.[28]

One or two cracks are visible in the wall of the traditional judicial view, just summarized, against public employee strikes. A conservative view of some comments appearing in recent cases might be that they are suggestions of how to overcome the traditional view, not deviations from it. Be that as it may, the judicial comments, mostly dicta, should not be overlooked.

In its 1957 opinion upholding an injunction prohibiting a teachers organization from striking, the New Hampshire Supreme Court said this:

In the light of the increase in public employment, the disparity existing in many cases in the salary of public employees as compared to similar positions in private employment, and the enactment in recent years of legislation guaranteeing the right of private employees to bargain collectively and to strike, it may seem anomalous and unfair to some that government should deny these same rights to its employees working in similar employment. However any modification in the common law doctrine that the sovereignty of the state should not be

24 *International Brotherhood of Electrical Workers, Local Union 976* v. *Grand River Dam Authority,* 292 P. (2d) 1018 (Oklahoma 1956).
25 *Board of Education of Community Unit School District No. 2* v. *Redding et al.,* 207 N. E. (2d) 427 (Illinois 1965).
26 *City of Pawtucket et al.* v. *Pawtucket Teachers' Alliance 930 et al.,* 141 A. (2d) 624 (Rhode Island 1958). *Norwalk Teachers' Association* v. *Board of Education of City of Norwalk,* 83 A. (2d) 482 (Connecticut 1951), decided before antistrike law enacted.
27 *Manchester* v. *Manchester Teachers' Guild,* 131 A. (2d) 59 (New Hampshire 1957).
28 *Pruzan et al.* v. *Board of Education of City of New York,* 209 N.Y.S. (2d) 966, aff'd. 215 N.Y.S. (2d) 718 (New York 1960); motion denied 212 N.Y.S. (2d) 416, aff'd. 217 N.Y.S. (2d) 86 (New York 1961).

hampered by strikes by public employees involves a change in public policy. It has been the consistent opinion of this court that such a change is for the Legislature to determine rather than being within the province of this court.

\* \* \*

There is no doubt that the Legislature is free to provide *by statute* that public employees may enforce their right to collective bargaining by arbitration or strike [emphasis supplied].[29]

A lower Minnesota court went even further. In a case involving noncertificated public school employees the court said that to hold that a public employee had no right to strike only because he is a public employee is

to indulge in the expression of a personal belief and then ascribe to it a legality on some tenuous theory of sovereignty or supremacy of government. . . . The right to strike is rooted in the freedom of man, and he may not be denied the right except by clear, unequivocal language embodied in a constitution, statute, ordinance, rule, or contract.

This decision was appealed to the Supreme Court of Minnesota and upheld.[30] In upholding the lower court, it was not necessary for the Supreme Court to approve or disapprove the lower court's words. Subsequently, an antistrike law applicable to public employees was passed by the Minnesota legislature. Despite the Minnesota case holding otherwise, it seems settled that if public employees, including teachers, are to be given the right to strike, it will be done by statute, not by judicial decision.

## Negotiation and Agreement

Is the negotiation process which leads to some type of agreement legally permissible? Do boards of education have the power and authority to negotiate? If they do, may they enter into a binding agreement? On these questions legal authorities, including courts, disagree.

---

[29] *Manchester* v. *Manchester Teachers' Guild,* 131 A. (2d) 59 (New Hampshire 1957).

[30] *Board of Education of City of Minneapolis* v. *Public School Employees Union,* 45 N. W. (2d) 797 (Minnesota 1951).

Where statutory authorization exists, where governmental units are specifically authorized to negotiate, there is little, if any, difficulty. There are pertinent statutes in at least eleven states of varying degrees of detail. Eight statutes were enacted in 1965 alone.[31] Negotiation and agreement statutory provisions in the eleven states are summarized below.

- *Alaska:* Governmental units may bargain with employee organizations and may enter into contracts with them.[32]

- *California:* Governmental units, including school boards, must meet and confer with representatives of employee organizations. No mention is made of agreements, but the governmental units are authorized to adopt rules and regulations to implement the statute.[33]

- *Connecticut:* Boards of education must negotiate with exclusive representatives of employee organizations and, on request of either party, a written agreement shall be executed.[34]

- *Florida:* Committees of the teaching profession may be involved with boards of education in arriving at a determination of policies, resolving problems, or reaching agreements affecting certificated personnel.[35]

- *Massachusetts:* Cities, towns, and school districts must bargain with employee organizations and may enter into agreements with them. State departments may enter into agreements with employee organizations.[36]

- *Michigan:* Boards of education must bargain collectively with exclusive representatives of public employees and, on request of either party a written agreement shall be executed.[37]

- *New Hampshire:* Towns may enter into collective bargaining contracts with unions of employees.[38]

- *New Jersey:* Boards of education must discuss matters of mutual

31 See Chapter 8, Table 8-1 for a detailed analysis of all eleven statutes.
32 *Alaska Statutes,* Title 23, secs. 23.40.010 and 23.40.030.
33 *West's California Government Code Annotated,* secs. 3500–3509 and *Education Code,* secs. 13080–13088.
34 *Connecticut Public Act* 298, 1965.
35 *Florida Statutes Annotated,* Chapter 230, sec. 230.23.
36 *Massachusetts General Laws Annotated,* Chapter 40, sec. 40:4c and Chapter 149, secs. 149: 178D–178N.
37 *Michigan Public Act* 379, 1965.
38 *New Hampshire Revised Statutes Annotated 1955,* Chapter 31, sec. 31:3.

concern with employees or recognized organizational representatives.[39]

- *Oregon:* Boards of Education must meet and confer, consult and discuss, in good faith, matters with a representative or committee elected by the certificated employees. No mention is made of agreements.[40]

- *Washington:* Boards of education must negotiate with the elected majority organization of certificated employees. No mention is made of agreements, except that existing agreements are not to be affected by the statute. Also, boards are authorized to adopt rules and regulations to implement the statute.[41]

- *Wisconsin:* Negotiations are permitted between employee organizations and governing boards. The law provides that agreements reached shall be reduced to writing.[42]

In a few states negotiating or bargaining with public employee organizations is specifically prohibited.

- *North Carolina:* Contracts between any governmental unit and any labor union as bargaining agent are void and against public policy.[43]

- *Texas:* It is against public policy for governmental units to enter into collective bargaining agreements or to recognize labor organizations of public employees as bargaining agents.[44]

- *Virginia:* It is against public policy for governmental units to recognize or negotiate with any labor union. Governmental units may discuss matters with employee organizations not affiliated with labor unions.[45]

In a few states there are statutes which provide that public employees or school employees may "present grievances" to their employers. These are not included in the "negotiation rights" list above since they do not add much to employees' rights, as citizens, to present matters to public bodies.

[39] *New Jersey Assembly Bill,* No. 439, 1965.
[40] *Oregon Revised Statutes,* Chapter 342, secs. 342.450–342.470.
[41] *Laws of Washington 1965,* Chapter 143.
[42] *West's Wisconsin Statutes Annotated,* Chapter 111, secs. 111.70(1)–111.70(4)(L).
[43] *General Statutes of North Carolina,* Chapter 95, secs. 95-97–95-100.
[44] *Vernon's Texas Civil Statutes,* Article 5154c.
[45] *Laws of 1946,* Virginia Joint Senate Resolution, No. 12.

The judicial view, in absence of statute providing negotiation and agreement authority to governmental units, is not clear. Part of the difficulty in determining the courts' view arises since, as mentioned earlier, collective bargaining agreements have been thrown out because of the strike issue. This issue, the right of public employees to strike, should not be so closely connected to the right to negotiate. But, since it has been in *private* employment, there is a tendency to assume that any *public* employee group seeking negotiation rights is also seeking the right to strike. Of course, this is not necessarily so. Nevertheless, in the following judicial analysis the strike problem must be kept in mind. In absence of statute, unless otherwise indicated, here is what the courts have said on the negotiation and agreement issue.

- *New Mexico (1965):* The court held that a municipality has the authority to enter into a collective bargaining agreement with a union of utility employees.[46]

- *Kansas (1964):* In holding that the state labor relations act did not apply to a governmental unit, the Wichita Board of Education, the court stated that "public employment cannot become a matter of collective bargaining and contract."[47]

- *Pennsylvania (1964):* In a decision involving the public employees antistrike act, the court expressed serious doubt whether a school board had authority to bargain exclusively with an organization elected by a majority of the teachers employed by it, but it did not need to decide that issue.[48]

- *Florida (1963):* The court stated that a municipality is not authorized to enter into a collective bargaining agreement, but it made the statement in a case enjoining a union from striking to *force* the municipality to engage in collective bargaining and where an antistrike law was applicable.[49]

- *Colorado (1962):* Under a city home rule charter providing that working conditions are a legislative function of the government, the

---

[46] *IBEW Local 611* v. *Town of Farmington,* New Mexico Supreme Court, No. 7694, August 23, 1965.

[47] *Wichita Public School Employees Union* v. *Commissioner of Labor,* 397 P. (2d) 357 (Kansas 1964).

[48] *Philadelphia Teachers' Association* v. *Labrum,* 203 A. (2d) 34 (Pennsylvania 1964).

[49] *Dade County* v. *Amalgamated Association of Street Electric Railway & Motor Coach Employees of America,* 157 So. (2d) 176 (Florida 1963).

court held that the city is without authority to enter into a collective bargaining agreement with a fire department employees' labor union.[50]

- *Georgia (1962):* The court stated that a ports authority is not authorized to enter into a bargaining agreement, but it made the statement in a case enjoining the union from striking and picketing to force the authority to bargain collectively.[51]

- *New York (1962):* An ordinance authorizing a union or employee organization as a bargaining agent for city employees was not held invalid for lack of prescribed standards.[52]

- *Connecticut (1951):* In a decision enjoining teachers from striking, the court also stated that the board of education had authority to negotiate with the teachers association.[53]

- *Missouri (1947):* A city is not authorized to enter into a collective bargaining contract with a union of its employees.[54]

- *Texas (1941):* A local tenure plan negotiated by the classroom teachers association and the board of education which was to be effective "year after year" is not valid because it violated a state statute which limited teacher contracts to 3 years.[55]

Almost all the decisions just summarized involved some issue other than negotiation and agreement. Three of the cases in which the court remarked that negotiation and agreement were beyond a board's authority, involved strikes by public employees to *force* negotiation and agreement. The Texas case involved a statutory provision on the term of employment; the Kansas case involved interpreting a labor relations act. Thus, only five cases are clearly on the point of negotiation and agreement. Three upheld negotiation and two did not.

It is necessary on this issue particularly to notice practice. Certainly, negotiation in absence of final written agreement signed by both parties is extensive. Also, memoranda of agreement are not

---

[50] *Fellows* v. *LaTronica,* 377 P. (2d) 547 (Colorado 1962).
[51] *International Longshoremen's Association, AFL-CIO* v. *Georgia Ports Authority,* 124 S. E. (2d) 733 (Georgia 1962); certiorari denied 370 U. S. 922 (1962).
[52] *Lipsett* v. *Gillette,* 187 N. E. (2d) 782 (New York 1962).
[53] *Norwalk Teachers' Association* v. *Board of Education of City of Norwalk,* 83 A. (2d) 482 (Connecticut 1951).
[54] *City of Springfield* v. *Clouse et al.,* 206 S. W. (2d) 539 (Missouri 1947).
[55] *Froman* v. *Goose Creek Independent School District,* 148 S. W. (2d) 460 (Texas 1941).

unusual. And, undoubtedly the result of negotiations in hundreds of school districts is an effective salary schedule or other provision which is adopted by the board of education as policy. These factors were specifically mentioned by the court in the Connecticut case, cited earlier, and decided in 1951 when there was no statute permitting or prohibiting negotiations. The court stated:

> The statutes and private acts give broad powers to the defendant [board of education] with reference to educational matters and school management in Norwalk. If it chooses to negotiate with the plaintiff [teachers association] with regard to the employment, salaries, grievance procedure and working conditions of its members, there is no statute, public or private, which forbids such negotiations. It is a matter of common knowledge that this is the method pursued in most school systems large enough to support a teachers' association in some form.

> \* \* \*

> The claim of the defendant [board of education] that this [negotiation] would be an illegal delegation of authority is without merit. The authority is and remains in the board.

Undoubtedly, if the question of legality is ever raised in the districts where negotiation is practiced, the view will be that the governing boards *do* have the power. Boards of education have the power and authority to set educational and personnel policies for the school district. Within this power, they may devise procedures to carry out their duties. Under this power, the board should be able to participate in negotiation procedures, even in the absence of statute.

If it is held that the board cannot bind itself to a professional negotiation agreement or contract with a local association under its general powers, there is nothing legally to prohibit the board from adopting negotiation procedures and abiding by them as it abides by its other rules and regulations. In the absence of fraud, statute violation, or abuse of discretion, the courts will not interfere with reasonable regulations adopted by a board for the government of the schools.

In absence of statute, it may be true that a board's resolution for professional negotiation or adoption of a professional negotiation agreement could be cancelled at any time by the board. But to assume this would be done is unrealistic and shortsighted, and supposes bad faith on the part of the board at the outset. The same is true regarding many board regulations adopted to assist in running the schools. That the board has the legal power to eliminate or change many of its long-standing personnel policies and regulations does not mean that the board will do so.

In the *Magenheim* case cited earlier in the discussion of compulsory union membership, the Missouri court expressed its views on the broad powers of a school board under its general statutory authorization to govern the schools:

The Legislature of this State has given Boards of Education the broad power to make all needful rules and regulations for the organization, grading and government in their school district.

*   *   *

In view of [this] broad authority . . . the provisions of the Salary Schedules [requiring teacher membership in professional organizations] must be regarded as prima facie reasonable. . . . We believe that the provisions of the Salary Schedules are reasonable and refuse to interfere with the judgment and discretion of the defendant Board. . . .

Under this view, it is quite likely the Missouri court would uphold the right of a board of education to negotiate if it desired to do so.

In absence of statute, it is unlikely that any court would hold that a board of education could be *forced* to participate in negotiations. The cases discussed earlier are quite consistent in enjoining strikes to force recognition and negotiation. But there seems to be nothing illegal in a board's voluntary participation in negotiation procedures.

### Exclusive Negotiation Rights

Exclusive negotiation rights or exclusive recognition accorded the organization representing the majority of the professional employees of the school district is seldom the subject of statute or judicial decision. The concepts are often the subject of lively debate as to their legality and appropriateness in public employment.

There is no legal stipulation requiring a board of education that desires to formalize its relationships with teacher organizations to ignore the number of professional employees supporting those organizations. According the organization representing the majority of professional employees exclusive recognition and negotiation rights does not "discriminate" against minority organizations, if they exist, or against individual staff members. In absence of statute no board can be forced to recognize the majority organization, nor is it prohibited from doing so. By according exclusive negotiation rights, the board acknowledges that the collective voice of the members of the majority organization is entitled to be given much greater weight than the voices of minority organizations.

Since boards of education are public bodies, they cannot deny a hearing to minority employee organizations or individuals. When the organization representing the majority is accorded exclusive negotiation rights, the minority organizations and individuals must be guaranteed testimony rights. That is, they must be given the opportunity to present views to the governing board. If testimony rights are protected, there is nothing illegal in the board's negotiating with the majority organization exclusively, so long as the results of the negotiations apply equally to all the professional staff, regardless of membership or nonmembership in the organization representing the majority.

Six of the eleven negotiation statutes now in force provide that the board shall negotiate with representatives elected by a majority of the employees concerned. The Connecticut, Massachusetts, Michigan, Washington, and Wisconsin statutes provide that organizations shall be elected representatives; the Oregon law provides that the representative may be an organization or a committee elected by the certificated personnel. Also, the New Jersey statute implies that there will be an exclusive representative by use of the term "recognized organizational representative." The Florida statute provides that boards of education may recognize existing committees of the teaching profession, and the Alaska and New Hampshire statutes do not provide for the selection of an organization to bargain.

In those states which authorize the board or other governmental units to negotiate, it can be implied that this process would include recognition of and dealing with the organization of the majority. The question of whether or not a board may voluntarily grant exclusive negotiation rights to the organization of the majority of its employees has not been decided in any reported court case.

As mentioned earlier, in the *Labrum* decision the Pennsylvania court held that the refusal of the Philadelphia school board to participate in the selection of an exclusive teachers' representative was not a "grievance" under the Pennsylvania mediation law. Since it was not, the court refused to require the issue to be mediated. During the course of its opinion, the court expressed serious doubt that the board had authority to negotiate exclusively with an exclusive representative, but it merely prohibited the board from participating in the selection. And it said this:

The school teachers of Philadelphia are not foreclosed from conducting their own election for the purpose of selecting a bargaining agent to represent them.[56]

Subsequently, an election was held to select the representative of the teachers and the Philadelphia Board of Education is negotiating with the Philadelphia Federation of Teachers, the organization which won the election. So despite the court's "doubt," its decision left the door open for a representation election, and an exclusive representative is negotiating with the board as a result. The only other pertinent mention of the exclusive negotiation representative issue has been in one or two of the cases in which unions were enjoined from striking to *force* the board to grant exclusive recognition.

In absence of statute, several attorneys general have ruled that governmental units cannot be forced to grant exclusive recognition. In a recent ruling involving schools, issued before the 1965 bargaining law was enacted, the Michigan attorney ruled that, although it could not be forced to, a school board *could* grant exclusive recognition to an association of teachers which received a majority of the teachers vote at a representation election.[57]

Exclusive recognition is authorized at the federal level. Presidential Executive Order 10988,[58] which deals with relationships

---

[56] *Philadelphia Teachers' Association* v. *Labrum,* 203 A. (2d) 34 (Pennsylvania 1964).
[57] *Michigan A. G. O. No. 4306,* March 18, 1964.
[58] See Appendix I for the full text of the Order.

between organizations of federal employees and the employing agencies of the federal government, distinguishes between employee organizations on the basis of membership. Although, of course, this Order does not apply to public school employees, its provisions are bound to have, and as a matter of fact have had an effect on the legal view of public employer-employee negotiation at the state level. In this Order, exclusive recognition is reserved for the organization that enjoys majority support, and *only* the organization accorded exclusive recognition has the right to negotiate in an effort to reach agreement with public officials on the formulation of policies. In support of exclusive recognition which grants exclusive negotiation rights to the majority organization, the President's Task Force on Employee-Management Relations in the Federal Service said:

The essence of exclusive recognition is that it makes it possible for management officials and employee representatives by the process of collective negotiations to reach agreements on personnel policies and practices. An agreement with an organization having exclusive recognition applies to all of the employees in the unit and agreement must be approved by the head of the agency, or an official designated by him ... The task force accepts the view that in appropriate circumstances exclusive recognition is wholly justifiable and in such circumstances will permit the development of stable and meaningful employee-management relations based upon bilateral agreements.

Thus, the federal government has officially approved the idea of exclusive negotiation rights for organizations which represent and have been selected by the majority of the employees in question.

## Mediation and Appeal Procedures

Seven of the eleven negotiation statutes provide for the resolution of disagreement through the use of some third party. Of the six statutes applicable exclusively to school personnel, those in Connecticut, New Jersey, Oregon, and Washington provide mediation through educational channels. Mediation is not provided in the California and Florida laws.

The Massachusetts, Michigan, and Wisconsin collective bargaining laws which are applicable to public employees, including teachers, provide mediation through labor channels. The Alaska and New Hampshire statutes do not contain mediation provisions, although it is possible that private labor mediation channels might be available to public employees.

Of all of the provisions of professional negotiation, these appeal procedures are most often cited as being a process in which a board of education cannot "legally" participate. Yet, many of the reasons in support of the "legality" of other professional negotiation procedures can be applied here. That is, that boards of education may participate legally in mediation and appeal procedures under their general powers to govern the schools. Mediation and appeal procedures are simply an orderly method which the board can use to assist it in resolving impasses. At the present time most boards request information and advice from outside sources. Similarly, they can obtain assistance in using orderly mediation and appeal procedures which are set out in a negotiation agreement. The recommendations which may result from mediation and appeal procedure must be advisory only and not binding either upon the board or upon the employee organization. It appears unlikely that recommendations could be made binding upon a board in the absence of statute. All of the negotiation statutes providing impasse procedures specifically state that resulting recommendations are advisory, and not binding on board or employee organization.

Several states have statutes which provide some form of appeal machinery. Of these, several concern "grievances" and it is sometimes difficult to ascertain whether the machinery provided could be used by an employee organization or school board to resolve a negotiation impasse or whether its use is confined to individual employees with grievances. Table 2-1 is a comparison of the statutory appeal machinery available to public school employees. Note that in a few states the machinery is limited to use by certain categories of employees. These statutes are included for comparative purposes although they do not apply to teachers.

Several court decisions were decided on the issue of mediation and appeal for public school employees:

- In Kansas, custodial and maintenance employees appealed to the state labor commissioner to compel him to hold a representation election. The state labor relations act did not mention public employees, and there was no other type of mediation and appeal statute on the books. The court held that the board of education is not an "employer" under the terms of the labor relations act, and that, therefore, the labor commissioner could not be compelled to act.[59]

- The Connecticut court, in absence of an authorizing statute, stated that mediation was permissible to settle or adjust disputes between a teachers association and a board of education.[60]

- Under the Michigan statute providing that public employees may have grievances considered under labor mediation, the court held that the labor mediation board could mediate a dispute between teachers and a board of education regarding salary and working conditions.[61] A similar ruling, with regard to regents and employees of a university, was made by the attorney general.[62]

- The Minnesota state labor conciliator was appealed to with a request to hold a representation election. The court held he was barred from acting because in order to have jurisdiction a "controversy" had to exist and the court ruled none existed.[63]

- In Pennsylvania, under its mediation statute for public employees, the courts held that a city must submit to the procedure upon request and must appoint a member to the mediation panel.[64] Also, it has been held that the statute does not require a city to carry out the recommendations of the panel.[65] And the refusal of a board of education to participate in the selection of an exclusive teachers' representative was held not to be a "grievance" which could be mediated under the statute.[66]

- The Wisconsin Employment Relations Board, under a statute giving it authority to mediate disputes between boards of education and

[59] *Wichita Public Schools Employees Union* v. *Commissioner of Labor,* 397 P. (2d) 357 (Kansas 1964).
[60] *Norwalk Teachers' Association* v. *Board of Education of City of Norwalk,* 83 A. (2d) 482 (Connecticut 1951).
[61] *School District of the City of Garden City* v. *Labor Mediation Board,* 99 N. W. (2d) 485 (Michigan 1959).
[62] *Michigan A.G.O. No. 1293,* August 31, 1950.
[63] *In re Investigation and Certification of a Bargaining Agent: Richfield Federation of Teachers and Richfield Board of Education and Richfield Education Association, Minnesota Education Association,* 115 N. W. (2d) 682 (Minnesota 1962).
[64] *Pittsburgh City Firefighters Local No. 1* v. *Barr,* 184 A. (2d) 588 (Pennsylvania 1962).
[65] *Erie Firefighters Local No. 293* v. *Gardner,* 178 A. (2d) 691 (Pennsylvania 1962).
[66] *Philadelphia Teachers' Association* v. *Labrum,* 203 A. (2d) 34 (Pennsylvania 1964).

school employees has ruled that the Wisconsin Education Association is a labor organization as defined in the statute. A labor organization is defined as one which furnishes advice and guidance to local affiliated organizations representing teachers in efforts to obtain recognition and in conferences and negotiations with their school boards.[67]

Of the courts just mentioned, the Connecticut court spelled out the rights of boards of education to mediate in absence of statute most clearly:

If it is borne in mind that arbitration is the result of mutual agreement, there is no reason to deny the power of the defendant [board] to enter voluntarily into a contract to arbitrate a specific issue.

The court did not believe a blanket agreement to arbitrate all issues to be permissible—but, remember, it was speaking of binding arbitration.

From what has been said, it is obvious that, within the same limitations, mediation to settle or adjust disputes is not only permissible but desirable. The answer to question (g) is "Yes."

\* \* \*

(g) Is mediation a permissible method under Connecticut law to settle or adjust disputes between the plaintiff [teachers association] and defendant [board]?

## Summary of Legal Status of Professional Negotiation

The foregoing detailed legal analysis can be summarized in rather brief form by stating some generalizations and noting some of the exceptions to them. Most of the generalizations are applicable in all jurisdictions with a few exceptions.

- There is little legal doubt today that certificated school employees have the right to organize and join employee organizations. There had been some doubt in the past, and several states have enacted statutes which specifically state that public employees have the right to join unions and employee organizations.

[67] School District No. 1, City of West Allis, Decision No. 6545, Wisconsin Employment Relations Board, November 1963.

**TABLE 2-1.** Comparison of Statutory Mediation and Appeal Procedures

| STATE | CODE CITATION | PUBLIC EMPLOYEES COVERED | ISSUE |
|---|---|---|---|
| 1 | 2 | 3 | 4 |
| Connecticut | *Connecticut Public Act* 298, 1965. | School employees. | Disagreements as to terms and conditions of employment. |
| Illinois | *Smith-Hurd Illinois Annotated Statutes,* Chapter 127, sec. 63b108c. | State employees. | Grievances. |
| Massachusetts | *Annotated Laws of Massachusetts,* Chapter 149, sec. 178G. | School employees specifically included among other employees. | Grievances, contract disputes, disputes over unit determinations. |
| Michigan | *Michigan Statutes Annotated,* Title 17, sec. 17.454(7). | Public employees. | Grievances, including compensation and conditions of work. |

| LOCAL LEVEL PROCEDURES | STATE APPEAL AGENCY | STATE LEVEL PROCEDURES | EFFECT OF RECOMMENDA-TIONS |
|---|---|---|---|
| 5 | 6 | 7 | 8 |
| | Secretary, State Board of Education. | Secretary is authorized to mediate. If he fails, the board of arbitrators is established at request of either party. Each selects one member and the two members select a third. | Advisory. |
| | State Director of Personnel. | State Director of Personnel is to establish a plan for resolving grievances. | Advisory. Compulsory arbitration is specifically excluded. |
| Arbitration tribunals other than state's may be used. | State Board of Conciliation and Arbitration and State Labor Relations Commission. | Labor Relations Commission makes unit determinations and may direct that representation elections be held. Board of Conciliation initiates fact-finding in negotiation dispute and at request of either party where no agreement exists 60 days prior to final budget date; also available to conciliate grievances and contract terms disputes. | Advisory, except that Labor Relations Commission determines unit in representation controversies. Fact-finders make written statements of fact and recommendations for resolution to parties. |
| | Labor Mediation Board. | Mediation service may be obtained on request of bargaining representative or of majority of employees or the employer. | Advisory. |

| State | Code Citation | Public Employees Covered | Issue |
|-------|---------------|--------------------------|-------|
| *1* | *2* | *3* | *4* |
| Minnesota | *Minnesota Statutes Annotated,* Chapter 179, sec. 179.57. | Public employees. | Grievances, including conditions of work. |
| Nebraska | *Revised Statutes of Nebraska, 1943,* Chapter 48, sec. 48-810. | Public employees engaged in proprietary functions or employed in public utilities. This does not include school employees. | Industrial disputes. |
| New Jersey | *New Jersey Assembly Bill,* No. 439, 1965.* | Certificated school employees. | Controversy over formulation or modification of policy, including grievances and matters of mutual concern. |
| New York | *New York General Municipal Law,* secs. 681–685. | School employees specifically included among other public employees. | Grievances, including violation or mismanagement of employee health and safety; supervision; but not compensation or retirement. |

* This legislation was vetoed by the governor of New Jersey.

**TABLE 2-1.**  Comparison of Statutory Mediation and Appeal Procedures

| LOCAL LEVEL PROCEDURES | STATE APPEAL AGENCY | STATE LEVEL PROCEDURES | EFFECT OF RECOMMENDATIONS |
|---|---|---|---|
| 5 | 6 | 7 | 8 |
| A mediation panel consisting of one member selected by the employees, one by the governmental unit, and a third by these two may be established to adjust grievances. | | | Advisory. If no agreement is reached, the panel shall send copies of its findings to the governor, the legislature, and the parties involved. |
| | | Arbitration. | Compulsory. |
| If state mediator fails to effect a solution, either party may cause an *ad hoc* board of review to be established. One member is appointed by each party and these two select a third, who is chairman. | State Commissioner of Education. | On mutual agreement, recognized organizational representative and board of education may request the State Commissioner to appoint a mediator.

The mediator shall be selected from a list of 10 persons experienced in public education. | Advisory. |
| The board of education shall establish grievance procedures providing for at least two procedural stages and an appellate stage. | | | Advisory. Recommendations shall be sent to the employee, his representative, if any, the unit head, and the chief executive involved. |

51

**TABLE 2-1.** Comparison of Statutory Mediation and Appeal Procedures *(Continued)*

| STATE | CODE CITATION | PUBLIC EMPLOYEES COVERED | ISSUE |
|-------|---------------|--------------------------|-------|
| *1* | *2* | *3* | *4* |
| North Dakota | *North Dakota Revised Laws,* Chapter 34-11, secs. 34-11-01–34-11-05. | Public employees. | Grievances, including disputes on working conditions and employment problems. |
| Oregon | *Oregon Revised Statutes,* Chapter 342, sec. 342.470. | Certificated school employees. | Persistent disagreement on matters of salaries or economic policies. |

| LOCAL LEVEL PROCEDURES | STATE APPEAL AGENCY | STATE LEVEL PROCEDURES | EFFECT OF RECOMMENDA-TIONS |
|---|---|---|---|
| 5 | 6 | 7 | 8 |

Stage 1: Employee's presentation of grievance to his supervisor.

Stage 2: Review and determination by governmental head.

Stage 3: Three-member grievance board appointed by governmental unit.

School employees have the right to be represented at all stages.

| | | |
|---|---|---|
| At the request of either the employee or employer a mediation board, consisting of the employee organization representative of the employee, a representative of the employer, and a third selected by these two, shall be established. | | Advisory. |
| Either party may cause consultants to be appointed. | | Advisory. |
| One person selected by each party and a third by those two. | | |

| STATE | CODE CITATION | PUBLIC EMPLOYEES COVERED | ISSUE |
|-------|---------------|--------------------------|-------|
| *1* | *2* | *3* | *4* |
| Pennsylvania | *Purden's Pennsylvania Statutes Annotated,* Title 43, sec. 215.1. | Public employees. | Grievances, including conditions of work and compensation. |
| Rhode Island | *General Laws of Rhode Island 1956,* Title 28, secs. 28-9, 1-7–28-9, 1-11; secs. 28-9, 2-7–28-9, 2-11. | Policemen and firemen. | Wages and terms and conditions of employment. |
| Washington | *Laws of Washington 1965,* Chapter 143. | Certificated school employees. | Matters of joint concern including but not limited to curriculum, textbook selection, in service training, student teaching programs, personnel, hiring and assignment practices, leaves of absence, salaries and salary schedules and noninstructional duties. |
| Wisconsin | *West's Wisconsin Statutes Annotated,* Chapter 111, sec. 111.70. | School employees specifically included among other public employees. | Wages, hours and conditions of employment. |

**T A B L E  2 - 1 .**  **Comparison of Statutory Mediation and Appeal Procedures** *(Continued)*

| Local Level Procedures | State Appeal Agency | State Level Procedures | Effect of Recommenda-tions |
|---|---|---|---|
| 5 | 6 | 7 | 8 |
| A mediation panel consisting of one member selected by the public employees, one by the governmental unit and a third by these two. | If professional school employees are involved the third member of the panel shall be the State Superintendent of Public Instruction or his nominee. | | Advisory. If panel cannot effect agreement, copies of its recommendations shall be sent to the governor, legislature, and the parties. |
| Disputes *must* be submitted to arbitration board. | | | Advisory. |
| | State Superintendent of Public Instruction. | Either party may request the advice and assistance of a committee of educators and school board members to be appointed by the State Superintendent of Public Instruction. The committee shall make a written report within 15 days of the request. | Advisory. |
| Local employers may establish fact-finding procedures. If they are substantially in compliance with this statute, state Employment Relations Board shall not initiate fact-finding. | Employment Relations Board | Both parties may request a mediator from the Employment Relations Board. Either party may request fact-finding if negotiations are deadlocked or if either party refuses to meet and negotiate in good faith. | Advisory. |

- Most legal writers agree that compulsory membership in employee organizations, the closed or union shop in school districts, will not be upheld by a court of record; and, there are no statutes specifically permitting compulsory membership for school employees. There are two cases in point involving school employees, and the courts went in opposite directions.

- The traditional judicial view is that teachers do not have a legal right to strike. There is indication the right would be upheld by courts if provided by statute. Statutes in several states prohibit public employees from striking, and some mention teachers specifically. No statutes provide that teachers may strike.

- The questions of teacher-board negotiation resulting in an agreement signed by representatives of the teacher organization and the school board has rarely been the primary subject of court decision. However, in several decisions, often enjoining public employee strikes to compel boards to negotiate, there are dicta indicating that boards may not have authority, in absence of statute, to negotiate and sign agreements. In other decisions, there are statements that boards have the right to negotiate under their general power to run the schools. It seems certain that without statute boards of education may not be *forced* to participate in negotiations.

- Several statutes authorize boards to negotiate. Negotiations are being carried on, and agreements are being signed or adopted as board policy in almost every state in the United States. This is evidence that, in absence of prohibiting legislation, boards may use the professional negotiation process.

- Exclusive negotiation rights and exclusive recognition have seldom been the subject of court decisions. Six of the eleven negotiation statutes provide for them. Such procedures are accepted in federal employment. Whether granted in absence of statute, or under statutes, provision must be made to guarantee testimony rights—the right to present views to the board—to individual employees and to minority organizations of employees.

- Mediation, fact-finding, and appeal procedures for public employees are provided for by statute in at least 14 states. There are few court decisions on the issue decided in absence of statute. In absence of statute, boards of education cannot be forced to participate in such procedures, but there seems to be nothing to prohibit them from voluntarily participating in most jurisdictions, if recommendations resulting from them are advisory. No existing statutory provisions authorizing such provisions for school employees provide that recommendations be binding.

# Chapter 3. Elements of Professional Negotiation Agreements

ALTHOUGH several hundred written professional negotiation agreements are known to be in existence, this process in education is still a relatively new one. It has only been since the 1962–63 school year that the National Education Association and its state affiliates began actively promoting the development of written agreements by local professional associations.

The *Guidelines for Professional Negotiation*[1] furnishes the following definition of the process:

Professional negotiation is a set of procedures, written and officially adopted by the local association and the school board, which provides an orderly method for the school board and the local association to negotiate, through professional channels, on matters of mutual concern, to reach agreement on these matters, and to establish educational channels for mediation and appeal in the event of impasse.

Written professional negotiation procedures should contain certain basic elements. These are:

*Recognition:* The board of education recognizes the local association as the representative of the professional staff.

*Channels:* The local association uses professional channels in the negotiation process.

*Negotiation:* Representatives of the local association and the board of education negotiate in good faith.

*Agreement:* A written document containing the matters agreed to is signed by the local association and board of education at the conclusion of negotiations.

---

[1] *Guidelines for Professional Negotiation,* Rev. ed., Washington, D. C.: Office of Professional Development and Welfare, National Education Association, 1965, p. 1.

*Impasse:* Educational channels are established for appeal in the event of an impasse.

While professional negotiation agreements vary considerably in scope and relative effectiveness, an examination of the Level II and III agreements filed with NEA reveals several common elements:

1. They provide for board of education recognition of a single organization to represent the classroom teachers, or entire professional staff, in negotiations on matters of policy.

2. They designate the subjects which are negotiable.

3. They provide guidelines for the structure and conduct of negotiations.

4. They specify ways in which agreement on any matter shall be reached and reported.

In addition, Level III agreements contain provision for advisory mediation and/or fact-finding in the event of failure to reach agreement during negotiations.

Many agreements, both Level II and III, contain some reference to the role of the superintendent of schools. This topic is dealt with separately in Chapter 5.

## Recognition of Single Organization

Most authorities on the subject agree that for meaningful negotiations to take place, a single organization must be recognized officially as speaking for the staff in matters of policy determination. The choice of such an organization is vastly simplified when only one staff organization exists in a school district. In such cases, a recognition clause similar to the following is usually found:

The Board of Directors of _____ School District recognizes the _____ Education Association as the exclusive and official organization to represent all certificated employees of the School District for the purpose of negotiations on all matters of mutual concern.

Since there is only one organization speaking for the staff in the above example, the organization is mentioned by name in the agreement. Similar recognition clauses, which mention organizations by name, are to be found in agreements granting negotiating rights on the basis of secret ballot elections.[2]

In most school districts in which two organizations compete for the membership of staff personnel, recognition is granted on the basis of relative membership strength, rather than secret ballot elections. Two general patterns of recognition are to be found in such cases, one of which mentions the organization by name and one which does not:

*Example 1.* The Board of Directors of the _____ School District recognizes the _____ Teachers Association which enrolls a majority of the certificated personnel of this District, as the exclusive and official organization to represent all certified employees for the purposes of joint consideration. This agreement shall be renewed annually unless another group presents to the Board of Directors a certified list of its members equal to or greater than 50 percent of the certificated personnel of the District.

*Example 2.* The Board of Education will recognize for the purpose of negotiating proposals the classroom teacher organization which has as its members a majority of contract teachers employed by the _____ Public Schools and which submits a list of names of its members to the Board of Education not later than January 1 of each year.

In each of the above examples the organization enrolling a majority of the negotiating unit is certified as the exclusive negotiating representative. It should be noted, however, that the concept of exclusive representation is confined solely to the negotiating process. In no case on record does it operate to prejudice the right of an individual teacher or minority staff organization to make its views known to the superintendent or the board of education.

An interesting method of granting exclusive recognition is being used by a school district in California. "Official" recognition is granted to the one staff organization which enrolls a majority of the certificated staff, while "informal" recognition is granted to those organizations which enroll 10 per cent or more, but less than a majority. The following is an excerpt from the agreement in effect in Orcutt Union School District, California:

2 For example, Milwaukee, Wisconsin; New Rochelle, New York; Bremerton, Washington.

The Board of Education shall recognize professional teacher associations and shall accord them rights and privileges in accordance with the provisions of this statement. Professional teacher associations may apply for recognition according to the following classifications:
A. Official
B. Informal

Negotiating rights shall be accorded only to a professional teacher association qualifying for official recognition on the basis of enrolling in its membership a majority of the certificated employees of the district.

Informal recognition shall be accorded professional teacher associations not accorded official recognition and which enroll ten per cent or more of the certificated employees of the district.

Official and informal recognition of professional teacher associations will be accorded on the basis of verified membership in the applying association.

According to the provisions of this agreement, the informally recognized organizations are entitled to many of the same privileges as the officially recognized organization, including the use of school facilities, being listed in the school directory, and having access to nonconfidential school district records. Only the officially recognized organization, however, is entitled to negotiate for members of the certificated staff.

In most districts with written agreements organizations which include all levels of staff personnel in their membership represent the entire staff in negotiations. Districts in which there are no all-inclusive staff organizations present another problem in negotiations, since no one group can speak for the entire professional staff. In such districts, the problem of representation for the administrative-supervisory staff is usually handled in one of two ways: (a) No negotiations take place on behalf of the administrative-supervisory staff; such personnel depend upon unilateral board action for any policy changes that are made. (b) Administrative-supervisory personnel are represented by their own organizations, and either negotiate separately from classroom teachers or by means of a districtwide negotiation committee whose membership is composed of proportionate representation from various organizations speaking for different classifications of professional personnel in the district.

The patterns of staff representation to be found in operation in school districts across the nation usually reflect local preferences and the methods by which former, informal negotiations have taken place.

## Designation of Subject Matter

Almost without exception, the designation of subject matter in professional negotiation agreements leaves wide latitude in the choice of subjects to be negotiated. Such designation goes far beyond the subjects usually termed of a "welfare" nature. The following list, included in the Wantagh, New York, agreement, may be considered illustrative:

. . . recruitment of teachers, community support for the school program, budget preparation, curriculum, inservice training, class size, teacher turnover, personnel policies, salaries, working conditions, communications, and other mutually agreed upon matters which affect the quality of the educational program.

Other agreements do not mention specific subject matter at all, yet remain comprehensive in scope by including in the recognition section a statement similar to the following:

The Board of Education recognizes the _____ Education Association, affiliated with the State Education Association and the National Education Association, as the official organizations through which the teachers of the district develop and present their considered opinions on matters of concern to them. The Board will give consideration to proposals and representations made on behalf of the _____ Education Association.

One of the criteria of a profession is its concern for the welfare of its clients and for the improvement of services to its clients. The philosophy underlying professional negotiation, as stressed in all NEA literature on the subject, is that the case for improved teacher welfare rests upon the necessity for improving the quality of public education generally. Agreements already adopted, to the degree that they designate broadly the subjects considered appropriate for negotiation, reflect this philosophy.

## Structure and Conduct of Negotiations

All Level II and III agreements contain guidelines for carrying out the negotiation process. In brief outline, or more extensively, these guidelines delineate (a) the composition or structure of the negotiating committee, and (b) the procedural rules for conducting negotiations.

### Structure

Two patterns are evident in the structure of negotiating committees, and they seem to be found in agreements with equal frequency. The first calls for a comprehensive committee, which includes in its composition representatives of the board and the administration as well as the recognized staff organization. In most cases the number of members is spelled out specifically, as in the following example:

There is hereby established a Negotiating Council consisting of three representatives of the officially recognized teacher association, two representatives or designees of the Board of Education, and the Superintendent of Schools or his designee.

Some agreements call for a comprehensive committee, but include no specifications governing the number of representatives from each group, as in the following example:

There shall be a Professional Negotiation Committee consisting of members of the Board of Education, the _____ Education Association, and the administrative staff. A chairman and secretary shall be elected from these members.

The second pattern of committee structure is one which specifies the members of the association only, thus leaving unclear the composition of board and administrative representation:

The Board will recognize a committee of three members of the teachers' association as the negotiators for the teaching staff.

There is little uniformity of practice with respect to committee designation. An interesting sidelight is that many agreements specify "representatives" when referring to board members or administrators on committees but restrict teacher participation on the committee to a "members only" basis. As a practical matter, this means that boards of education are free to employ professionals skilled in employer-employee relations techniques to negotiate with the teachers, while the teachers are confined to using members from their own ranks in the negotiation process. More recently adopted agreements, however, are specifying "members *or* representatives" for all parties in the negotiation process.

*Procedural Rules*

Meetings of the negotiation committee are handled in one of two ways in most agreements: (a) either they are scheduled on a regular basis at the beginning of each school year (for example, "At the beginning of each school year the committee will arrange to publish a calendar of its regular meetings, these meetings to be supplemented as needs may require"); or (b) they are called only upon the request of one of the parties, and only for a specific reason (for example, "Meetings composed of the Board of Education, the ———— Education Association Negotiation Committee, and the Superintendent shall be called upon the written request of any one of the parties involved. A request for the meeting should contain a specific statement as to the reason for the request"). In the latter case, when scheduled meetings are not arranged beforehand, there is usually some stipulation concerning the setting of a mutually convenient meeting date within a reasonable period of time.

Since negotiations usually cover a wide variety of topics, most of which can be extremely time-consuming, several agreements make provision for the appointment of subcommittees to make preliminary studies and recommendations concerning specific matters under discussion. The following excerpt is illustrative of this point:

If both parties concur, the Professional Negotiation Committee may, at its discretion, appoint joint study committees to engage in cooperative research, study, and development of projects, programs, reports, and recommendations in matters under consideration by the Professional Negotiation Committee. Each joint study committee shall operate under procedures approved by the Professional Negotiation Committee and shall report directly to the committee.

Several other procedural rules are frequently spelled out in professional negotiation agreements. Most such rules are designed for the purpose of facilitating and expediting the work of the committee. Following are examples of these rules as they appear in various agreements:

The participants may call upon competent professional and/or lay representatives to consider the matters under discussion and to make suggestions.

\* \* \*

All participants have the right to utilize the services of consultants in the deliberations.

\* \* \*

With the approval of all parties, periodic progress reports may be made.

\* \* \*

Official summary minutes will be kept of all meetings, and clerical assistance will be provided for the purpose by the Board of Education.

\* \* \*

The committee will have available to it any additional clerical assistance necessary to the performance of its duties.

\* \* \*

Teacher members of the committee shall be released in reasonable number and at reasonable times from school duties without loss of salary when negotiation meetings are scheduled during the school day.

\* \* \*

The Board and the Superintendent agree to furnish to the Association's members of the Professional Negotiation Committee, in accordance with their reasonable requests, all available information concerning financial resources of the district, tentative budgetary requirements, and allocations, and such other information as will assist the Association in developing intelligent, accurate, and constructive programs on behalf of the teachers and their students.

\* \* \*

Facts, opinions, proposals, and counterproposals will be exchanged freely during the meeting or meetings (and between meetings if advisable) in an effort to reach mutual understanding and agreement.

## Reaching and Reporting Agreements

An inspection of adopted agreements reveals a variety of methods used for implementing the decisions reached during the negotiation process. Excerpts from four representative agreements will serve to illustrate the procedures currently in use.

*Example 1.* When the Board and the teachers' representatives reach agreement, it should be prepared as a written recommendation for both groups.

If the Board and the teachers' representatives are unable to agree, they should seek further instruction from their respective groups. All reasonable means, including expert guidance, should be employed in an effort to reach agreement.

When an agreement has been approved by both groups, it should be adopted by a formal board vote as official policy.

*Example 2.* When the participants reach agreement, it will be reduced to writing and submitted to the Board of Education for formal adoption, whereupon it will become a part of the official minutes of the Board of Education. When necessary, provisions in the agreement shall be reflected in the individual teacher contract. The agreement shall not discriminate against any member of the teaching staff, regardless of membership or nonmembership in any teachers' organization.

*Example 3.* If agreement is reached between the parties, the necessary action shall be taken by the Board of Education at its next regular meeting implementing the specifics of the agreement.

*Example 4.* Reporting: When the participants reach a consensus, a joint written report will be prepared, one copy for the Board and one for the Association.

Reports may be presented to the Board or the Association by either party.

Action: When a joint report is presented, and the representatives of the Association affirm final acceptance of a report and the Board accepts the report, the recommendations of the report will be put into effect by the Superintendent.

When the representatives of the Association and the Board cannot reach agreement and have presented their separate reports, the representatives of the Association, the Superintendent, or the Board may call a regular or special meeting. If an appeal is made and if requested by the representatives of the Association, the Board shall meet together with the Association representatives and the superintendent in executive session to negotiate. Upon mutual agreement, other persons may be called in to act as consultants. Final decision of the Board on this subject, or a decision to appeal, will be made at a regular or special meeting of the Board.

## Provisions for Mediation

Level III agreements, in addition to specifying the procedures to be used in the negotiating process, also make provision for resolving disagreements in the event that they occur. While the provisions for mediation in the various agreements vary considerably in substance and form, they have one element in common: in no case are the recommendations officially binding upon the parties concerned. While it is legally permissible in specific instances for a board of education to agree to abide by the recommendations of an impartial third party or panel, to date there is no professional negotiation agreement on record that contains such a provision. Nor, it should be noted, do any of the statutes presently in effect provide for binding arbitration in the event of impasse. The mediation provided for in these statutes is purely of an advisory nature. However, no party may refuse, under the statutes, to submit to mediation or fact-finding.

Appeal and mediation provisions range from the most simple and informal of one step operations to complex and formal multi-step procedures utilizing state resources for assistance. The following resources are those most often used in resolving disagreements that arise during negotiation:

### At the Local Level

1. The board of education, if the entire board has not been involved in initial negotiations. When the board of education is mentioned as an appeal resource in Level III agreements, it is always used as the first step in a multi-step procedure.

2. An individual acceptable to both parties. Such individuals

may be local residents with experience in educational matters or they may be staff members of state and/or national educational organizations—e.g., education associations, school board associations, school administrator associations.

3. A panel of individuals acceptable to both parties. Usually, the board selects one panel member, the association selects another, and the first two select a third who serves as chairman. Such panels may consist of local association and board members, local residents selected from the staffs or memberships of state education, school administrator, and school board associations. Such groups are variously called boards of review, agreement assistance panels, mediation boards, advisory boards, or review committees.

*At the State Level*

1. The state superintendent (or commissioner) of education or state board of education.

2. Individuals or panels, acceptable to both parties, designated by the state superintendent of education.

As previously stated, agreements may call for using only one of the above resources in settling impasses, or they may call for the use of two or more mediatory or fact-finding levels in seeking to effect reconciliation of viewpoints. In addition, time limits are sometimes placed upon various steps in the appeal procedure. The following excerpts from existing agreements, ranging from simple to complex, furnish examples of the various approaches being employed to mediate impasses:

*Example 1*

DISAGREEMENT

When the Board of Education and representatives of the official negotiating organization cannot agree, other professional or educational groups or individuals may be called in to act as consultant.

*Example 2*

RESOLVING DISAGREEMENT

Recognizing, as they do, their respective responsibilities for the education of the children of the community, the parties accept their obligation to assure the uninterrupted operations of the school system.

To this end the parties pledge themselves to negotiate in good faith such matters as may appropriately be included in an agreement between them, and, in the event of failure to reach agreement, to utilize in good faith such mediatory facilities as may usefully contribute to arriving at agreement between them. In this connection the parties recognize that, in the event that they call upon any third party to assist them in arriving at agreement, such person shall be qualified by general background in the educational field and special understanding of the issue at hand. The report of such person shall be advisory only and shall not be binding on the parties. Although the parties include the provisions of this paragraph for the purpose of indicating their pledge to the community to prevent the interruption of the operation of the school system, they nevertheless reiterate that each of them will make every effort to reach agreement at the local level where important details of the needs of the school system can most clearly and thoroughly be understood.

*Example 3*

When the representatives of the BEA and the Board cannot reach agreement and have presented their separate reports, the representatives of the BEA, the Superintendent, or the Board may call a regular or special meeting. If an appeal is made and if requested by the representatives of the BEA, the Board shall meet together with the BEA representatives and the Superintendent in executive session to negotiate. Upon mutual agreement, other persons may be called in to act as consultants. Final decision of the Board on this subject of the appeal will be made at a regular or special meeting of the Board.

In case of disagreement about the meaning or application of this agreement, or if an impasse is reached during professional negotiations, the matter will be submitted to an Advisory Board within thirty days after the request of either party to the other. The Board will name one adviser, and another will be named by the BEA. A third member, who shall be the chairman, shall be named by the first two named members.

The Advisory Board will be expected to report recommendations for settlement within fifteen days. The recommendations will be submitted to both parties and shall be made public.

*Example 4*

REFERRAL

1. To the Board of Education:

In the event that agreement is not reached, and members of the Board of Education have not participated directly in the deliberations, the Community Teachers Association representatives and the Superintendent or his representative may present separate reports stating their points of agreement and disagreement to the Board of Education. The procedure outline in II will be followed in an effort to reach understanding and agreement, with the full Board—or Board members selected by the Board—participating in the deliberations.

2. To a Board of Review:

In the event that agreement is not reached with the Board either the Board or the Community Teachers Association may request that a Board of Review be created in the following manner.

One member will be nominated by the Board of Education or its designated representatives, one member will be nominated by the teacher association representatives, and a third member will be selected by the first two and will serve as chairman.

If the first two members cannot agree on the third member, the State Commissioner of Education will appoint a third member.

The Board of Review will have authority to hold hearings and to confer with any parties deemed advisable in seeking to effect a settlement.

If an agreement is not reached within a specified time after selection of the Board of Review, the Board of Review will prepare a public report with written recommendations and shall submit it to the Board of Education and teacher association representatives.

3. To the State Commissioner of Education:

In the event that agreement is not reached with the Board, either the Board or the Community Teachers Association representative may request the State Commissioner of Education to appoint a competent individual to seek to bring about a mutually acceptable settlement. The person chosen will have the authority to confer separately or jointly with the Superintendent of Schools, official representatives, or to utilize any other source of information. He may make public any data or recommendations that he may deem advisable.

*Example 5*

1. When the representatives of the Ashtabula Area Education Association and the Superintendent cannot reach agreement and have presented their separate reports to the Board of Education, or when the Board of Education rejects a joint report, the representatives of the Ashtabula Area Education Association or the Superintendent may appeal to the Board at a regular or special meeting. If an appeal is made and if requested by the representatives of the Ashtabula Area Education Association, the Board of Education shall meet together

with the Ashtabula Education Association representatives and the Superintendent in executive session. Upon mutual agreement, professional persons selected by the National Education Association, the Ohio Education Association, the Ohio Association of School Administrators, the Ohio School Boards Association, may be called in to act as consultants. The decision of the Board of Education on the subject of the appeal will be made at a regular or special meeting of the Board of Education.

2. Board of Review:

a. In the event that agreement is not reached with the Board as per section 2 above, either the Board or Ashtabula Area Education Association may request that a Board of Review be created.

The Board of Review will be created within fifteen days unless both parties agree to a later date.

(1) The Board of Review will be created in the following manner:

(aa) The Board will select its member from a list of nominees submitted by any one of the organizations, as follows: National Education Association, Ohio Education Association, Ohio School Boards Association, Ohio Association of School Administrators.

(bb) The Ashtabula Area Education Association will select its member from a list of nominees submitted by anyone of the organizations as follows: National Education Association, Ohio Education Association, Ohio Association of School Administrators, Ohio School Boards Association.

(cc) The two members selected shall select a third member from one above-named professional organization who will serve as chairman.

(2) The Board of Review will have authority to hold hearings and to confer with any parties deemed advisable in seeking to effect a recommendation to the Board of Education and the Ashtabula Area Education Association.

(3) All hearings conducted by the Board of Review shall be in closed sessions and no news releases shall be made concerning progress of hearings.

(4) Whatever conclusion that the reviewing board might reasonably arrive at can only be advisory or in the nature of recommendations to the Board of Education.

3. State Superintendent:

a. If an agreement is not reached within a reasonable time after selection of the Board of Review, and the problem is within the jurisdiction of the State Superintendent of Public Instruction, either the Board of Education or the Ashtabula Area Education Association may request the State Superintendent of Public Instruction to review and make recommendations.

## Miscellaneous Provisions

While not yet widespread, the following provisions are increasingly becoming evident in negotiation agreements. Taken together, they represent a much more sophisticated approach to the negotiation process and are therefore to be encouraged.

### Policies Agreed Upon in Writing

Several agreements, notably those in New Rochelle and Rochester, New York; Milwaukee, Wisconsin; Newark, New Jersey; and Bremerton, Washington provide that policies jointly developed be reduced to written form and actually made a part of the agreement itself. This practice leaves no doubt concerning the results of the negotiation process. The entire document, then—procedural sections as well as substantive—becomes the agreement to which the association and the board of education are parties. Theoretically, the procedural sections remain constant from year to year since they constitute the ground rules for negotiation; the substantive sections, however, such as salary schedules, leave policies, working conditions, and the like, are subject to periodic negotiation and modification. It should be noted, too, that several statutes require that negotiated policies be reduced to writing.

Examples of this type of provision are as follows:

*Example 1.* The salary schedule and policy statements, attached hereto in the form of Articles, are hereby made a part of this agreement and shall be negotiated in conformance with the dates listed in the next section and with the procedures outlined above.

*Example 2.* When the Committee has arrived at a consensus with regard to any matter, it shall from its agreement in the form of a written recommendation to be submitted to the Board and the governing body of the Association. Upon acceptance of the committee's recommendation by both, its recommendation shall be publicly announced and put into effect as official policy, and shall constitute a modification of the Articles of this Agreement.

The New Rochelle, New York, agreement, reproduced in Appendix C, serves as a good example of one type of document which includes in writing the agreed-upon policies.

## Costs of Mediation

Some agreements provide for a sharing of the costs of mediation among the parties as follows:

Any costs and expenses which may be incurred in securing and utilizing the services of any person or persons in a consultative or mediatory capacity will be shared equally by the Board and the Association.

## Use of Specified School Facilities

Some California agreements stipulate the facilities that may be used by the recognized association in the conduct of its affairs. Such facilities as the following are listed:

1. Use of school mail and bulletin boards for official organizational communications.
2. Opportunity to announce building membership meetings and matters under consideration at regularly scheduled faculty meetings.
3. Permission to use school facilities when not otherwise used for educational purposes for appropriate activities of the recognized association.
4. Reasonable access to teachers at their place of assignment when such access will not interfere with assigned duties of the teachers.
5. Listing in the school district's official directory of the addresses and telephone numbers of the association and its officers.

## Changing or Amending Agreements

In addition to negotiating the substantive sections of the agreement, several agreements contain provisions for amending the procedural sections thereof. This type of provision is very desirable since it recognizes that procedures that appear clear cut in writing frequently turn out to be difficult to follow in practice, thus requiring modification. Also, it is sometimes found desirable to strengthen the provisions of an agreement, changing it, for example, from Level II to Level III.

Examples of such provisions follow:

*Example 1.* Either party desiring changes in this agreement must notify the other party in writing at least thirty days prior to May 1 of any year; however, changes may be made at any time by mutual consent.

*Example 2.* This shall be a continuing agreement from year to year. If changes are to be made, thirty days' notification shall be given by the party proposing the changes, in which case the same procedures as outlined heretofore will be followed.

## *Renewal of Agreement*

While the majority of agreements do not contain provisions for renewal from year to year, many do. For example: "This agreement shall take effect July 1, 1965, and will remain in effect until June 30, 1966. It shall be renewed automatically for a period of one year unless changed as herein provided."

## *Signatures of the Parties*

Many agreements conclude with the signatures of association and board representatives. While such signatures do not alter the voluntary nature of an agreement, they are nonetheless looked upon as evidence of good faith on the part of the parties, and as such are to be encouraged.

For example:

IN WITNESS WHEREOF, the parties have hereunto set their hands and seals this _____ day of _____, 196____.

BOARD OF EDUCATION OF
THE CITY OF _____
BY _____
_____ EDUCATION ASSOCIATION
BY _____

## Sample Negotiation Agreement

In its *Guidelines for Professional Negotiation* the NEA has provided a sample Level III agreement.[3] Included in the agreement are many features which purport to illustrate best practice derived

---

[3] *Guidelines for Professional Negotiation, op. cit.*, pp. 43–47.

from agreements currently in effect throughout the country. While no individual existing agreement embodies all of the features of the sample, it does serve to illustrate a composite of desirable provisions. Following is the text of the sample agreement:

The Board of Education of ABC and XYZ Education Association do hereby agree that the welfare of the children of ABC is paramount in the operation of the schools and will be promoted by both parties. The parties do hereby agree as follows:

## I. RECOGNITION

The Board of Education of ABC, hereinafter referred to as the Board, recognizes that teaching is a profession. The Board recognizes the XYZ Education Association, hereinafter referred to as the Association, as the exclusive representative of all the certificated personnel employed, or to be employed, by the Board for the purpose of negotiation on matters of mutual concern.

The Association recognizes the Board as the elected representative of the people of ABC and as the employer of the certificated personnel of the ABC School District.

The purpose of this recognition is the mutual agreement that the parties will negotiate with regard to all matters of common concern and will use professional and educational channels for appeal in the event of impasse.

## II. PRINCIPLES

### A. Attaining Objectives

Attainment of objectives of the educational program of the district requires mutual understanding and cooperation between the Board and the professional teaching personnel. Free and open exchange of views is desirable and necessary, with all parties participating in deliberations leading to the determination of matters of mutual concern.

### B. Professional Teaching Personnel

Teaching is a profession requiring specialized qualifications, and the success of the educational program in the district depends upon the maximum utilization of the abilities of teachers who are satisfied with the conditions under which their services are rendered.

Teachers have the right to join, or not to join, any organization for their professional or economic improvement, and membership in any organization shall not be required as a condition of employment.

### C. Representation

The Board, the Board and superintendent, or their designated representatives shall meet with representatives of the Association to negotiate and to reach agreement on policies governing the recruitment of teachers, community support for the school program, budget preparation, curriculum, in-service training, class size, teacher turnover, personnel policies, salaries, working conditions, communications, disposition of funds received pursuant to the Federal Elementary and Secondary Education Act of 1965, and other mutually agreed upon matters which affect the quality of the educational program.

Individuals and minority organizations may present their views and recommendations to the Board at regularly scheduled meetings of the Board.

### III. PROCEDURES

### A. Directing Requests

Requests for meetings from the Association normally will be made directly to the superintendent or his representative. Requests from the superintendent or the Board or their representatives will be made to the president of the Association. A mutually convenient meeting date shall be set within 15 days of the date of the request.

### B. Meetings

Meetings composed of members of the Association Negotiation Committee, the Board, and the superintendent shall be called upon the written request of any one of the parties. Requests for meetings shall contain the reasons for the request. Teacher members of the Committee shall be released from school duties to attend meetings. Meetings shall be scheduled to interfere the least with school schedules. Official summary minutes shall be kept and clerical assistance provided.

### C. Assistance

The parties may call upon competent professional and lay representatives to consider matters under discussion and to make suggestions. Educational consultants may be used in the deliberations. Necessary clerical assistance shall be provided.

### D. Study Committees

The parties may appoint *ad hoc* study committees to research, study, and develop projects, programs, reports, and to make recommendations on matters under consideration. The committees shall report findings to the parties.

### E. Progress Reports

With the approval of the parties, periodic progress reports may be issued.

### F. Exchange of Information

The Board and superintendent agree to furnish the Association Negotiation Committee upon reasonable request, all available information concerning financial resources of the district. Such information will include the tentative line budget on or about December 1, as well as preliminary budgetary proposals, requirements, and allocations, and such other information as will assist the Association in developing intelligent, accurate, and constructive programs on behalf of the teachers, the students, and the educational program.

### IV. AGREEMENT

When agreement is reached, it shall be reduced to writing and when approved by the Association and the Board, signed by the parties, and become a part of the official minutes of the Board. The agreement shall constitute a modification of the Articles of this Agreement, and when necessary, provisions in the agreement shall be reflected in individual contracts. The agreement shall not discriminate against any member of the staff regardless of membership or nonmembership in the Association.

### V. MEDIATION AND APPEAL

### A. Board of Education

If agreement is not reached, and members of the Board have not participated directly in the deliberations, the Association representatives and the superintendent or his representative may present separate reports to the Board. The procedure outlined in Section III will then be followed to reach agreement, with the Board, or a majority of Board members, participating in the deliberations.

## B. Advisory Board

In case of disagreement about the meaning or application of this Agreement, or if an impasse is reached during negotiations, the matter will be submitted to an Advisory Board within 30 days after the request of either party to the other. The Board will name one adviser, and the Association will name another. A third member, who shall be the chairman, shall be named by the first two named members.

The Advisory Board shall report recommendations for settlement within 15 days. The recommendations shall be submitted to both parties and shall be made public.

## C. State Commissioner of Education

If the Advisory Board fails to make a recommendation acceptable to the parties within the specified time, either the Board or the Association may request the State Commissioner of Education to appoint an individual or committee to recommend a settlement. The person or committee shall have authority to confer separately or jointly with the superintendent, representatives of the Board and the Association, and to utilize any other source of information. Data or recommendations may be made public.

If the parties refuse to accept the proposed settlement, the Commissioner shall so notify the State Board of Education.

### VI. COSTS

Costs and expenses which may be incurred in securing and utilizing the services of any individual or Advisory Board shall be shared equally by the Board and the Association.

### VII. ARTICLES

The salary schedules and policy statements, attached hereto in the form of Articles, are made a part of this agreement, and shall be negotiated in conformance with the dates listed in the next section and with the procedures outlined above.

### VIII. DURATION

The provisions of each Article attached hereto shall be effective as of July 1, 196___, and shall continue in full force and effect until June 30, 196___.

Either party desiring changes in this Agreement shall notify the

other party in writing at least 30 days prior to April 1 of any year.
Changes may be made at any time by mutual consent.

ATTEST:                          BOARD OF EDUCATION OF
                                 THE ABC SCHOOL DISTRICT
                                 BY _____
                                 XYZ EDUCATION ASSOCIATION
                                 BY _____
                                 DATE _____

\*   \*   \*

Following is a list of the Articles attached to the Agreement:

Article I        — Salaries
Article II       — Teaching Conditions
Article III      — Teacher Assignments
Article IV       — Transfers
Article V        — Promotions
Article VI       — Summer School
Article VII      — Protection of Teachers
Article VIII     — Leave Pay
Article IX       — Leaves of Absence
Article X        — Improvement of Curriculum and
                   Instructional Services
Article XI       — General
Article XII      — Grievance Procedures

# Chapter 4. Methods of Securing Professional Negotiation Agreements

BOARDS OF EDUCATION, administrators, and teacher organizations are striving in a variety of ways, and with varying degrees of success, to develop satisfactory patterns of staff relationships. In many instances genuine cooperative effort is made, with all parties striving together to achieve suitable accommodations. In such situations a high degree of receptivity on the part of boards and administrators to the philosophy of professional negotiation is usually to be found. Such unity of purpose, however, is not universal, and there is frequently a great deal of resistance toward the adoption of written agreements.

While such negative attitudes are unfortunate, they are nonetheless understandable; boards of education and administrators are not likely to embrace eagerly a process which they perceive, rightly or wrongly, as threats to their traditionally exercised authority. Too often such perceptions are based not upon the facts, but upon unfounded rumor, faulty understanding, and apprehension, concerning the elements of professional negotiation.

Through officially adopted resolutions and policy statements, massive public relations efforts, written guidelines, special schools and seminars, direct consultative assistance, and legislative activity, state and national education associations are mounting ever-increasing campaigns of information and assistance to local affiliates in support of their efforts to secure adoption of written professional negotiation agreements.

Three levels of action are successfully being employed in achieving agreements: (1) cooperative work with school boards and administrators at the local level by local associations; (2) state association activity in support of local efforts to secure recognition and the adoption of agreements; and (3) activity of the NEA in support of the efforts of its local and state affiliates to achieve negotiation agreements.

## Local Action

Several procedures may be described that have met with success in securing agreements at the local level.[1]

- In one large city a series of informal conversations was organized by the local association. The board of education, officers of the local teachers association, and administrative representatives met informally from time to time without a rigid agenda or specific problem to solve. They discussed their mutual goals and concerns, the need for a written procedure for conducting negotiations, and the types of specific items that could be included in an agreement. It was agreed in advance that the conversations would continue over a sufficiently long period of time to enable the groups to arrive at acceptable understandings. There was no deadline. After a series of these meetings, extending over several months, an agreement was finally approved and officially adopted by the board and the teachers association.

- In another school system, at the request of the local association, a joint study committee with teacher, board, and administrative representatives was appointed to work out proposals for a negotiation agreement. These proposals were then submitted to the respective larger groups for study; revisions were made, and a satisfactory agreement was eventually evolved.

- In still another system, officers of the local associations met first with the superintendent of schools to work out an agreement, the superintendent keeping the board of education informed of progress. When completed, the document was submitted officially to the board of education with recommendations made jointly by the association officers and superintendent.

- In still other systems, local associations draw up proposed agreements beforehand, presenting the completed agreements to the

---

1 Adapted in part from *Guidelines for Professional Negotiation,* Rev. ed., Washington, D. C.: Office of Professional Development and Welfare, National Education Association, 1965, pp. 9–10.

boards and superintendents for consideration and discussion. A series of meetings then ensue in which the parties negotiate on the agreement itself. Proposals and counterproposals are made both by the boards and local associations, with superintendents participating in the discussions, until satisfactory agreements are worked out.

- In some systems, signed authorization cards or petitions are presented to boards of education, with the signatures of a majority of the staff naming the local association as their representative and requesting that an agreement be reached. If the authorization cards are accepted in good faith, an agreement is worked out. In some cases, boards of education promulgate procedures which must be followed for an employee organization to be recognized as negotiating agent for the staff. Recognition in these cases is generally based upon strength of membership.

- In increasing numbers of systems, secret ballot elections are being held to determine which organization will represent the staff in negotiations with the board. These elections are sometimes preceded or accompanied by other elections to determine whether the staff wishes to be represented by a single organization, or by multiple organizations negotiating on behalf of their respective members. Almost without exception teachers elect to be represented by a single organization. The position of the National Education Association is that when organizations enjoy clear-cut majorities in their membership no elections are necessary, that recognition should be granted on the basis of verified membership lists. Six of the eleven pertinent state statutes call for secret ballot elections to determine negotiating representatives. It would be reasonable to assume that the future will bring more rather than fewer elections to determine negotiating representatives.

## Use of Persuasive Measures

Most of the procedures mentioned above depend for their success upon boards of education and administrators who display open-mindedness toward the question of collective negotiations, who are willing to listen to and discuss in good faith the proposals coming from their professional staffs. Even in those instances in which elections have been held (except where mandated by law), they have been held at the discretion of willing boards of education —admittedly, sometimes under considerable pressure, but always voluntarily.

The drive to secure adoption of written agreements is increasing steadily, as is indicated by the following excerpt from the NEA *Guidelines for Professional Negotiation,* in the section entitled "Achieving Professional Negotiation":[2]

An approach which utilizes good human relations skills and factual documentation in support of professional negotiation, will not guarantee success, but it should preclude arbitrary rejection of the association's proposal.

Obviously, the final development of an acceptable agreement may require a good deal of give and take. The association should not realistically expect that its original proposal will be accepted "as is." It can and should expect, however, that its request will be considered and negotiated in good faith.

If the board of education refuses to meet with association leaders to discuss the request, if a decision on the matter is unreasonably delayed, if the proposal is rejected out-of-hand, the local association may have to devise other technique to obtain negotiation rights. State and national advice and assistance should be sought. In most cases, outright refusal to consider the legitimate requests of teachers is symptomatic of other, more deeply seated problems affecting the efficient operation of the schools. Such cases might call for an investigation by a state or national professional rights and responsibilities commission. A source of information in this area is the publication, *Guidelines for Professional Sanctions.*[3]

Clearly, the sanctions *Guidelines* specifically suggest the possibility of imposing national sanctions upon those boards of education not willing to meet with their staffs to engage in discussions in good faith concerning the adoption of agreements.

## State Action

State education associations can be extremely powerful forces in the achievement of professional negotiation agreements. Regional differences and even differences within states, make necessary a

[2] *Guidelines for Professional Negotiation,* Rev. ed., Washington, D. C.: Office of Professional Development and Welfare, National Education Association, 1965, p. 11.

[3] *Guidelines for Professional Sanctions,* Washington, D. C.: National Commission on Professional Rights and Responsibilities, National Education Association, 1963, 19 pp.

wide variety of approaches. Most state associations, however, are supporting in various ways the efforts of their local affiliates for recognition and negotiating rights.

## Specific Methods of Support

Specific ways in which state associations are of direct service to local organizations in securing and carrying out agreements may be enumerated as follows:

State associations

1. seek passage of legislation mandating negotiation between boards of education and representatives of their professional staffs, such legislation designed specifically for educational employees;

2. adopt, through their representative assemblies, resolutions calling for the formalization of relationships between their local affiliates and school boards;

3. provide resource material in the form of guidelines and policy statements for the use of their local affiliates in securing agreements;

4. send specially trained field personnel into local districts to assist in securing the adoption of negotiation agreements;

5. develop in cooperation with other concerned agencies, such as school board and administrators' associations, guidelines for strengthening staff relationships at the local level. These often include models to be used or adapted by local affiliates and school boards in developing their own agreements;

6. maintain liaison with various lay organizations concerned with education in the state, and attempt through their publications and various mass communications media to develop a greater awareness and understanding of professional negotiation;

7. sponsor workshops and conferences for the information and training of local association leaders in the principles and techniques of professional negotiation;

8. provide staff members to assist local negotiation committees in developing proposals and, when necessary, in presenting them to boards of education;

9. provide staff members to assist in the satisfactory resolution of impasse situations that sometimes develop between local affiliates and boards of education.

Obviously, not all state associations are pursuing the achievement of professional negotiation agreements with equal enthusiasm. In fact, several, appear thus far to have taken no cognizance of the fact that there is such a process as professional negotiation. However, considering the fact that the NEA did not formally endorse the concept of professional negotiation until 1962, when the official resolution on the subject was adopted by NEA's Representative Assembly, progress since then has been remarkable.

As pointed out in Chapter 1, there are presently several officially adopted, written agreements in existence throughout the country, and one with the Federal Government. It is significant that the great majority of these agreements are to be found in only seven of the states: Connecticut, Ohio, Oregon, California, Washington, Michigan, and New Jersey. Equally significant is the fact that in six of these states—Connecticut, Oregon, California, Michigan, Washington, and New Jersey—the state associations have in 1965 supported state legislation *mandating* negotiation between teachers and school boards. It should be noted that the agreements mentioned above were all adopted voluntarily, before legislation was passed.

The passage of state legislation establishing formal negotiating procedures between school boards and their professional staffs is probably the most significant breakthrough yet to occur in this relatively new field. Laws were introduced in the legislatures of more than a dozen states in 1965, and in eight states they were passed (one was vetoed). In the future there doubtless will be a substantial increase of activity in the legislative area, for this avenue is most promising for the development and the adoption of agreements at the local level.

## Resolutions and Guidelines

Short of the actual passage of legislation, the following actions appear to be characteristic of state education associations in the states that lead in the number of local agreements officially adopted, according to a recent study conducted jointly by the National Association of Secretaries of State Teachers Associations and the Office of Professional Development and Welfare, NEA:[4]

[4] Study as yet unreleased.

1. Passage of resolutions by delegate assemblies evidencing an interest by the parent organization in the adoption of agreements. Twenty-three of the 50 responding state associations have adopted resolutions on the subject of professional negotiation.[5] Staff assistance is frequently provided to local associations in those states which have adopted resolutions.

2. Publication of guidelines by 18 state associations for the use of their local affiliates in establishing negotiation procedures.[6] In some cases, the guidelines consist of little more than generalized principles underscoring the importance of establishing good communication. In other cases, the guidelines are concrete and specific, outlining step-by-step procedures to be employed in securing recognition, developing the agreement, and carrying out negotiations. As pointed out previously, workshops and conferences as well as direct staff assistance are often also provided.

3. Development of joint recommendations or guidelines in cooperation with state school board and/or administrator organizations. Nine states thus far have published such guidelines and three states are in the process of developing them at the present time.[7] As might be expected, these guidelines differ considerably in their approaches to staff relationships and in the procedures for consideration and adoption in local districts. All, however, are characterized by a common purpose: to bring teachers, school boards, and administrators closer together in seeking solutions to common problems.

One of the most comprehensive of these documents is to be found in Connecticut. Developed by representatives of the education, school boards, and superintendents' associations, and revised several times since its first publication in 1952, it is called *Report of Committee on Working Relations Between Boards of Education*

---

5 Colorado, Connecticut, Delaware, Idaho, Illinois, Indiana, Iowa, Kansas, Kentucky, Maryland, Massachusetts, Michigan, Minnesota, Missouri, New Hampshire, New York, New Jersey, New Mexico, North Carolina, Ohio, Pennsylvania, Utah, and Wisconsin.

6 Connecticut, Delaware, Florida, Illinois, Iowa, Kansas, Massachusetts, Michigan, Minnesota, Missouri, New Jersey, New Mexico, New York, Ohio, Oregon, Pennsylvania, Utah, and Washington.

7 Connecticut, Kansas, Massachusetts, Minnesota, Missouri, New Jersey, New York, Utah, and Vermont. States in the process of developing guidelines at the time of this writing are Delaware, Nebraska, and Virginia.

*and Teachers Organizations*. The Connecticut document has been officially adopted by the state board of education in addition to being approved in principle by the executive boards of the state education, school boards, and superintendents' associations. Sixty-eight Connecticut districts have adopted the procedures outlined in the publication, which includes specific provisions for resolving disagreements that may arise in negotiations. Interestingly, the publication also contains recommendations concerning the conduct of secret ballot elections for the purpose of determining the negotiating organization, such elections being open to all members of the professional staff. As a result, Connecticut has been one of the few states in which staff representation elections have included all staff members rather than just classroom teachers.[8] The 1965 legislation will likely supersede provisions of the guidelines, but they are reproduced here as an example of the fine cooperative action that can be achieved among various interested groups in a state.

### WORKING RELATIONS BETWEEN BOARDS OF EDUCATION AND TEACHERS ORGANIZATIONS[9]

#### PREFACE

On November 7, 1962, the State Board of Education voted its approval of this revision of the bulletin on working relations between boards of education and teachers organizations. The revisions, recommended by a representative committee, should make the bulletin an even more useful guide for local boards and teachers groups. They are based on sound judgment drawn from experience with the original bulletin and reflect recent developments in the area of working relations in this and other states. It should prove useful for boards of education and teachers organizations not only in Connecticut but in other states.

---

[8] Laws passed in Connecticut, Oregon, and Washington in 1965 call for elections to be held among all professional staff members below the rank of superintendent.

[9] *Report of Committee on Working Relations Between Boards of Education and Teachers Organizations,* Bulletin 85, Hartford: Connecticut State Board of Education, 1962 revision.

Local boards should note that this bulletin is offered as a guide to assist them in the development of good working relations with their professional staff. They should feel free to make whatever adaptations are desirable to "promote understanding, confidence and agreement" between boards of education and teachers. This is the purpose of the report.

*William J. Sanders,*
Commissioner of Education and
Secretary, State Board of Education

### INTRODUCTION

This revision of the bulletin on "Working Relations" appears more than a decade after the declaratory judgment of the Connecticut Supreme Court of Errors in 1951 that teachers may organize but may not engage in strike.[10] Subsequent to this decision, and on the suggestion of the executive committee of the Connecticut Association of Boards of Education, the then Commissioner of Education, Finis E. Engleman, named a committee to study working relations of boards of education and teachers organizations. Membership of the committee changed from time to time but always included members of the Connecticut Education Association, the Connecticut State Federation of Teachers, the Connecticut Association of Public School Superintendents, and members of the State Department of Education.

The Committee issued a preliminary report on September, 1952. After consideration by the groups represented on the Committee, the preliminary report was revised several times until it was in such form that it was endorsed in principle by the Connecticut Association of Boards of Education, the Connecticut Association of Public School Superintendents and the Connecticut Education Association. On March 21, 1957, William J. Sanders, Commissioner of Education, submitted the report to the State Board of Education. The report was approved by the State Board on April 3, 1957. Later, it was printed and distributed to boards of education, teachers and other Connecticut groups and citizens.

This report received wide recognition and many boards of education adopted policies based on its recommendations. Experience with the recommended practices and policies, particularly those in Part

---

[10] *Norwalk Teachers' Association* v. *Board of Education of the City of Norwalk,* 138 Conn. 269.

Three, has shown the need for still further revision. In May 1961, Commissioner Sanders, on the suggestion of the Board of Directors of the Connecticut Education Association, appointed a committee to study current problems in this area and to suggest revisions of the 1957 bulletin. The following report is a result of that study.

Teachers organizations have gained greater recognition of their role in developing good working relations between teachers and boards of education. The term "Teachers Organizations" is used to refer to local associations or federations of teachers, i.e., board of education employees who hold certificates issued by the State Board of Education. The 1961 General Assembly incorporated the teachers' right to join professional organizations in the general statutes. Section 10-153a now reads:

"Members of the teaching profession shall have the right to join or refuse to join any organization for professional or economic improvement without prejudice."

This report is based on belief in the importance of teachers groups in helping to formulate sound principles and procedures for effective working relations. These "working relations" primarily include such matters as personnel policies, salaries and conditions of employment. The policies and practices described herein are not to be taken as a substitute for proper administrative procedures for the operation of the school system. The board must operate the schools through its superintendent and administrative staff. Nor are these policies and practices intended to deprive an individual teacher of the right of selecting his own representation before the school administration or the board of education on matters relating to that teacher alone. Further, these recommendations are offered as one means, but certainly not the only means, for boards of education and teachers to establish and maintain good working relations.

PART ONE

*Policy Statements on Working Relations Recommended to Boards of Education, Superintendents of Schools and Teachers*

    I. In their consideration of problems of working relations, the board of education, the superintendent of schools and the teachers should keep paramount the interests of the students.

   II. The superintendent of schools, with responsibilities to the board and the teachers, should be expected to advise both groups in accordance with his best professional judgment, and should be actively involved in all proceedings between the two groups.

  III. The board of education and the teachers should establish and follow procedures which will promote understanding, confidence and agreement.

IV. The board of education and the teachers have a responsibility to confer about problems of working relations.

V. Teachers should participate in discussions with the board through a committee of the organization chosen by the professional staff for purposes of representation.

VI. The board of education and the teachers should cooperate in identifying and studying problems which may affect working relations before either group takes an official position.

VII. The board of education and the teachers should work together in good faith to reach agreement in the solution of these problems.

VIII. The board of education should have due regard for the professional status of the teachers.

IX. The board of education must recognize its obligation to fulfill its statutory duties, including its responsibility for employing teachers and determining teachers' salaries.

X. The teachers should recognize that the board of education has statutory powers, duties and obligations which it may not surrender.

PART TWO

*Recommended Procedures for Good Working Relations Between Boards of Education and Teachers*

If a board of education and the teachers are to work together harmoniously, procedures should be established for orderly, free and thorough discussion of working relations. These procedures should be flexible enough to meet the many different situations which may arise. The following procedures are suggested as one means of seeking agreement between the teachers and the board of education on such matters as salaries and other personnel policies.

I. Selection of Representatives

A. The board of education as a whole or a committee to represent the board should work with teachers representatives in the consideration of working relations.

B. The committee representing the teachers should be selected through their organization or organizations.

1. Where there is only one teachers' organization, the board of education should negotiate with representatives of that group.

2. Where there is more than one teachers' organization, the

board of education should negotiate with representatives of the group which it determines constitutes a majority of the professional staff (except as provided in 3 or 4).

3. If the organizations reach an agreement on the composition of the committee to represent the teachers, the board should recognize the committee for that purpose.

4. Upon written request by at least twenty percent of the professional staff, the board of education should arrange for a referendum to determine which organization should represent the teachers in negotiations with the board.

   The referendum should be under the supervision of the board. Rules for the conduct of the referendum should be determined in consultation with teachers' representatives. Voting should be by secret ballot, and should be open to all members of the professional staff. The organization receiving a majority of the votes cast should be recognized as the group to represent the teachers in negotiations with the board.

   The referendum result should be accepted until in any subsequent year a referendum is requested and conducted in accordance with the procedures described above, or until the teachers agree upon a committee to represent them as provided in PART TWO, Section I (B-3) above.

C. Prior to reaching a final decision on matters under negotiation the board should provide opportunity for any teacher, group of teachers, or other teachers' organizations to be heard.

II. The Superintendent's Role

   The superintendent should be present at all meetings and participate in all negotiations between the teachers and the board.

   Out of his knowledge of his own school system and practices elsewhere, the superintendent should be expected to provide information and counsel to both the board and the teachers.

III. Meetings and Procedural Policies

A. The initial meeting of the board with the teachers representatives should be arranged through the superintendent early in the school year.

B. The board and the teachers representatives should together review and discuss pertinent information prior to taking a final position.

C. All members of the board and all of the teachers should be kept informed of the progress of the discussions.

D. There should be agreement on policies regarding press relations and public information.
E. On occasion it may be desirable to invite observers or consultants to attend the meetings. Such invitations should be extended only with agreement of both the board and the teachers' representatives.

IV. The Reaching of Agreements
A. When the board and the teachers' representatives have reached a proposed agreement, it should be prepared as a written recommendation for both groups.
B. If the board and the teachers' representatives are unable to agree, they should seek further instruction from their respective groups. All reasonable means, including expert guidance, should be employed in an effort to reach agreement.
C. When an agreement has been approved by both groups, it should be adopted by a formal board vote as official policy.

V. The Establishment of Teachers' Salary Schedules
A. The establishment of the teachers' salary schedule is an integral part of the budget procedure of the board of education. If the board is to submit valid estimates to the town fiscal authorities, it must base these upon a firm salary schedule which it has adopted. Consequently, the board of education and the teachers should seek to reach agreement on the salary schedule prior to the time when the board of education is required to submit its budget estimates. When such agreement has been reached, the board of education should take official action to adopt the schedule and should issue binding contracts which are based on the schedule and are not contingent upon subsequent action by other agencies.
B. In the event such agreement has not been reached, the board of education must, nevertheless, adopt a schedule in order to issue contracts on such terms as it believes necessary.

PART THREE

*Procedures in Cases of Persistent Disagreement*

I. Final Local Effort.
A. After every effort has been made to resolve the dispute at the local level and the suggested procedures have not produced an agreement, the two groups should secure a review by an outside person or agency to analyze the points at issue and

the position of each party, and to recommend a basis for settlement.

    1. The outside person or agency might be a college or university faculty member who is an expert in this field, a retired superintendent of schools, a representative of a state educational organization or any person with appropriate qualifications.

    2. A review committee might be established by each group naming one member of the committee and these two naming the third member.

II. Referral to the Secretary.

  A. If either group concludes that an appeal to the Secretary of the State Board of Education (hereinafter referred to as "the Secretary") is warranted, the board or the teachers, preferably through their state organization, should inform the Secretary of the dispute and request him to take action.

    The requesting group should submit documentary evidence to support the contention that the educational interests of the state are in jeopardy.

  B. Some Criteria for Referral.

    1. Before referring their disagreement to the Secretary, the board and the teachers should consider carefully whether such an appeal is justified. The criteria to be applied might include:

      a. Are the points in dispute sufficiently serious?

      b. Are the positions of the groups widely divergent?

      c. Does the recent record of teacher-board relations reveal unreasonable action on either side?

      d. Is there evidence that the disagreement has resulted in significant deterioration of morale?

III. Action by the Secretary.

  A. The Secretary will determine whether the educational interests of the state are in jeopardy.

    1. If he finds that these educational interests are not in jeopardy, he will so notify the parties involved and inform them of the reasons for his decision.

    2. If he finds that these educational interests are in jeopardy, he will so notify the parties involved and impress upon them the necessity to cooperate with him in seeking an agreement.

  B. The Secretary will appoint a representative or a committee to meet with the board, the superintendent of schools, the teachers representatives and, if it seems desirable, any other official, and to take any other measures which may help to bring about an agreement.

C. If an agreement cannot be reached in a reasonable time, the representative or the committee will notify the Secretary who may call together the board members, the superintendent of schools and the teachers representatives or follow other procedures which seem most likely to achieve an agreement.

D. If agreement is not achieved, the Secretary will so report to the State Board of Education and will give public notice of his findings. The Secretary will take such other steps as are necessary to protect the educational interests of the state.

Cooperatively developed guidelines, if put to use in various states will be of extreme benefit to all organizations concerned with maintaining stable staff relationships in the schools. Such action holds great promise for spreading the adoption of negotiation agreements on a voluntary basis. Concurrent with increased drives for the passage of legislation on the subject it is to be expected that the years immediately ahead will witness a significant movement by state associations to develop guidelines in cooperation with their school board and administrator association counterparts. The philosophy inherent in such cooperative endeavors is summarized well in the guidelines published cooperatively by the Kansas Association of School Boards and Kansas State Teachers Association. Although Kansas is one of the more politically conservative of the nation's states, it was early seen by officials of these two organizations that some reconciliation had to be made between the traditional authority of boards of education and the legitimate demands of teachers for increased participation in making educational decisions. Hence the development of cooperative guidelines was begun, culminating in their official publication in 1965. While they do not, understandably, go as far as those in Connecticut, they do make provision for third party mediation of disputes, and they have been responsible for the adoption of at least six written agreements, four of them Level III. They are reproduced here to illustrate the sort of guidelines that are increasingly being adopted in states throughout the nation.

GUIDELINES FOR STRENGTHENING TEACHER-ADMINISTRATOR-
BOARD RELATIONSHIPS IN KANSAS[11]

INTRODUCTION

*Need.* When the 1962 strike of the New York City teachers hit the
front pages of the nation's newspapers, the problem seemed far away
to many Kansans. When relationships between teachers, superintendents and school boards were disrupted at Gary, Indiana; East St.
Louis, Illinois; Cleveland, Ohio; Conway, Arkansas; Jefferson County, Idaho;
Waterbury, Connecticut; and Carter County, Kentucky, the com-
placency of many Kansans began to disappear. When the entire state
of Utah was in trouble, with every school in the state affected, people
began to ask themselves whether or not there was some basic defect in
relationships between the teachers and the school systems of our country. The recent unrest in Louisville, Kentucky, and in Oklahoma has
cleared away every doubt that something is wrong.

The great need is for teachers to sit down with their superintendents
and when necessary with their school boards, to discuss the points of
misunderstanding. The difficulties need to be replaced by mutual respect and joint commitment to a common goal—the best possible
schooling for the children and youth of the district. Creating conditions under which such discussions can take place is the purpose of
these *Guidelines.*

*Advisory.* These *Guidelines* are advisory, not mandatory, in nature.
They represent the careful consideration of a selected group of board
members, superintendents, and teachers who now submit them to all
Kansas board members, superintendents, and teachers for consideration.

WE BELIEVE

*We believe*—that classroom teachers, administrators and school
boards must together seek pathways for mutual development of policies and practices.

*We believe*—that these groups have common interest and a common
goal.

*We believe*—that effective communication among classroom teachers, administrators and school boards is essential.

*We believe*—that the welfare of children is paramount in the operation of the schools.

---

[11] *Guidelines,* Topeka: Kansas Association of School Boards and Kansas
State Teachers Association, May 1965, p. 10.

### PRINCIPLES

1. *Build on Present Practices.* Effective teacher-administrator-board relationships should be developed by utilizing and improving any procedures of communication which in the current practice of a school system, are useful in developing school policy on matters of common concern.

2. *Service to Youth Paramount.* The local association which expects to improve its communication and develop confidence with administrators and school boards must seek professional goals such as teacher excellence and professional ethics, as well as good personnel practices.

3. *Contribution by Teachers.* Professionally prepared teachers are uniquely qualified to make important contributions to the formulation of recommendations for school policies which are related to the work of teachers.

4. *Involvement of Teachers.* The legal responsibility for the adoption of school policies belongs to the board exclusively. However, before arriving at a decision with respect to important policies which affect the work of teachers, the board should make sure that teachers have participated cooperatively in the preparation of the recommendation which it will have under consideration. In the event the board feels the recommendation to be unwise, it will engage in good faith discussions with representatives of the teachers before taking action on the recommendation.

5. *Policies in Writing.* A cooperatively developed school board policy handbook is fundamental to good board-staff relationships. Written policies should be revised regularly, should be made available to the school staff, and should be used consistently by the school board as the basis for its action.

6. *Role of Superintendent.* The role of the superintendent of schools is of utmost importance because he must function both as the chief administrator for the board and as head of the professional staff. With this dual role goes the responsibility for leadership. The superintendent's leadership should result in mutual respect between the board and the professional staff. It should result also in steps by which differences can be resolved.

7. *Scope.* Only matters of broad professional concern are within the scope of professional negotiation. Although the proper handling of personal grievances of teachers is of utmost importance to the maintenance of staff morale, such grievances are not within the scope of professional negotiation unless they have been evaluated by a respon-

sible committee of the teachers association and found to be of such broad significance that the association by official action decides to make common cause with the teacher in question.

### PROCEDURES

1. *Board Recognition.* The organization representing the majority of teachers in a school system should reach a written agreement with the school board which recognizes that this organization is the official agency for those teachers. This does not preclude the right of other groups or individuals to be heard by the school board.

2. *Responsibility of the Teachers Association.* The association designated as representing the majority of teachers must have a well informed, responsible membership. It is essential that there be competent research committees to compile evidence as the basis for whatever the association presents as the needs and desires of the professional staff. The association has a duty to educate its own membership with respect to those realities of school system operation with which their proposals are related. The local teachers' association should file a copy of its constitution and bylaws with the school board.

3. *Requests for Conferences.* When the official organization wishes to discuss a matter or make a proposal, it should make its request to the superintendent or his representative. Accompanying the request for a conference should be a written statement setting forth the nature of the concern of the professional staff. Such a request will result in discussions between the superintendent and representatives of the teachers association within a reasonable period of time. It is probable that in nearly all such conferences, there will be a meeting of the minds, resulting in a recommendation to the board by the superintendent with the full support of the teachers association.

In those rare cases in which there can be no meeting of the minds, the teachers association may choose to request the superintendent to arrange a conference with the board.

Requests for conferences may move in the opposite direction. Whenever the superintendent or the board desires to discuss a matter of importance with the teachers association, a request for a conference should be directed to the president of the local teachers association. Accompanying such a request should be a written statement setting forth the concern of the superintendent and/or the board. Such a request will result in a conference within a reasonable period of time, with a committee representing the local teachers association.

In school systems where the rapport is so good that written requests and statements are not desirable, such requests and statements may be made orally.

4. *Conferences.* Facts, opinions, proposals and counter proposals should be exchanged freely during conferences in an effort to reach mutual understanding. Participants in these conferences may wish to utilize the services of consultants.

5. *Policy.* When the participants reach an understanding, such understanding should become a matter for policy action by the board. The policy shall not discriminate against any member of the teaching staff regardless of membership or nonmembership in any teachers' organization.

6. *Persistent Disagreement.* When the school board and representatives of the association officially recognized by the board cannot come to a mutual understanding on matters of great importance, some impartial fact-finding body should be called in by both parties jointly to review the situation and to make recommendations publicly to the board, to the professional staff and to the citizens of the school district. After having selected the fact-finding body the school board and representatives of the association should prepare a statement of issues of fact, for the guidance of the fact-finding body. The welfare of children and youth of the school district should be regarded as paramount by all parties concerned. After reviewing the recommendations of the fact-finding body, the legal responsibility for making a final decision rests with the local school board.

### WORK TO CONTINUE

Committees of the Kansas Association of School Boards and the Kansas State Teachers Association will continue jointly to seek ways of strengthening teacher-administrator-board relationships. In this way it may be possible to improve the schools of Kansas by demonstrating that school boards and teachers should regard themselves and each other as public servants who are bound together by a common goal— that of providing the best possible schools for the children and youth of the district. There should be no differences between them excepting honest differences over how best to achieve their common goal.

### MORE INFORMATION AVAILABLE

Additional information may be secured free of charge by writing to:
Dr. Marion A. McGhehey, Executive Director
The Kansas Association of School Boards
825 Western Avenue
Topeka, Kansas 66606

or to
Wendell R. Godwin, Asst. Secretary for Lay Relations
Kansas State Teachers Association
715 West 10th Street
Topeka, Kansas 66612

## National Action

As far back as 1938 NEA publications were promoting the desirability of cooperative determination of school policies. In an early Educational Policies Commission report, referred to in Chapter 1, the following paragraph is found:

The formulation of school policy should be a cooperative process capitalizing upon the intellectual resources of the whole school staff. This participation in the development of educational policy should not be thought of as a favor granted by the administration but rather as a right and an obligation. Some plan should be provided through which the constructive thinking of all the workers in a school system may be utilized. After policies have been developed by the staff they should be submitted to the board of education for final review and approval. When approved, every member of the school system for whom it has implications becomes responsible for carrying into effect the adopted policy. The procedure promotes efficiency through individual understanding of policies and through the acceptance of joint responsibility for carrying them into effect. What is far more important, it provides a democratic process through which growth in service is promoted and the school service itself profits from the application of heightened morale and of group thinking to school problems. It makes the school in reality a unit of democracy in its task of preparing citizens for our democratic society.[12]

Other NEA publications through the years have consistently upheld the importance of joint development of school policies, and the democratic principle that those affected by these policies should have some voice in their formulation. Although hundreds of NEA affiliates had for years been negotiating informally with their em-

---

12 *The Structure and Administration of Education in American Democracy,* Washington D. C.: Educational Policies Commission, National Education Association and the American Association of School Administrators, 1938, pp. 67–68.

ploying boards of education, without benefit of written agreements, the adoption in 1961 of an NEA resolution entitled *Teacher-Board of Education Relationships* formally set the stage for the efforts of teachers everywhere to achieve recognition as participants in every phase of the educational decision-making process. The words "professional negotiation" first appeared in an official NEA resolution at the 1962 convention, when the 1961 resolution was amplified and strengthened.

## Specific Methods of Support

The national association, through its publications, conferences, workshops, and varied types of consultative assistance, has played an important supportive role in efforts to secure written agreements in school districts throughout the nation. Significant action has taken place on many fronts.

1. National and regional NEA-sponsored salary schools have since 1962 stressed the importance of professional negotiation.

2. *Guidelines for Professional Negotiation* was published in 1963 and went through seven printings with a total distribution of 125,-000. Thousands of copies have been distributed to local association leaders, state associations, school board and administrators' organizations, professors of educational administration, and interested citizens. A revised version of *Guidelines* was published in the summer of 1965. In addition, a Research Division publication entitled *Professional Negotiation with School Boards: A Legal Analysis and Review,* was published in 1962 and revised in 1965. Numerous pamphlets and smaller brochures are also made available.

3. In the fall of 1964 the NEA sponsored a national conference on the principles and techniques of professional negotiation for state association staff members.

4. NEA staff members have appeared at local, regional, and state sponsored workshops and conferences dealing with professional negotiation, and have made frequent presentations on the subject at regional and state school board and administrators' conferences.

5. NEA staff members regularly consult with local, regional, and

state associations in the development of negotiation agreements and guidelines appropriate to existing conditions.

6. Legal advice, consultation, and assistance in drawing up agreements and proposed legislation are continually being provided to local and state affiliates upon request.

7. The NEA maintains a clearing house for the collection, maintenance, and dissemination of negotiation agreements that have been adopted in local school districts. Collections of sample agreements are also distributed upon request.

8. NEA assistance, in cooperation with state associations, is furnished to assist local affiliates in the conduct of representation elections.

9. The NEA maintains liaison with other national organizations concerned with education, and attempts through various communications media to develop an understanding of the principles and procedures of professional negotiation.

It seems clear that vastly increased emphasis is being placed upon the strengthening of local associations and the improvement of staff relationships at the local level. National and state funds and assistance are being provided as never before in the direct support of local efforts to achieve professional negotiation rights. These efforts will continue; indeed, they will increase in the months and years ahead. It is evident that no one association—local, state, or national—working alone can accomplish what all three levels are able to accomplish working in concert. Team approaches will increasingly be utilized in securing for teachers a full partnership role in the development of educational policies.

# Chapter 5. The Role of the Superintendent in Professional Negotiation

FEW ASPECTS of professional negotiation have been as widely discussed and debated as the role of the superintendent of schools in the process. From the mass of written material on this subject one fact is emerging clearly: some new form of accommodation must be found to balance the superintendent's traditional authority with the increasing insistence of teachers for a share in educational decision-making, through organizations of their own choosing. For many superintendents this will not be a difficult transition. Indeed, in many school districts, negotiations between staff organizations and school boards have been taking place for years, with the superintendent assuming the same role that is currently being advocated by NEA and its state and local affiliates. However, for many other superintendents—those who traditionally have served as sole agents between their staffs and school boards—the vigorous thrust of staff organizations for recognition is a distinct threat to the exercise of unilateral authority.

This chapter will deal with the superintendent's role in professional negotiation (a) as set forth in the resolutions and publications of NEA and other national organizations; and (b) as treated in state association guidelines, state legislation, and locally adopted professional negotiation agreements. Suggestions for the future development of the superintendent's role will also be discussed.

## Positions of National Organizations

*The National Education Association*

The superintendent of schools was not mentioned in the resolution adopted by the NEA Representative Assembly in 1962 and 1963. Not until the 1964 resolution (at Seattle) was he mentioned by name. The Association has maintained, however, that the expression "using professional channels," used in the 1962 resolution, was meant to imply the active participation of the superintendent in the negotiating process. The 1962 and 1963 resolutions contained the following paragraph:

> The National Education Association insists on the right of professional associations, through democratically selected representatives using professional channels, to participate with boards of education in the determination of policies of common concern, including salary and other conditions of professional service.[1]

Doubtless recognizing the fact that many factions in the profession were concerned about this issue, the Representative Assembly in 1964 amended the resolution to include specific reference to the superintendent's role. While retaining the above mentioned paragraph, the following was added:

> Recognizing the legal authority of the board of education, the administrative function of the superintendent, and the professional competences of teachers, matters of mutual concern should be viewed as a joint responsibility. The cooperative development of policies is a professional approach which recognizes that the superintendent has a major responsibility to both the teaching staff and school board.[2]

The 1965 revision of NEA's *Guidelines for Professional Negotiation* made little mention of the suggested roles and responsibilities of the various parties to professional negotiation. This was so primarily because the subject was dealt with exhaustively in the original, 1963 publication. The 1963 edition emphasized

---

[1] *NEA Handbook, 1963–64,* Washington, D. C.: National Education Association, 1963, p. 63.

[2] *NEA Handbook, 1964–65,* Washington, D. C.: National Education Association, 1964, p. 66.

strongly the concept of the superintendent's dual role as executive officer of the board of education and member of the school staff. Following are excerpts from this official NEA publication:

[The superintendent's] role in professional negotiation is a dual one. He is the executive officer of the board, responsible for administering adopted policy. At the same time, he has a responsibility as a member and leader of the professional staff. . . .

In the negotiating process, the superintendent's role is a central one. Since he is probably in possession of more facts about school revenue and needs than anyone else, it is imperative that he be deeply and actively involved. In the initial data-gathering stages, the board may delegate to the superintendent the responsibility of working with the association committee. But in the middle and latter stages of negotiation the association committee should work out a solution with the board and superintendent with ample opportunity for give and take aimed at reaching a cooperative determination.

The superintendent has the responsibility in the negotiating process to provide information to both teachers and the board, to help clarify issues, and otherwise stimulate both groups to put forth their best efforts to achieve agreements which are in the best interests of the total school program. These are complex responsibilities, requiring great skill and educational statesmanship. The effective superintendent will strive to fulfill them in the best manner possible.[3]

## The Department of Classroom Teachers

Reference to the dual role of the superintendent of schools is made in the 1965 resolution on professional negotiation by the Delegate Assembly of the Department of Classroom Teachers, as follows:

. . .

The Department therefore urges local associations to strive for adoption of agreements with local boards of education that would (a) provide an orderly method of involving local classroom teacher representatives, administrators, and school board members in the cooperative development of mutually satisfactory policies, (b) *define the obligations of the superintendent in his dual role as member of the staff and*

---

[3] *Guidelines for Professional Negotiation,* Washington, D. C.: Office of Professional Development and Welfare, National Education Association, 1963, p. 14.

*adviser to the school board,* and (c) authorize a means of appeal through designated educational channels when agreement cannot be reached. . . .[4]

Two references are made to the role of the superintendent in the DCT publication, *Classroom Teachers Speak on Professional Negotiations.*[5] In the section entitled, "Basic Principles Which Should Be Written into Professional Negotiations Agreements" the following principle is found:

The superintendent has a dual role in professional negotiations. He is both a member of the profession and the executive agent of the board. His role and responsibility to each must be clearly identified.

Another section of the publication, "Reflections," contains this statement: "The new role of the superintendent is one of partner-ship, not boss."

It seems clear, then, that policy statement of the NEA and DCT are in agreement concerning the place of the superintendent in negotiations. Both organizations see him as playing a dual role in the process, as a facilitating and harmonizing agent rather than as a representative of the school board.

## The American Association of School Administrators

Two resolutions adopted by the American Association of School Administrators at its 1965 convention give evidence of increasing concern over the superintendent's role in professional negotiation. The resolution on "Staff Relations" contains this statement:

We believe that teachers, school boards, and administrators are all committed to the advancement of public education and that the goals and interests of these groups are highly inter-related. We believe strongly that the development of school policies and programs and the solution of school problems can best be accomplished by these groups working in harmony and with respect for the roles of each. We believe that effective policy development involves important contributions by each group.

[4] *The Platform and Resolutions, 1964–65,* Washington, D. C.: Department of Classroom Teachers, National Education Association, 1965.

[5] *Classroom Teachers Speak on Professional Negotiations,* Washington, D. C.: Department of Classroom Teachers, National Education Association, 1963, 16 pp.

... We believe that shared responsibility for policy development is a professional concept requiring a unique professional approach. We maintain that the superintendent of schools has a unique responsibility to provide leadership in these matters.[6]

In the AASA resolution on "The Role of the Superintendent" the following guidelines are provided:

The superintendent of schools is the chief executive officer of the board of education. He is the professional leader of the board, the leader of the staff, and the focal point of educational responsibility within the district. The superintendent occupies a unique position. He assists the board of education, the staff (singly and in groups), and the citizens of the community as they work through educational problems. He is the chief professional advisor to the board in policy development. He is responsible for developing appropriate educational opportunities to meet the needs of all children. He is a professional educator and a professional school administrator. That which strengthens his effectiveness in any of these roles automatically strengthens the schools.[7]

In addition, the resolution voices a warning against incursions into the centrality of his role:

We strongly urge that boards of education and professional groups insist upon the recognition of the role and responsibility of the superintendent. The association pledges to resist any effort to displace the superintendent and his authority in matters affecting the interest and welfare of school personnel.

In 1963 the American Association of School Administrators published a position document[8] which contained several statements bearing directly on the matter of professional negotiation. Because of its importance to a full understanding of the many ramifications of staff relationships, the document is reproduced in full in Appendix H. The following excerpt would appear to support the dual role concept of the superintendent of schools:

---

[6] *Resolutions, Platform, Constitution, Bylaws, Ethics,* Washington, D. C.: American Association of School Administrators, National Education Association, 1965, p. 12.

[7] *Ibid.,* p. 11.

[8] *Roles, Responsibilities Relationships of the School Board, Superintendent, and Staff,* Washington, D. C.: American Association of School Administrators, National Education Association, 1963, 15 pp.

Today, the superintendent of schools occupies a complex and demanding position. He is often torn between diverse alternatives, obligations, and responsibilities. Yet it seems clear that the professional superintendent has one allegiance that transcends all other commitments. Although he is a devoted member of his professional group and deeply concerned with the success of his associates, his allegiance to the learner supersedes all other loyalties. This commitment need not and should not place him in conflict with his colleagues. Its very nature makes him seek assiduously and vigorously to maintain environmental circumstances which his associates desire, need, and must have to work to best advantage. One of the major concerns of the superintendent always has been and always should be to help provide those conditions which enable teachers and all other staff members to achieve their professional goals.[9]

The policy statement also discusses the relationship of the superintendent to the board of education:

Neither does this freedom of operation by the superintendent suggest disloyalty to the school board. It is his professional judgment, wisdom, and leadership that makes him valuable to the board. School trustees should never seek nor achieve subservience from the school administrator. In fact, when controversy rages most violently, his role is one of independent, judicious statesmanship governed largely by his depth of professional insights and his primary commitment to improved educational service to pupils and to basic human values.[10]

---

[9] *Ibid.*, p. 8–9. Interestingly, the above paragraph appears to have been adapted from the following, more strongly worded excerpt from an editorial by Finis Engleman, then Executive Secretary of AASA, appearing in the December 1962 issue of *The School Administrator,* a periodical of the association: "This ideal of service [allegiance to the learner] does not place the superintendent in conflict with his colleagues; instead, it puts him on the same team in a very special role. His very concern for pupil development makes him a determined champion of those environmental situations which his associates desire, such as respectable and pleasant working conditions, satisfactory work loads, instructional materials and aids, living and saving salaries, security, and specialist assistance. If he ever loses his interest in the welfare of his colleagues, if he avoids taking up the cudgel for improved teacher welfare, including adequate salaries, if he is deflected from a statesmanlike and independent role in decision-making by any force from within the profession or without, his leadership role will decline to a low level."

[10] *Ibid.*, p. 9.

These statements of the AASA would seem to place the superintendent of schools squarely in the middle with respect to boards of education and their professional staffs: he owes primary allegiance to neither side, but operates in a manner calculated to bring both groups together in as harmonious a manner as possible. In this respect official AASA policy is quite similar to the policies of NEA and the Department of Classroom Teachers.

## The National School Boards Association

The NSBA has traditionally been opposed to "sanctions, boycotts, strikes, or mandated mediation against school districts," and has been passing resolutions against these actions since 1962. In its resolution concerning "Teacher-Superintendent-Board Relations" the NSBA has put forth its policy concerning the role of the superintendent of schools in this manner:

. . . NSBA urges each local board to review its policies, procedures, and activities and to give careful consideration to incorporating the following items if they are not included:

(a) Procedures which will actively involve school boards, administrative staff, and teachers in discussing total budget needs with particular emphasis on the determination of salaries and the handling of grievances.

(b) Written policies concerning the above procedures that are widely disseminated, and presented in such a way that they are clearly understood by all parties concerned—the teachers, administrative staff, the board of education, and the general public.

(c) Policies whereby the superintendent, as administrative officer of the board, can function as a channel and interpreter of teacher concerns to the board and the board responsibilities and concerns to the teacher. Direct hearings with the board should be arranged through the superintendent if this proves inadequate. . . .[11]

It may be observed that NSBA policy on the matter is not entirely incompatible with those of other national organizations. The superintendent's envisioned function as "channel and interpreter" might not be all that is desired by the NEA and its affiliates, yet such a function does place the superintendent in a position of

---

[11] National School Boards Association, "Resolution on Teacher-Superintendent-Board Relations," adopted April, 1963.

working with and between both parties. Many professional negotiation agreements tend to cast the superintendent into a similar role. So long as the superintendent is free to exercise independent judgment with respect to school matters, serving as advisor to both groups, and so long as free access is maintained between representatives of the staff organization and the school board, then such a procedure can be made to work successfully. It must be conceded, however, that NSBA's concept of good staff relationships, carried out in practice, too often amounts to nothing more than occasional conferences between staff representatives and the superintendent of schools.

## State Legislation, State Guidelines, and Local Professional Negotiation Agreements

### Legislation

As pointed out earlier in this volume, statutes governing relationships between staff organizations and boards of education have been enacted in eleven states. In none of the statutes is the role of the superintendent of schools spelled out. However, the three "educators-only" statutes which provide for staff elections to determine the negotiating representative (Connecticut, Oregon, and Washington) specifically exclude the superintendent, and only the superintendent, from the definition of "certificated employee" for election purposes. The statutes, therefore, leave great latitude to individual school systems for developing procedures and delineating the superintendent's role in a manner best suited to unique local circumstances.

### State Guidelines

The Connecticut State Board of Education in cooperation with the Connecticut Education Association, Association of Boards of Education, and Association of Public School Superintendents, has published guidelines governing working relations between boards of education and teachers organizations.[12] These guidelines refer to the role played by the superintendent of schools as follows:

[12] *Report of Committee on Working Relations Between Boards of Education and Teachers Organizations,* Bulletin 85, Hartford: Connecticut State Board of Education, 1962 revision.

The superintendent of schools, with responsibilities to the board and the teachers, should be expected to advise both groups in accordance with his best professional judgment, and should be actively involved in all proceedings between the two groups.

In a section entitled, "The Superintendent's Role" the Connecticut guidelines say this:

The superintendent should be present at all meetings and participate in all negotiations between the teachers and the board. Out of his knowledge of his own school system and practices elsewhere, the superintendent should be expected to provide information and counsel to both the board and the teachers.

The Connecticut guidelines also suggest that the initial meeting of the school year between the board and teachers representatives be arranged through the superintendent. Clearly, the Connecticut guidelines conform both to the spirit and letter of suggestions concerning the superintendent's role as made by the National Education Association. The guidelines are reproduced in Chapter 4.

*Guidelines for Strengthening Teacher-Administrator-Board Relationships in Kansas* were approved in May 1965 by the Kansas State Teachers Association and the Kansas Association of School Boards.[13] They differ in form and content from the Connecticut guidelines. In the section entitled, "Principles," the following paragraph delineates the role of the superintendent of schools:

The role of the superintendent of schools is of utmost importance because he must function as the chief administrator for the board as head of the professional staff. With this dual role goes the responsibility for leadership. The superintendent's leadership should result in mutual respect between the board and the professional staff. It should result also in steps by which differences can be resolved.

The procedures suggested in the Kansas guidelines call for initial conferences to take place between the official staff organization and the superintendent of schools:

---

[13] *Guidelines for Strengthening Teacher-Administrator-Board Relationships in Kansas.* Topeka: Kansas Association of School Boards and Kansas State Teachers Association, May 1965, 11 pp. See Chap. 4 for the Kansas *Guidelines* in full.

It is probable that in nearly all such conferences there will be a meeting of the minds, resulting in a recommendation to the board by the superintendent with the full support of the teachers association. In those rare cases in which there can be no meeting of the minds, the teachers association may choose to request the superintendent to arrange a conference with the board.

The Kansas guidelines also call for impartial fact-finding in those instances in which boards and associations are not able to resolve differences together. Such fact-finding bodies will "make recommendations publicly to the board, to the professional staff and to the citizens of the school district."

The state of New Jersey has also developed guidelines for the use of local boards of education and teachers organizations.[14] Included are sample individual grievance procedures, as well as those for the joint development of educational policy. In each of the two sample group negotiation agreements the superintendent of schools plays a key role. The first pattern calls for a Teacher-Board Relations Committee composed of three members designated by the local teachers organization; three members of the board of education, and the superintendent. Interestingly, the superintendent is designated as chairman of the Teacher-Board Relations Committee, with responsibility for calling meetings of the Committee. Despite the formal structure recommended in the sample agreement, it contains a statement saying that "the above procedures do not preclude the teacher representatives from carrying on conversations with and resolving problems through the superintendent of schools."

The second sample provides for initial meetings with the superintendent of schools in the hope that joint recommendations can be developed for submission to the board of education. Failing this, either party may request direct negotiations between the board and the teacher organization with the superintendent, if mutually agreeable, serving as chairman of the meetings. The sample agreement also includes this clause: "Throughout the period of negotiations with the board of education on any subject, teacher representatives or board members may meet and consult with the

---

14 *Developing Personnel Policies,* Trenton: New Jersey Education Association, New Jersey School Superintendents Association, State Federation of District Boards of Education of New Jersey, 1963.

superintendent in advisory discussions on the subject under consideration."

Although the second sample calls for initial discussions between the superintendent and teachers' organization, both samples cast the superintendent into the role of an intermediary, working with the teachers organization *and* the board in an effort to solve whatever problems may arise in negotiations.

Guidelines developed in Minnesota also delineate the role of the superintendent in the negotiation process.[15] In a section discussing the responsibilities of the various groups involved, the following is found:

*Superintendent of Schools.* The superintendent of schools should assume the responsibilities of the dual role he has as executive officer of the school board and as a member of the teaching profession:

1. To recognize that the achievement of educational goals requires a cooperative approach.

2. To support the efforts of local teachers associations to understand and achieve recognition of their appropriate role in the decision-making process relative to school district policies of professional concern.

3. To provide information to local teachers associations on all topics under consideration which are of legitimate professional concern.

4. To participate in discussions taking place between teacher representatives and the school board or its representatives.

5. To utilize effective human relations procedures.

In the "Procedures" section of the Minnesota guidelines, the following recommendations are made relative to the superintendent's participation in negotiations:

1. The superintendent shall be present at all meetings and participate in all discussions between the teachers and the school board.

2. Out of his knowledge of the school system, and in his role as a member of the teaching profession, the superintendent should be expected to provide information and counsel to both the school board and the teachers.

It may be seen that the Minnesota guidelines adhere quite closely to the Connecticut pattern in discussing the superintendent's role.

---

[15] *Guidelines for Working Relations Between School Boards and Professional Teachers Associations,* St. Paul: Minnesota Education Association and Minnesota School Boards Association, undated, 5 pp.

In this respect, they conform to the philosophy which delineates a dual role for the superintendent in the negotiation process.

*Local Agreements*

The superintendent of schools is mentioned by name in the vast majority of professional negotiation agreements on file at the NEA. His participation in the negotiation process may be classified in two basic patterns. The first pattern is one in which initial discussions are carried on between the teachers association and the superintendent or his representative. If agreement is reached in these discussions, joint recommendations are presented to the board, sometimes by the superintendent alone and sometimes by both the superintendent and the association. If agreement is not reached, negotiations are carried out directly between the board and the association. An example follows: "The policy negotiations will be carried out in two steps: the first will be preliminary negotiation with the administration. If the policy negotiation cannot be resolved in the first step, the second step will be taken: direct negotiation with the board of education."

The second most prevalent pattern is one in which the superintendent serves along with others on a joint negotiation committee composed of board, administrators, and teachers' representatives. This pattern is closer to the ideal than the previous one in that all parties including the superintendent participate in negotiations from the outset. For example, "Meetings composed of the community teachers association professional policies committee, the board of education, and the superintendent shall be called upon the written request of any one of the parties involved." In most agreements the superintendent is designated as the "channel" through which requests to the board or from the board are made. Such a practice conforms to accepted administrative operation and is specifically what "through professional channels" in the NEA resolution is meant to indicate.

The above patterns or variations are to be found in virtually every agreement in existence at the present time. Some agreements go so far as to spell out the function of the superintendent in the three-way negotiating process, similar to the Connecticut guidelines. The following example is representative:

The superintendent of schools is both the executive officer of the board, responsible for administering adopted policy, and the primary professional adviser to the board. He also has a responsibility to the staff as a member and leader of that staff. The superintendent has the responsibility in the process of joint study of matters of mutual concern to provide information to teachers and the board, to help clarify issues and to stimulate both groups to put forth their best efforts. The superintendent will be expected to offer his professional recommendations to both the board and the professional association.

## Discussion and Recommendations

Simply stated, there can be but three basic patterns governing the participation of superintendents of schools in the negotiating process: (a) They may refrain from taking *any* part in negotiations, leaving the field entirely to representatives of the staff and board of education; (b) they may participate in negotiations as representatives of the board of education, negotiating with teacher representatives on behalf of the board; and (c) they may participate in negotiations as a third party, serving as a resource both to the teachers and the board.

The first alternative, that of complete nonparticipation, is clearly unacceptable and undesirable, and may be discarded at the outset. No effective superintendent would wish to sit on the sidelines while matters of school policy are being discussed, nor should boards of education and teachers organizations have to make do without the professional advice and counsel that the superintendent can provide.

The second alternative, that of the superintendent serving as agent of the board of education, would appear to be a simple solution to the problem. It certainly leaves no doubt concerning the superintendent's role; neither does it permit the superintendent to serve as professional advisor or resource person to the teachers organization. Once and for all, it removes the superintendent from any sort of colleague relationship with other members of the professional staff and places him alongside the board of education in any negotiation situation. Admittedly, this interpretation of role has a certain conventional appeal to many. It vastly simplifies the question of staff relationships by making the superintendent analogous to the manager of a private corporate enterprise in a collective bargaining context. In education, however, as in most other fields, simple answers are seldom the best answers.

Such a role for the superintendent of schools is repugnant to the spirit of professional negotiation. Not only does it almost assure that the superintendent will become an adversary of the professional staff, it cuts down immeasurably his effectiveness as educational leader of the school system. It is too much to expect, as some have written, that the superintendent can act in some instances as colleague of the staff and in others as chief negotiator for the board. If the superintendent is to carry out his professional responsibilities effectively, he should not be forced to serve as an adversary of the professional staff. While such a position may be emotionally satisfying to some superintendents and board members, and indeed to many teachers, the school district's educational program will inevitably suffer. Only if the operation of a school system is looked upon as completely analogous to a corporate enterprise is such a position tenable.

The third alternative, that of participation together with teacher and board representatives as a third party in the negotiations, would appear to be the one most suited to professional negotiation in an educational setting. Such a role, of course, is the most difficult of the three to fill, but that it *can* be filled is attested to by the scores of agreements in which negotiations by this method are being carried on successfully.

Dr. John H. Fischer, president of Teachers College, Columbia University, and former superintendent of schools in Baltimore, Maryland, has said this about the superintendent's role:

> The superintendent should accept the duty to represent the viewpoint of his staff to his board and the viewpoint of the board to the staff and thus to help each group clarify its views and articulate them most effectively and most persuasively to the other. The superintendent also has the duty to establish and keep clear, open, active, and free the channels of communication within the staff, within the board, between the two.[16]

[16] John Fischer, "Board-Staff Relations: Issues and Alternatives," speech delivered to the Fall School Board Dinner of the Metropolitan School Study Council, New York, November 28, 1962, p. 7.

A bulletin recently published in the state of Washington[17] sheds light on the attitudes of a selected number of school administrators in that state concerning their roles in professional negotiation. The study consisted of confidential interviews with eight practicing school superintendents. Some felt that "the recent legal elimination [in Washington] of the superintendent as a certificated employee for bargaining purposes and the trend toward direct negotiations with school boards on a wide variety of detailed matters will throw the superintendent of the future completely into the employer's camp as the school board's representative in negotiations or will set him aside as a mere purveyor of information."

The majority of the superintendents interviewed, however, believed quite differently. In summarizing results of the interviews, the following generalizations bearing on this subject were made:

The superintendents interviewed believe it important that the teachers have the opportunity to present their case directly to the school board. They hold that improvements in teacher welfare must come in part through pressure and that pressure must be exerted where the final authority lies.

These superintendents see no great erosion of their own authority through the existence of direct bargaining between teachers and school boards. They look upon this as but one phase in the changing role of the superintendent from director to persuader.

Wildman,[18] on the other hand, sees the possibility of an erosion of the superintendent's traditional authority:

One result of the establishment of bargaining procedures which provide for direct access to or involvement of the board from the outset in negotiations may be the compromising of the superintendent's leadership position and the weakening of a proper degree of autonomy and freedom which he may legitimately enjoy within his system with regard to matters of professional expertise and administrative authority.

In sounding his warning, Wildman is careful to specify involvement of the board in negotiations *from the outset*. He states:

[17] E. J. McNamara, *The Superintendent's Role in Professional Negotiation*, Bulletin 1964–65:13, Seattle: School Information and Research Service, May 19, 1965. Mimeographed.
[18] Wesley H. Wildman, "Implications of Teacher Bargaining for School Administration," *Phi Delta Kappan*, December 1964, p. 156.

Whether, ultimately, recourse may be had to the board in the event of impasse, and aside from the fact that the board must ultimately ratify any agreement reached, the superintendent should consider the importance of having both working responsibility for and authority over the collective negotiations with the teacher group.

Wildman would appear to be taking a traditionally orthodox approach in viewing the superintendent as an "agent of management" in the negotiation process. This point of view need not necessarily become dominant in considering relationships which should exist in the field of education. Campbell, Cunningham, and McPhee, in discussing the superintendent's interaction in the relationship between teachers organizations and boards of education maintained that:

In most cases, the superintendent can become the spokesman for neither group. Instead, he may, with good fortune, become an agent to assist each group in understanding the position and reasoning of the other, he may see that relevant facts are made available to both groups, and he may actually evolve some recommended solutions not initially acceptable to either group.[19]

The position of the superintendent as resource person both to the teachers and the board has been expressed by Harry A. Becker, superintendent of schools in Norwalk, Connecticut—which has had a group contract between the professional association and the board of education since 1947. Dr. Becker speaks not as a theorist but as one who is actively engaged on a daily basis in negotiations. In a speech made at the 1964 convention of AASA, Becker said:[20]

NEA-affiliated organizations assign the superintendent to a dual role in which he serves as a resource person both to the board and to the teacher group. This dual role is difficult to fulfill, but it is not impossible. A superintendent can be of great value as a resource person to his board of education. His contributions can be even more valuable if he is held in such high esteem by the teacher organization that they, also, would utilize him as a resource person.

[19] Ronald F. Campbell, Luvern L. Cunningham, and Roderick F. McPhee, *The Organization and Control of American Schools,* Columbus, Ohio: Charles E. Merrill Books, Inc., 1965, p. 210.

[20] Harry A. Becker, "The Role of School Administrators in Professional Negotiations," *The American School Board Journal,* Vol. 150, No. 5, May 1965, pp. 9–10.

Some might question whether it is possible for a superintendent to serve as a resource person for both the board and the teacher organization. Is there a conflict of interest in serving in a dual capacity? I believe that there is no conflict of interest. A superintendent of schools is not comparable to a superintendent of a factory. The superintendent of a factory needs to produce goods and services as cheaply as possible, and hence he needs to purchase services at the lowest possible rates. The superintendent of schools, happily, is engaged in a profession dedicated to the social welfare. His job is to provide the best possible education and not the cheapest. Hence the superintendent is in a position to advocate what is good and yet feasible.

Just what does the superintendent do in his role as a professional resource person? As has already been suggested, one of his functions is to recommend that which is good and yet is feasible. Thus his recommendations to the board will include better salaries and his recommendations to the teacher organization may include better staff utilization through teachers' aides and television.

An important function for the superintendent and his staff is factfinding. How much will a certain proposal cost? What are the comparative costs of other school systems? What is the operational feasibility of a proposal? What available information is there on trends?

The superintendent also gives his judgment, but he tells why he holds a point of view. Often he can persuade both parties to reduce excessive demands. He may be able to get the negotiators to see a problem from a different point of view.

Discussions with the superintendent may be informal as well as formal. The superintendent has numerous opportunities to talk with the individuals who are the negotiators for both parties. There are opportunities in connection with other events such as school functions, civic meetings, and social occasions.

Forbes Bottomly, former superintendent of schools of Jefferson County, Colorado, has stated his views concerning the role of the superintendent in negotiations.[21] (Jefferson County has a Level II professional negotiation agreement.)

I think all the publicity this question receives tends to overshadow the relatively simple answer: The superintendent does what he has to do under the circumstances. I act as a supplier of information, as a

---

[21] Forbes Bottomly, "Negotiating with Teachers," *School Management*, Vol. 9, No. 5, May 1965, pp. 150–52.

liaison, as a referee, as a judge, as an active participant, as a mediator, as a "cajoler," as one who tries to seek a consensus.

I've made it clear from the outset that I am my *own* man, and having done so, do not anticipate getting into any compromising situations with either the board or the teachers. As the executive officer of the board, I must give it the best of my advice and support. However, I don't hesitate to side with either group on any question. And, when dealing directly with the teachers myself, I certainly represent my own views as to what's best for the district. The superintendent cannot satisfy everyone. If he tries, he will get into trouble. He can only react honestly to each situation as it arises.

There are those who hold that boards of education should not be involved in the time-consuming earlier stages of negotiations, when data are being gathered and proposals are being formulated and tested. This position is a valid one, especially when one considers that board membership is not a full time job and that there are a multitude of other pressures impinging upon board members in their official capacities. This does not mean, however, that the superintendent must be cast in the role of chief negotiator for the board. Several agreements employ the device of using subcommittees for the purpose of developing preliminary estimates, projections, and recommendations.

Many agreements seek a middle ground by calling for initial discussions between the superintendent and teachers organization, while providing for negotiations among all three parties if joint recommendations cannot be developed in the first instance. While this pattern may not be as satisfactory from the teachers' standpoint as one which calls for initial negotiations among all three parties, it does recognize the substantial time factor involved in preliminary stages of negotiation. So long as the superintendent exercises an independent point of view throughout the process, representing the interests of the educational program rather than the sometimes partisan interests of teachers or board, then this mode of operation can be made to succeed. Admittedly, however, whether or not the superintendent *wants* to be chief negotiator for the board, he is often forced into this role upon express instructions from the board. This is unfortunate, since the superintendent should not be put in a position requiring him to be an adversary of the staff.

Holders of extreme positions on either side of the issue believe that the superintendent will either (a) be cast aside and bypassed completely in the negotiation process, or (b) be placed in a role as active partisan for the "management" position. Neither end of the continuum need become the norm. Avoiding the extremes will be a relatively simple matter if all parties seek to do so in good faith when developing the agreement.

Regardless of the pattern of negotiation chosen, and patterns will inevitably vary depending upon size of district and upon former relationships and modes of operation, the superintendent need not represent one side or the other nor need he be reduced to a role as a "mere purveyor of information." Rather, his responsibility in the negotiating process should be to provide data and counsel to both teacher and board representatives, and to do whatever is needed to insure that agreements are made which reflect credit on the negotiators as well as contribute to the over-all good of the school program.

It should be clear from the foregoing that the superintendent of schools cannot be represented in negotiations by the local association, regardless of whether or not he is a member of the association. For the purposes of negotiation he must remain completely neutral, and this also holds true in respect to all association activities leading to the presentation of proposals to the board. This problem will not manifest itself in systems in which the chief school administrator does not belong or is not eligible to belong to the local association. Where the superintendent *is* a member, however, he must hold himself strictly aloof from any participation whatsoever in the negotiation process in his capacity as an association member. To do otherwise would be to jeopardize his position of independence in the negotiation process just as surely as if he were to proclaim himself as the agent of the board of education.

The superintendent's role can best be filled if he participates in all negotiations as an *ex officio,* nonvoting member of the negotiating committee. In this way he will be able to exercise independent judgment on all educational matters, to make recommendations to both sides based upon what is best for the educational program, and to be free from criticism concerning conflicts of interest based upon primary allegiance either to the school board or school staff. Education is unique, requiring unique approaches to the question of staff relationships; it should be possible to develop approaches which recognize that the superintendent of schools has a unique role to play in the process of negotiation. Effective superintendents have been playing such a role for years; increasingly, professional negotiation agreements are incorporating this concept into the procedures being developed.

# Chapter 6. Professional Sanctions

PROFESSIONAL NEGOTIATION, as used and defined by professional associations of teachers, will inevitably be viewed by some as the counterpart of collective bargaining in industry. Likewise, professional sanctions will be viewed as a substitute for the strike. That there are some similarities between the two clusters of processes is obvious. These similarities have induced the widely held concept that the teaching profession, as represented by the NEA and its affiliated state and local associations, have adopted the processes of organized labor in watered-down forms and under softer names.

Since the two processes (professional negotiation and sanctions) were officially adopted by NEA at the same convention, in 1962, it has been assumed that the two are companion pieces constituting one package. Actually, the two are not integral parts of one process. Although they may, indeed, be companion pieces in some instances, they are discrete processes.

## Relation of Sanctions to Professional Negotiation

In the package context, sanctions are generally viewed as the enforcer, the weapons supporting professional negotiation. As previously stated, they may have this value occasionally, but the use of sanctions is not so narrowly restricted. The purposes of sanctions are much broader than simply to act as a lever for professional negotiation. Actually, in no case in which NEA sanctions have been invoked, has there been a professional negotiation agreement in existence.

In the first place, sanctions are not weapons in the sense that they possess inherent power. They are a moral force, a persuader, backed by a reasonable degree of unanimity of the group utilizing them. As such, they become a means to an end, usually expressed in the form of a declaration; the purpose of such a declaration is to bring about conformance with a custom, law, or accepted standard. Sanctions impose rewards or penalties, such as recognition, approval, withdrawal of recognition, or loss of a reward, and from this they derive their force.

In public education, the power of sanctions as a tool rests upon two bases—the degree of unanimity of the invoking group, and public opinion. Real power comes with favorable public opinion, because the power of unanimity in a publicly employed professional group is dependent upon public support. Thus, the success of professional sanctions invoked against a given school district depends, in large measure, upon the good will of people in that district. These are people who want and demand high quality educational services for their children, who will not accept substandard services for them.

Again, as applied in public education, sanctions may be used to compel the improvement of undesirable conditions, to achieve a satisfactory educational program, to guarantee fair treatment of members of school staffs. Technically, all of these may be sought with or without the existence of professional negotiation agreements.

Sanctions do not necessarily require positive action. Sometimes, as with the strike, the threat of concerted action by the profession or the possibility of such action, influence remedial action or serve as a deterrent to proposed actions. Of course, positive action by the profession is often necessary. Whenever such action is invoked, its effectiveness will depend in large measure upon the extent to which the action expresses the will of the total profession. Just here is where the chief weakness of the process occurs—the fragmentation of the teaching profession into many interest groups and organizational groups makes it extremely difficult, if not impossible, for sanctions to be backed by the total profession. Not only are there multiple organizations within the teaching profession, but there are thousands of uncommitted teachers, who do not affiliate with any organization.

The nearest thing to an expression of the will of the total profession would be a hypothetical case of sanctions invoked jointly by the NEA and all of the respective state and local affiliates of NEA, some 8,000 in all. This has never been done; joint actions by NEA, a state association, and a local association have been taken. But such concerted action is possible. Should this combination ever be realized, it would represent about 90 per cent of the 1,800,000 public school personnel.

It is true that the NEA Representative Assembly adopted resolutions endorsing the invoking of sanctions against Utah and Oklahoma. Since the respective state education associations are heavily represented in this body, it can be assumed that such endorsement reflected the views of these associations, but it does not commit these associations to supporting actions. Only an action of their official bodies or delegate assemblies could do that.

To illustrate the weakness of the fragmentation in the profession, NEA was importuned by the Overseas Education Association in 1962 to invoke the sanction of withdrawal of services against the Department of Defense because of failure, since 1960, to meet salary commitments to the teachers in the Overseas Dependents Schools. But NEA has in its membership only slightly more than one half the nation's public school teachers. Obviously, such a sanction would have been only partially effective. Joined by the affiliated state associations, the proposed sanction could have been devastatingly effective, but not total. The Canadian Teachers Federation did invoke such a sanction in 1962, because of similar conditions, and made it stick by enlisting the cooperation of its 10 affiliated provincial associations, all of which had compulsory membership by law.

### The Functions of Professional Sanctions

As defined by NEA, professional sanctions are designed to prevent violation of a right or a responsibility, in the following statement:

... A community should support its schools; school boards should discharge their functions with integrity and impartiality; administrators should use the procedures essential for democratic administration of good schools; teachers should make every effort to provide the best possible learning experiences for students. Against those who fail to act by such standards, organizations of the education profession may impose sanctions.[1]

From the suggestion above, specific uses of sanctions can be enumerated as follows:

1. They can express the profession's serious disapproval of unsatisfactory conditions.

2. They can attract the community's attention to specific deficiencies which make quality education difficult or impossible.

3. They can be used to withhold further professional service or support when that service or support could be used to continue unacceptable conditions.

4. They are a process through which the profession can protect children from unacceptable educational practices.

5. They are a process through which the profession can protect its members from being forced to contract their services under conditions that are demeaning, compromising, or otherwise intolerable.

6. They are a process through which the profession can protect the public from unknowingly condoning and financing indefensible programs or unacceptable practices in education.

7. They are a process for exerting the profession's influence in areas where it has expertness and should have autonomy.

8. They can be used to protect the public and children from incompetent or unethical practices of members of the profession.

## Types of Sanctions

The use of professional sanctions in education is not a new development. In one form or another, they have been used for many years.

One of the most effective sanctions developed in higher education was the evolution of voluntary accrediting groups. Accredita-

---

[1] *Guidelines for Professional Sanctions,* Washington, D. C.: National Commission on Professional Rights and Responsibilities, National Education Association, 1963, p. 9.

tion, as used in the United States, is the act of a voluntary association of giving approval to the quality of the program of a school or college. Such approval is, in a very real sense, the lifeblood of an educational institution. Such approval enables its students to transfer to other institutions, to gain admission to graduate study, to seek legal licensure or admission to the profession. It is significant that this sanction has been left, almost completely, to professional groups in the United States. Only superficial or token legal participation is involved. States do exercise authority over approval of teacher education programs by the respective state departments, the power of which is certification of graduates of such programs. But this is only a mild form of accreditation.

To refuse to accredit, or to disaccredit, an educational institution is a powerful sanction. The institution so affected is dealt a severe blow in the loss of prestige and usually the loss of its clientele. To many institutions, such a sanction is, in fact, a mortal blow. This is the profession's way of protecting students and the public against weak, inferior, or fraudulent institutions. It is a profession's way of seeking to guarantee a floor of quality in educational programs. The public is still being defrauded by spurious schools offering phony high school diplomas or college degrees, because of its ignorance of the protecting aspects of accreditation. This defrauding of the public has been especially noticeable since the furor over high school dropouts arose.

There have been several instances of the disaccreditation of state university systems by the appropriate regional accrediting associations because of political interference. In most such cases, the interference has come from the governor of the state, who sought to make the state's higher education institution a part of his political power structure. Professors were often fired summarily because of some statement or some action displeasing to the governor. In such cases, appointments to the faculties, the administration, and tenure of such appointees tend to be at the pleasure of the governor. Of course, this kind of political interference can destroy the integrity and the quality of an educational program. This has happened in school districts, too. With the sanction of disaccreditation a college accrediting association can dramatically and forcefully shock the people of a state into militant and remedial action, to remove the higher education system from politics. This disaccreditation occurred in Georgia and Mississippi several years ago, by action of the Southern Association of Colleges and Secondary Schools. Similar disaccreditation actions were taken by the North Central Association of Colleges and Secondary Schools in two states. Here is the power of a voluntary professional association which, by disaccreditation, serves notice on the clientele and the controlling bodies, that existing practices are impairing the quality of the educational program beyond the limits of tolerance. Vested power structures will invariably bemoan the interference of an outside agency (as was the case in the declaration of sanctions by NEA against the states of Utah and Oklahoma) as unwarranted and untoward. But the record is clear that such sanctions, as a general rule, shock people into remedial action.

A second type of professional sanction is the disciplining of a profession's membership. A profession is obligated to guarantee not only the competence of members admitted to practice, but the ethical practice of each member. The first step in such discipline is for the profession to derive a code of ethics, to which its members subscribe when admitted to membership. The second step is to derive machinery for enforcing the code if violated. The penalties for violation are censure, suspension, or expulsion from membership.

In 1964, the NEA developed and adopted the "Code of Ethics of the Education Profession" which now has been endorsed by all of its state association affiliates. As a prerequisite to membership, all NEA members accept this code as binding on their conduct. Before the derivation of this code, there were many codes. Almost all state education associations had developed their own codes and despite the fact that many of these were patterned after the NEA code, wide dissimilarities existed.

There are several other types of professional sanctions. Examples are accreditation of professional schools, licensure restricted to graduates of the accredited schools, employment in the profession restricted to such graduates, and membership in professional associations restricted to such graduates. Such sanctions are employed by many of the private professions, but their use in a public profession has been widely resisted in the past. But for the purposes of this book, the types or degrees that cluster around the withdrawal of services of teachers from a school district should be the focus of discussion.

The withdrawal of services of teachers is the weapon that is widely equated in the public mind with the strike. This concept will be discussed below.

There are several steps, or degrees, involved in the sanction of withholding or withdrawing of the services of teachers. The mildest form is the issuance of an advisory by the professional association or associations involved, alerting members to the existence of unsatisfactory conditions in a given school district. Strictly speaking this is not a sanction, since no request is made that members refuse to accept positions in the school district. But of course, the advisory may have some influence toward this end. Actually, the advisory simply publicizes a current dispute between employed teachers and the employing school district, or it publicizes conditions in the district which tend to preclude the rendering of teaching services of professional quality. The advisory presumes that teachers will make their own decisions regarding employment in the district.

An example of the use of the advisory is the "Urgent Advisory" issued by the NEA in February 1963, with reference to conditions in the Overseas Dependents Schools, operated by the Department of Defense, some excerpts of which are quoted below:

*This letter is to inform teachers who are considering teaching positions for the 1963–64 school year in the Overseas Dependents Schools operated by the Department of Defense about the serious problems that exist in these schools. We are taking this step in the interests of the teaching profession in general and of the Overseas Dependent Schools in particular.*

*Teachers in the Overseas Dependents Schools have not had a salary schedule increase since September 1960. At that time, their starting salaries were fixed at rates equal to those paid teachers in the large U. S. school systems in September 1959. . . . This directive, the Salary Determination Procedures, has not been followed because funds have not been provided. . . . If the salary directive had been fully implemented, the starting salaries of overseas teachers would be at least 9.6% higher in 1962–63 than they are. As a group, overseas teachers have lost more than $4 million in the past three years by the failure of the Department of Defense to pay the salaries rightfully due them. During the period* that teachers' salaries have stood still, other civilian federal employees have had two pay raises averaging 13%.[2]

The second step in invoking the sanction of withholding teacher services is for the association to request its members, employed elsewhere, not to seek or accept positions in a given school district until the specified, unfavorable conditions are corrected. This step does not apply to teachers already employed in the district. It is aimed at reducing or shutting off the supply of new teachers. This was the type of sanction invoked by NEA against the State of Utah in 1964.

The third step would involve both the withdrawal and the withholding of teacher services by an association requesting its members already employed in the district, as well as those members currently teaching elsewhere, not to accept employment in the district for the ensuing school year unless existing conditions are rectified.

The ultimate step, which has not as yet been fully employed, and doubtless will be rare, is to accompany the request (to presently employed teachers and outsiders) with the declaration that members violating the request will (or may) be judged by the association as guilty of unethical conduct, punishable by censure, suspension, or expulsion from membership. This type of sanction was invoked, in part, by NEA against the State of Oklahoma in 1965. Teachers employed in the state were not asked to withdraw service, but NEA set up five relocation centers in the state to find jobs for teachers who elected to leave the state. The unethical charge possibility was invoked against teachers outside of Oklahoma who took jobs in that state. The language was not categorical; it simply warned that such teachers *might* be judged guilty of unethical conduct.

The only known cases in which this full action was voted by the official bodies of an association occurred in Connecticut. In cases involving the West Haven School District (1958) and the Waterbury School District (in 1963), the Connecticut Education Association did vote such actions. But, in both cases the disputes between the districts and their teachers were resolved before such extreme measures had to be applied.

2 "Urgent Advisory, to Affiliated Associations," issued by William G. Carr, NEA Executive Secretary, February 1, 1963.

There is a companion step to the invoking of sanctions which has not, as yet, been widely used, but which will probably be extensively used in the future. That step is to withdraw placement services of education associations (about 20 state associations have such services) and to request college and university placement agencies to refuse to refer candidates for positions in the offending districts. Such a step cannot be effective until sanctions have been used extensively enough to demonstrate beyond question the integrity and validity of the procedures by which they are invoked.

## Sanctions versus Strikes

The general public, some superintendents of schools, some school boards, and some teachers have difficulty in seeing any difference between professional sanctions and strikes by teachers. The argument is that withdrawing or withholding of the services of teachers is tantamount to a strike.

There are essential differences. The sanctions of withdrawing or withholding services by teachers do not violate existing contracts. Teachers fulfill their contracts for the current school year.

NEA has frequently been criticized for not having a categorical no-strike policy. Actually it does not, as such. But the Code of Ethics for the Education Profession contains an indirect no-strike prohibition, by requiring that members observe the conditions of a contract, until it is discharged or terminated by mutual agreement.

As a general rule, sanctions are invoked effective the following school year. The offending school district is given several months notice in which to correct conditions which interfere with or prevent adequate educational services. If public opinion in the district is willing to tolerate these inferior conditions, schools can be maintained. There is no picketing by teachers to prevent this. Standards can be lowered and teachers of some kind can be recruited, some with substandard preparation.

But here is the power of sanctions. If the facts supporting the profession's judgment are clear that high quality services to children cannot be provided under existing conditions, parents will not often support the shortchanging of their children. Whether the courts will equate professional sanctions with teacher strikes in the public schools, and thus declare the former illegal under the law of certain states, probably cannot at present be predicted. There are some precedents but they are not extensive enough to be definitive.

In the Little Lake (California) sanctions case, the district asked the court to enjoin the California Teachers Association from withholding teacher placement services from the district, and from discouraging its members from seeking employment in the District. The court declined to issue such injunctions. An informal comment of the court expresseed the point of view that criticism of public agencies is a part of the concept of a democratic society.

Also, when the Oklahoma Education Association and NEA refused to lift sanctions against Oklahoma, in the summer of 1965, after the Legislature had made an appropriation of $28,800,000 for the schools, and in advance of a pending referendum on a proposed change in the state constitution on September 14, to authorize local districts to vote higher millage rates on schools, the governor reacted angrily. He requested the state's attorney general to file damage suits against OEA and NEA. Nothing came of this request. Thus, it can be assumed that valid legal grounds for such a suit could not be found.

A decision of the National Labor Relations Board, with reference to a case in private industry, indicates there are three essential elements in a strike: (1) an employer-employee relationship must exist; (2) there must be a refusal by employees to perform all or part of the work which they were hired to do; and (3) the refusal to perform the work must be concerted. This decision said:

> The broadest definition of a strike includes "quitting work" or "stoppage of work." Men cannot quit work before they are hired; they cannot stop work before they start. We reject, therefore, the contention that the alleged refusal to refer employees [by the union involved] should be construed as a strike.[3]

This decision would seem to have some analogy to the withdrawal of services of teachers currently employed in a school district, and the withholding of services of outsiders for the ensuing

[3] Glaziers Union (Joliet Contractors Association), 30 LRRM 1174 (1952).

school year. These sanctions, also, would not appear to embrace all of the three essential elements in a strike, as delineated above. In several recent cases teachers under contract have refused to supervise extracurricular activities. The question then is whether such supervision is covered by contract and, if so, whether this action constitutes a strike.

## Procedures for Invoking Sanctions

The invoking of professional sanctions is a serious step by the nature and power of the action. Thus, the teaching profession must exercise extreme care in their use. Precautions must be observed to prevent capricious or hasty use, or use on frivolous grounds. Nothing would so quickly destroy the power of sanctions as injudicious and unwarranted use of them. Thus, the resolution officially endorsing the use of sanctions, adopted by NEA in 1962, specified:

The National Education Association calls upon its affiliated state associations to cooperate in developing guidelines which would define, organize, and definitely specify procedural steps for invoking sanctions by the teaching profession.[4]

These guidelines recognize that there will be cases in which sanctions are invoked by a local association alone, a state association in conjunction with a local association, or by the local and state association in conjunction with NEA. The latter course is recommended wherever possible and justified, since such concert tends to reflect the will of the total profession. This assumes, of course, sympathetic support by other state and local affiliates, even though they may not formally declare sanctions.

The guidelines specify that national sanctions are to be imposed by the NEA Executive Committee after a "comprehensive and objective investigation" by an official agency, usually the National Commission on Professional Rights and Responsibilities.

While acknowledging that in extreme emergencies, the NEA Executive Committee might declare sanctions without such investigation, the guidelines stress adherence to the above procedure.

---

[4] *Addresses and Proceedings* (100th Annual Meeting of NEA, Denver), Washington, D. C.: the Association, 1962, Resolution 19, p. 398.

Investigating committees are chosen with great care, and two or more laymen (usually school board members) and a university professor are usually included.

To illustrate the case with which NEA seeks to safeguard the integrity of this procedure, the NEA Executive Committee refused to invoke sanctions against the state of Utah in the spring and summer of 1963, as requested by the Utah Education Association, because the PR&R Commission had not had time to uncover facts which would indicate intolerable educational conditions. In the face of pressure to impel the annual NEA Representative Assembly (consisting of about 7000 delegates) to vote the sanctions anyway, the Executive Committee stood its ground. It refused to invoke the sanctions on the grounds that it did not have the facts to assert that intolerable conditions existed. It is ironic that neither the National School Boards Association nor the AASA commended the NEA Executive Committee for this stand.

In the spring of 1964 it did invoke sanctions in Utah, because the investigation had been completed and the use of sanctions recommended. The following excerpt from the Guidelines[5] will indicate the process of invoking sanctions by NEA, and the powers used to enforce them:

Following a formal request from a state or local affiliated association or from a member of the NEA, an investigation or field study will be made by an appropriate NEA agency, usually the Commission on Professional Rights and Responsibilities, before sanctions are applied. If at any time in the investigation there appears to be a likelihood of successful mediation or of negotiation of the controversy, the investigation may be suspended or cancelled.

When in the course of an investigation an official investigating committee finds conditions to be so clearly unsatisfactory that application of sanctions by the NEA appears likely, notice of such likelihood may be sent by the NEA Executive Secretary, or his deputy, to the principal parties affected by the application of sanctions. The usual procedure would not include any notice to the press or other publicity from the national office.

Since a request for application of sanctions by the NEA will indicate an emergency condition, expeditious but precise procedures will be

5 *Guidelines for Professional Sanctions, op. cit.,* pp. 16–17.

used. This means that the usual procedures for full scale investigations by the NEA may be set aside and the usual printed report may not be issued or may be delayed until the crisis has been ended.

*Types of sanctions applied against a school district or a community and their official bodies may include:*

1. Censure through public notice including release of investigation report, articles in national and state journals, reports through various mass media of communication.

2. Notification to state departments of education of findings concerning unsatisfactory conditions.

3. Notification to certification and placement services of unsatisfactory conditions of employment for educators.

4. Warning to members that acceptance of employment as a new teacher in the school district would be considered as unethical conduct and could lead to discharge from and future refusal of membership in the national professional association.

5. Advice to members, presently employed that, if their private arrangements permit, they should seek employment elsewhere.

*When the application of sanctions has been approved by the NEA Executive Committee, the following steps will be taken:*

1. A statement will be authorized to include (1) the name or names of the district, schools, agencies, and persons against whom the action is taken, (2) the cause or causes of the action, and (3) conditions or actions that would be conducive to action lifting the sanctions by the Executive Committee of the National Education Association.

2. The authorized statement, with a covering note, will be sent by the NEA Executive Secretary or his deputy to the members of the school board, the superintendent of schools, the president of the local teachers association, the mayor or city manager of the community, the chief state school officer, the president and executive secretary of the state education association, the newspapers of the community, the national wire services, the public and private placement services for educators and such other individual and agencies as may appear to be appropriate in the particular case.

3. Sanctions will be lifted *upon* recommendation of the Commission on Professional Rights and Responsibilities *or by* the investigating committee that originally recommended their application, and by action of the NEA Executive Secretary, or his deputy, and confirmed by the NEA Executive Committee. Such action will occur only when there is

clear evidence that conditions have materially improved and there is assurance of a continuance of conditions that promote an effective program of education. In some instances the evidence of improvement may be so clear that it will not be necessary to have the recommendation of the investigating committee. When professional sanctions are removed, notice will be sent to the same persons and agencies as were addressed when sanctions were applied.

## Case Examples of Professional Sanctions

Since the use of sanctions was first officially endorsed in a resolution by the NEA Representative Assembly in 1962, it has been generally assumed that this marked the origin of the process for the teaching profession. This is not the case. Sanctions had been used by NEA, and some state associations, for more than a decade under authority of the NEA Executive Committee and the executive committees of the state associations involved. The idea for the use of sanctions by the teaching profession probably was borrowed from the "censure of administration" procedures of the American Association of University Professors, with modifications to fit the needs of public school teachers. This is the belief of Dr. Richard Barnes Kennan who, as executive secretary of the NEA Defense Commission (now the NEA Professional Rights and Responsibilities Commission), borrowed and modified the AAUP procedure to bring about a solution of the North College Hill case, described below.

THE NORTH COLLEGE HILL CASE.[6]   The NEA, in conjunction with the Ohio Education Association, first invoked the sanction of withdrawal of teaching services in the case of the North College Hill School District, in June 1947. This district, a suburb of Cincinnati, had become embroiled in a bitter controversy stemming from arbitrary actions of the three majority members of the school board.

The focus of the controversy was the injection of sectarian con-

---

[6] *North College Hill, Ohio: An Example of Some Effects of Board of Education Interference with Sound Administration of Public Education,* Washington, D. C.: National Commission for the Defense of Democracy Through Education, National Education Association, November 1947.

siderations into school policies. The election of three members of a particular religious group to the school board gave that faith a majority of the five member board. The majority group began to make decisions based on church affiliation. Personnel decisions were made upon such a basis. The majority began a campaign to strip the superintendent of his prerogatives under the law, by rejecting his personnel nominations, to force him to make nominations they desired. Finally, they declared that none of the nominations of the superintendent would be approved until he submitted to the board all applications for a given position. The superintendent offered to submit such a list but only with names, ages, and qualifications of the applicants. This did not satisfy the board majority; and, after a year of turmoil over appointments, they charged the superintendent with insubordination. In February 1947, by a 3 to 2 vote, the decision was made not to renew the superintendent's contract when it terminated in July of that year.

This action brought to a head animosities and grievances in the community which had been accumulating due to the high-handed methods of the majority members. Twenty-eight teachers signed a petition protesting the dismissal of the superintendent. High school students threatened a strike, being dissuaded at that time by the superintendent.

At its March meeting, the board ignored popular petitions to reinstate the superintendent. There was a general student strike, high school students remained out for a month, and 400 elementary school children remained out for most of the remainder of the school year. Parents and children picketed the schools daily. The community vigorously supported the superintendent. A board meeting was attended by 1,000 citizens. Feelings were running so high that police protection had to be provided for these board meetings. At one meeting two of the board majority were physically assaulted by indignant citizens. The 28 teachers who had petitioned the reinstatement of the superintendent resigned, effective with the end of the school year. The school system was in disarray and on the verge of disintegration. During the turmoil, the Ohio Education Association and the NEA Defense Commission were asked to investigate the situation. On June 17, 1947, a joint statement by the executive committees of the two associations invoked sanctions against the North College Hill School District requesting all members of the profession to refuse to accept positions in the district as long as it remained under the control of the board majority.

Within hours after this declaration of sanctions, the entire board resigned (although the action was against the three majority members). Under Ohio Law, the school system was placed under control of the probate court until a new board could be selected. The court immediately renewed the contract of the superintendent, and the sanctions were lifted.

THE KELSO, WASHINGTON CASE.[7]   The first case of invoking of sanctions backed up by withdrawal of placement services by a college was that of the Kelso, Washington School District, in 1950. In March of that year, 17 teachers and principals were threatened with dismissal, without cause or proper notice. This action involved teachers in each of the five schools in the district, in a total staff of 120.

The local association, supported by citizens, requested an investigation by the Washington Education Association and the NEA Defense Commission. The joint investigating committee recommended (1) the immediate removal of the superintendent of schools, (2) the immediate issuance of contracts to teachers and principals, (3) the employment of an acting superintendent, and (4) the development of school policies to create a proper educational climate in the district.

The board seemed bent on ignoring the recommendations of the investigating committee; and in April a mass meeting of citizens was held which demanded the reinstatement of the teachers and principals threatened with dismissal. The mass meeting also demanded the resignation of three board members. The School of Education of the State College of Washington issued a statement on April 25 declaring that since the board had seen fit to disregard the recommendations of the investigating committee, the school would not recommend a candidate for the superintendency. Further, the school stated that it would advise its graduates of conditions in the

---

[7] *Report of the NEA-WEA Investigation Committee on Kelso, Washington,* Washington, D. C.: National Education Association and Washington Education Association, June 1950.

district. In the meantime, members of the Kelso Education Association adopted a resolution demanding that the board put into effect the recommendations of the investigating committee, threatening resignation by July 15, if these conditions were not met. In the face of all these demands, the board agreed on April 22 to accept the recommendations of the investigating committee.

THE POLSON, MONTANA CASE.[8] The Polson, Montana case marked the first one in which a professional association spelled out the criteria for applying and lifting sanctions. This was a case involving dismissal of the superintendent of schools without following due process. The school board was within its legal rights, since the tenure law did not apply to superintendents in that state; but the superintendent must be notified that his contract will not be renewed on or before February 1 of the year in which his contract expires. The Montana Education Association felt that the board had been arbitrary and unfair in its dismissal of the superintendent and joined with the local teachers association and the state congress of parents and teachers in requesting the NEA to join in an investigation. The result of the case was that the Montana Education Association issued a step-by-step process as follows: First, the MEA stated that until the board of education adopted policies looking toward better relationships for the professional staff that it could not consider the Polson School System as a desirable place for its members to seek positions.

Second, the Montana Education Association declared that it would immediately make known to all its members, to the state department of education, the appropriate regional accrediting association, and the education associations and the teacher education institutions in nearby states of the conditions in Polson.

Third, the MEA spelled out requisite conditions for lifting the sanctions, such as renewal of the superintendent's contract, adoption of a better salary schedule, the holding of public meetings by the school board, and the replacement of the current members of the school board.

[8] *Report of an Investigation of School Controversy in Polson, Montana,* Washington, D. C.: National Commission for the Defense of Democracy Through Education, National Education Association, April 1951.

THE WEST HAVEN, CONNECTICUT CASE.[9] This case arose from the repeated veto over several years by the Board of Finance of the Board of Education's proposals for teachers' raises. In the spring of 1958, the teachers finally rebelled and refused to sign salary agreements for the ensuing year, submitting instead written notices of their intention to return to their jobs in the fall. The Board then took the overt step of notifying teachers that unless they returned the signed salary agreements they would be denied any raise.

The Connecticut Education Association immediately voted drastic sanctions against the district, including the unethical conduct indictment against teachers outside the district who accepted positions there. Before the sanctions were actually applied, a settlement was worked out by involving the state board of education.

THE WATERBURY CASE.[10] This case involved invoking the sanctions of withdrawing extracurricular service and was among the first, if not the first, of this type. But the Waterbury teachers did not count exclusively on the effect of expected sanctions, which had already been voted but not yet applied by the Connecticut Education Association. NEA had completed its study of conditions and stood ready to invoke sanctions. The Waterbury Education Association organized a political campaign to defeat the incumbent mayor who had repeatedly vetoed teachers' raises and funds for badly needed school facilities and services. The local association was successful in the election, and the new mayor quickly resolved the controversy by securing an increase in the tax levy.

STUDENT NEA SANCTIONS. Powerful collateral actions to invoke sanctions have been taken by at least two state associations of teacher education students.

For the first time, in the spring of 1962, the Connecticut Student Education Association, an affiliate of the NEA, voted sanctions

9 *Report of an Investigation of West Haven, Connecticut: A Study of Community Inaction,* Washington, D. C.: National Commission for the Defense of Democracy Through Education, National Education Association, September 1959.
10 *Report of an Investigation, Waterbury, Connecticut: A Study of the Inhibiting Effect of Political Control on the Quality of Education,* Washington, D. C.: National Commission on Professional Rights and Responsibilities, National Education Association, May 1963.

against two school districts in the state, by requesting its membership to refrain from accepting jobs in the two districts unless and until the disputes between the boards and the local associations were settled. This was significant because these students were graduating as teachers from the colleges and universities of the state, and their action had the effect of shutting off from these two districts the in-state source of supply.

The Michigan Student Education Association caused a furor in that state, in the spring of 1965, by adopting a resolution calling upon its members to refuse to accept positions in school districts offering less than $5,000 as a starting salary for new teachers and a maximum of less than $8,000.

In view of the fact that NEA and its affiliated state associations have student chapters on virtually all campuses eligible to qualify for them, and a total membership of about 125,000, such activism by newly graduating teachers could become extremely significant.

In 1964 NEA joined the Utah Education Association,[11] and the Oklahoma Education Association[12] in 1965, in invoking statewide sanctions in those two states, after exhaustive studies revealed a steady deterioration in the quality of the school programs in those states. The Utah sanctions were lifted in the spring of 1965, at the request of UEA, after the Utah Legislature had appropriated substantial increases in school founds.

## THE UTAH AND OKLAHOMA CASES

Since the invoking of sanctions by NEA against two states—Utah and Oklahoma—has been so widely publicized, these two cases should be described in some detail.

First, there should be some comment on the question: "Why a whole state?" The import of such action is that the financing of public education is rapidly shifting away from the local school district to the state; and, in 1965, it appears that the shift in a

---

[11] *Report of an Investigation, Utah: A State-Wide Study of School Conditions,* Washington, D. C.: National Commission on Professional Rights and Responsibilities, National Education Association, March 1964.

[12] *Report of an Investigation, Oklahoma: A State-Wide Study of Conditions Detrimental to an Effective Public Educational Program,* Washington, D. C.: National Commission on Professional Rights and Responsibilities, National Education Association, February 1965.

substantial degree, may go all the way up to the federal government. Second, because of this dramatic shift, the states, in these two cases at least, were the only recourse for remedial action. The local districts were, as a general rule, powerless to effect the needed changes. Certainly there were in these two states some local school districts with the wealth and power of action to rectify unsatisfactory conditions, but they were few in number.

Third, a fair question is: "Were not the levels of quality of the public school programs in these two states above those of some other states not placed under sanctions?" The honest answer to this question is that of course there were. Then, the logical question that follows is, "Why these two states?"

There are at least two answers to this question: (1) Each state must be evaluated on the basis of its own potential to provide for education; in effect, its effort must be measured against its potential, its will against what it could do if the prevailing power structure would permit. (2) The judgment of a state's own public school staff as to the adequacy of its effort. The teachers in both states overwhelmingly voted that their states were falling far short of their potential to support schools, or of reasonable effort to do so.

In the case of Utah, the revolt in 1963 of the state's teachers was not a new thing. The state had been in a turbulent condition over school support since about 1950, with the advent of a very conservative governor who defeated every effort of the school people to adjust to rapidly increasing enrollment, to the need for new school buildings, additional teachers, curriculum additions, and for teaching materials. Instead, the governor persuaded the people that they were doing all right—that the state was in the forefront of quality programs among the states. This was true— in 1948—when Utah was close to number one in the nation in terms of per capita expenditures for education. But it overlooked what was to come—the population explosion, the rising price index, the rapidly increasing burden on the schools. Thus, Utah's position began to deteriorate, while the state power structure was adamant in its drive to retain as nearly as possible the status quo regarding the financing of its schools. There was a revolt against this skidding situation in 1953. The teachers in desperation decided to "stack" their contracts for the school year

1953-1954. Enlightened public school supporters persuaded the teachers to resume service in September on the promise that a special session of the legislature would provide additional support for the schools. The teachers went back and this promise was in part made good. But the power structure still dragged its feet in making really significant adjustments.

By 1963 the situation had so deteriorated that Utah had fallen from number one in per capita expenditures in 1948, to thirty-sixth. The teachers, fortified by careful studies and endorsement of the CAPS group program (the Cooperative Associations Program for the Schools, consisting of recommendations of the associations of the teachers, the school superintendents, the school boards, and the parent-teacher group). The CAPS program recommended a state appropriation of $24.5 million to meet the growing needs of the schools. The incumbent governor permitted only a $11.5 million appropriation, at which the teachers rebelled, as grossly inadequate. The Utah Education Association, in the spring of 1963, requested the invocation of sanctions by NEA. The UEA was advised that sanctions are invoked only after a careful, thorough, objective study of conditions, so the NEA Commission on Professional Rights and Responsibilities came in with a study committee, which included two school board members and a university professor of school administration. By the time of the annual summer convention of NEA, at Detroit, the Utah teachers made an emotional appeal to the 7500 delegates to vote sanctions, despite the fact that the PR&R Commission had not yet had time to complete its study. The NEA Representative Assembly refused to take this hasty action. During the school year 1964-1965, the PR&R Commission completed its study. In the meantime the Utah governor had appointed his own study committee, which announced its findings shortly after the report of the PR&R Commission study. Both studies confirmed the inadequacy of school support; and the governor's committee recommended an immediate special session of the legislature to make emergency appropriations for the schools. The governor summarily dismissed both studies, and refused to act. The Utah teachers staged a two-day recess in violent anger, and held a mass meeting to air their rebellion.

Sustained now with the PR&R Commission's comprehensive

study, the NEA Executive Committee declared sanctions against the state. Only NEA members outside the state were enjoined from accepting positions in Utah. During the summer of 1963, the teachers of Utah decided to add another string to their bow (in addition to the sanctions). The Utah Education Association, through a separate organization, developed an all-out political campaign to elect a governor and members of the legislature known to be friendly to the teachers cause. This campaign was highly successful, with results that school appropriations in the spring of 1965 substantially met the demands for adequate financing of the schools. Thus, on March 15, 1965, NEA and UEA lifted the sanctions against the state, after 300 days.

How effective were the sanctions? Did they win the victory as described above? The answer is that they were effective, but not the sole cause forcing remedial action. The political activity of the Utah teachers was certainly a powerful factor. Apparently the NEA sanctions were most effective in forcing a shift in the adamant opposition of the state's economic forces. The report is that many industries invited to build plants in the state refused to do so while the schools were under the ban of NEA.

Governor Rampton, after the sanctions were lifted, probably gave the fairest assessment of the effect of the sanctions. He said in a public speech (in effect): If I were asked if sanctions forced me and the legislature to provide more money for the schools, I should have to answer "no." However, if I were asked if the sanctions influenced the people to form the conviction that school support was inadequate, I should have to answer "yes."

A sequel to the Utah story was the dispute that developed between the teachers and the school board of Box Elder County at the beginning of school in Steptember 1965. (This was the only district of 42 in the state that resisted the settlement of the state-wide controversy.) Unable to agree upon the salary schedule for the ensuing school year, the Box Elder Education Association invoked local sanctions against the district and called upon the UEA and NEA to invoke state and national sanctions. The UEA acted immediately to declare sanctions, but before NEA could act, the dispute was settled by negotiation. Opening of the schools was delayed six days, which the teachers agreed to make up during the year, thus losing no pay.

There were many similarities between the Utah and Oklahoma sanctions cases. The common ingredient was the skidding support of the public schools over a period of years. The chief difference in the two situations was a difference in tactics. In Utah the economic power structures exerted their vetoes on increased school support through the governor and the legislature. In Oklahoma, the same effective controls existed, but the heat was diffused by the gimmick of referral of proposals to referenda, to a popular vote. The power structure was able to persuade the people that they were already supporting the schools generously, which was contrary to the facts revealed in the NEA study.

In Oklahoma the trouble really began when the Republican governor vetoed, in 1963, an act to raise teachers' salaries. Seeing no hope of legislative action to help the skidding school situation, the Oklahoma Education Association sponsored four remedial referenda to increase school support for a vote of the people. Again the economic interests wheeled out their public relations programs opposing the proposals. The governor aided their opposition by refusing to call a special election on the school support proposal, but chose (as the law permitted him to do) to have the vote in the general election on November 3, 1964. This seems reasonable enough. But the device here is that referenda in Oklahoma in a general election must carry a majority vote of all those voting for the President of the United States, whereas in a special election only a majority of those voting on the referenda was required.

In the general election, the people were persuaded to defeat the school proposal by not voting at all on the referenda. Thus the "silent vote" made it impossible to secure a majority of all votes cast for president. Each of the school measures received a majority of the votes cast on them but not a majority of all votes cast in the election.

This clever maneuvering so angered the teachers of the state that a near statewide walkout of teachers was narrrowly averted. Immediately following the general election, on November 3, 1964, a "professional holiday" was declared by school boards in several of the school districts to permit a mass meeting of teachers—an indignation meeting to decide upon a course of action. At this meeting, the teachers demanded an immediate investigation by NEA and the invoking of sanctions if the facts warranted. The

PR&R Commission moved in quickly with a study team, completed its study and issued a report in April. In the meantime, the Oklahoma legislature had taken no action to remedy the boiling situation. The legislature had resorted to the old ploy of proposing an increase in the state sales tax from two to three per cent but instead of taking the action itself, referred the proposal to a vote of the people in April. The proposal was defeated. NEA therefore invoked sanctions against the state, adding a provision which it had not previously invoked, enjoining outside teachers from accepting jobs in the state with the warning that violators might be judged guilty of unethical conduct, and that possible expulsion from membership might result. Another provision was also included. NEA announced the establishment of five relocation centers to expedite the placement of Oklahoma teachers who elected to leave the state for positions in other states. NEA did not urge teachers to leave the state; it simply sought to help them if they desired to leave.

Quickly requests from other states for about 10,000 Oklahoma teachers were received by NEA. These lists of vacancies were transmitted to the five relocation centers. The evidence seems to indicate that relatively few (about 600) Oklahoma teachers sought to leave the state.

In late June the state legislature passed a $28,800,000 appropriation for the schools. This provided salary increases of about $800 per teacher in the larger cities and raises ranging from $400 to $1,000 throughout the state, an average per teacher statewide of about $550, plus considerable general funds for the school program. In addition, the legislature authorized a referendum by which local school boards would be enabled to raise the millage levy by 10 mills.

On August 10, the Oklahoma Education Association's Board of Directors voted 84 to 77 to endorse lifting only that portion of the sanctions relating to the relocation centers and transmitted this request to NEA. The refusal of the OEA and NEA to lift all sanctions at this time provoked bitter reactions from the Governor and others in Oklahoma. The reason for this refusal was that only the teacher salary demands had been met and that the over-all needs for school improvements had not been met.

On September 14, 1965, the people of Oklahoma voted overwhelmingly to amend the state constitution to permit electors in local school districts to vote an additional 10-mill levy for support of the schools.

This action, combined with enactments of the legislature, substantially met the demands for school improvements which prompted the invoking of statewide sanctions by OEA and NEA. Thus, on September 18 the OEA Board of Directors voted to lift sanctions and requested NEA to do likewise.

In addition to the $28,800,000 increase in appropriations for the schools, the legislature had enacted several other significant pieces of legislation, including mandatory social security coverage for all teachers; mandatory sick leave provisions of 10-days per year cumulative to 60 days, for all teachers; improved teacher retirement benefits; and several other provisions to improve the conditions of teachers. In addition, a professional practices act was passed, placing certain responsibilities for developing criteria for admission to teaching and continuation in practice in a commission of teachers and administrators.

Out of the Oklahoma case again came a demonstration of the effectiveness of state and national sanctions, in reversing a deteriorating school program and assuring steady improvement in the quality of education for all of the state's children. An interesting and significant by-product was the overhauling of the structure of the Oklahoma Education Association to guarantee broader participation of teachers in policy making for the Association.

THE IDAHO STUDY. A constructive outcome of the sanctions controversy in Utah was the comprehensive study and report of the NEA PR&R Commission of school conditions and support in Idaho.

Idaho was the one state among the seven surrounding states where school support fell consistently below that of Utah. Naturally, the repercussions of the 1963-65 wrangle over the schools in Utah had their impact upon Idaho teachers and the public. Therefore, when the PR&R study of the Utah situation was completed in the spring of 1964, the Idaho Education Association requested that a similar study be made in that state. There was connected with this study no hint that its outcome would result in the invoking of sanctions. At no point was there such a proposal or threat.

As a result of the study, the Idaho governor and legislature supported, in the 1965 session, the largest percentage (42 per cent) increase in school funds in the history of the state. This experience suggests again the persuasive power of an impartial analysis of the facts, by a group respected for its fairness and integrity.

A fortunate legacy of the Oklahoma, Utah, and Idaho cases may well be to encourage efforts at developing peaceful and constructive actions to remedy inferior school conditions, rather than increasing such bitter, statewide controversies.

### Quick Action Procedures in Local School Crises

It has been pointed out that sanctions have been effective, but that they are slow acting, requiring relatively long periods of time to get desired results. Circumstances sometimes arise in school districts of such crucial nature that teachers demand immediate action of some kind. They are unwilling to wait out the period required to invoke sanctions.

This situation developed both in the Louisville School District and in the State of Oklahoma after the general election in November 1964. The voters, for the fourth time, rejected a tax raise in Louisville, in the face of desperate conditions in the schools, in regard to both teachers' salaries and school support in general. In anger, without a design or plan, several hundred teachers stayed at home for a couple of days. The temper of the teachers was such that a concerted, full-scale strike could have eventuated. In Oklahoma, the voters rejected four separate referenda designed to rectify the deteriorating school system. The reaction of the state's teachers was violent and immediate. In fact, the foresight of a few superintendents and school boards in arranging a "professional holiday" so that a mass meeting of teachers could be held to discuss what should be done probably prevented a spontaneous mass walkout, at least in Oklahoma City and Tulsa.

Crises such as these demand a psychological equivalent of the strike. They demand quick action both as an emotional catharsis and as a remedy or to ameliorate the situation.

To meet this need, the NEA Commission on Professional Rights and Responsibilities has developed a cluster of 19 proposed procedures geared to quick action, to prevent spontaneous walkouts or strikes.[13] These procedures are not sanctions, but they may be considered as supplements to sanctions, or as forerunners of sanctions. The 19 suggested quick action procedures in this cluster are as follows:

1. Petitions for redress of grievances—teacher petition to school board.
2. Use of mass media—newspaper, radio, and TV appeals to the public.
3. Mass attendance at board meetings—teachers and laymen converge in such numbers that the school board is compelled to secure a larger meeting room.
4. Demonstration of professional solidarity—mass meeting of teachers to protest conditions.
5. Mass meeting of citizens—at which teachers explain their grievances.
6. Massive motorcade—this is a drive-in to call attention of public to teachers' grievances.
7. Community alert—publicizing of a secret or public ballot of teachers to alert community to teacher unrest.
8. Legal action—court injunction or mandamus. (This was used by NEA in the Louisville crisis, resulting in a court decision mandating assessment of property at full value.)
9. Stacking contracts—teachers select an official of the local association to hold all contracts until unsatisfactory conditions are remedied.
10. Stacking resignations—as a threat to resign before legal deadline of entering into contract for the ensuing school year.
11. Immediate limited withdrawal of services—particularly of extracurricular services.
12. Application of sanctions by a local association—without waiting for action of state association and NEA.

---

[13] *Action Programs When There Is a Local School Crisis,* Washington, D. C.: Commission on Professional Rights and Responsibilities, National Education Association, 1965, 10 pp.

13. Emergency Defense Fund—raising such a fund alerts community and school officials to seriousness of the situation.
14. Appeal to higher authority—soliciting help of mayor, state commissioner of education, or the governor.
15. Staff statements—a mild form of censure by an official of the state association or the PR&R Commission, with proposals for improving conditions.
16. Statement by intermediate authority—refers to a warning statement of the Interim Committee of the Commission on Professional Rights and Responsibilities.
17. Warning by NEA or state association executive secretary —a publicized statement alerting public to unsatisfactory conditions.
18. Urgent advisory—by the executive secretary of NEA or a state association advising members of unsatisfactory conditions in a given school district.
19. Temporary enjoinment—NEA Executive Secretary could urge members to refrain from performing certain duties (not covered by contract) for a specified period of time.

## Factors in Effectiveness of Sanctions

While sanctions, in their relatively short history, have indeed worked rather well for the teaching profession, the results are often so slow in emerging that they do not have the breathcatching appeal of the strike. A group of indignant teachers, as with any other group, want release for their pent-up emotions, want positive and dynamic action *now,* not next month or next year. The crucial question then (again ignoring the legality of each) is which in the long look is better for the teaching profession. There is evidence on both sides, and the question will continue to be debated in the future. Are sanctions effective? Yes. NEA and its affiliates have won, fully or partially, every case in which the sanction of withdrawing of service has been applied.

The great handicap of sanctions is the time element. The process often, though not always, requires an extended time period to produce results. In the first place, if sanctions are to mobilize formidable public opinion, the integrity of the procedures for applying them must be carefully protected. This revolves around a careful, objective study of educational conditions, which clearly reflects unsatisfactory or intolerable conditions. Such a study must demonstrate clearly that children cannot receive a first rate education under existing conditions; that teachers cannot perform professional services of a high caliber under existing conditions. Such a study takes time. It cannot be done overnight. In the Utah case, for example, a full year was required to assemble and evaluate the facts. Of course, this was an extraordinary case, since it involved an entire state. But even in a single good-sized district, several months are generally required. Then there is the time lag between the declaration of sanctions and the date when their effectiveness will be observable. As a general rule, sanctions are applied effective the ensuing school year; that is, in a case affecting all teaching positions of a whole district. There have been cases of local associations immediately withdrawing services in extracurricular fields. (Examples: Waterbury in 1962–63, and a threatened action in Denver in the spring of 1965; also threatened actions in Dade County, Florida, in the spring of 1965 and in Duval County, Florida, in the fall of 1965.)

The basic factor in the effectiveness of sanctions, as has been observed previously, is public opinion. When the educational program of a given school district is declared substandard by a respected profession, such declaration is a powerful weapon. The first reaction of the people is likely to be one of outrage. Their pride is hurt. They tend to look for some conspiracy to bludgeon more tax money out of them, by attacking the reputation of their community and their schools. Here is where the integrity of the investigative study is at stake. If the facts are there, have been found and revealed, have not been distorted or angled to prove a preconceived, biased position, the ultimate reaction of the people will be favorable. Nobody wants a second rate school system. No parent wants the onus of shortchanging his children. No community wants the reputation of condoning inferior educational conditions. At least enlightened, unselfish people do not want these things, and they are in the majority—if they do not constitute the power structure of virtually all communities. Here is the great power of sanctions—carefully guarded and prudently used.

The second power factor in sanctions, as previously stated, is that, whenever possible, they should reflect the will of the total profession. This is why it is desirable that the national, state, and local associations should, in most cases (there are exceptions when this is neither necessary nor desirable), act in concert. Obviously, in cases where teachers are requested not to seek positions in a given school district, if the associations making the request represent only a minor segment of the total profession in their membership, the boycott cannot be fully effective and may be only partially so.

A new provision to strengthen the enforcement of sanctions was added to the resolution on professional sanctions, by the New York NEA Convention, in the summer of 1965. The passage is as follows.

> Further, a violation of sanctions by a member of the profession is a violation of the Code of Ethics of the Education Profession. Therefore, the offering or accepting of employment in areas where sanctions are in effect should be evaluated in terms of the Code, and local, state, and national associations should begin developing procedures for disciplining members who violate sanctions.[14]

The word "offering" (of employment) clearly had reference to the superintendent who seeks to fill vacancies from the pool of teachers enjoined from accepting employment in the sanctioned district or state. Usually (as in the cases of the sanctions against Utah and Oklahoma), this applies to teachers outside the state or, in the case of a given sanctioned school district, to teachers outside the district.

There was little discussion of the reasons for proposing this amendment. It apparently stemmed from the conviction that all members of the profession—administrators as well as teachers—should be bound by the restrictions of sanctions. While nothing was said in the discussion about the Oklahoma situation, it was common knowledge that there was deep resentment against a few superintendents in that state who were quoted in the press—during the bitter fight to enforce the sanctions and during a time when the situation was touch and go as to whether the profession in Okla-

---

[14] *NEA Handbook for Local, State and National Associations, 1965–66,* Washington, D.C.: National Education Association, 1965, p. 63.

homa could win its case—that they were employing teachers from outside the state. In other words, these statements were interpreted as sneers at the impotence of sanctions.

The NEA, with its affiliated state associations and its more than 8,000 affiliated local associations, represents about 90 per cent of the 1,800,000 public school personnel. This coalition can be very effective in the enforcement of sanctions.

OTHER FACTORS.  The enforcement of sanctions is usually accompanied by factors other than public opinion and the will of the total profession. Political activity on the part of the teachers in the affected areas is one. In the Utah case, sanctions alone (applied only to teachers outside the state) were effective, but not dramatically so. They served to alert the people of the state to the fact that school conditions were not as rosy as had been assumed. The sanctions had some adverse impact upon the drive to bring industry into the state. But the state's power structure did not move to correct conditions with vigor. So the Utah Education Association organized a political arm in the summer of 1964 and sought the support of other sympathetic groups. The UEA conducted a vigorous campaign to elect a sympathetic governor and legislature. This activity was successful, and the Utah situation was resolved in the spring of 1965 by action of legislature.

The teachers of Waterbury really won their case by actively and successfully campaigning to defeat the incumbent mayor who had repeatedly vetoed or drastically cut items in the school board's annual budget, including proposed salary raises for the teachers.

Another significant factor in the success of sanctions is the willingness of college and university placement services to refuse to refer applicants for teaching positions in sanctioned school districts. Here again enters the integrity of the process of invoking sanctions. The placement services must have great confidence in the objectivity, validity, and honesty of investigative studies which result in the application of sanctions. They will not support preconceived and biased invocations of sanctions.

# Chapter 7. Major Issues in Professional Negotiation

SEVERAL ISSUES related to professional negotiation have been the cause of considerable concern and diversity of opinion among school board members, administrators, and teachers. Some of the issues, such as the legality of professional negotiation and the role of the superintendent of schools in the process, are discussed fully elsewhere in this volume and will receive only cursory treatment in this chapter. Other issues, such as composition of the negotiating unit and the role of administrative-supervisory personnel in the negotiation process, will be dealt with in a more comprehensive manner. The following issues will be discussed: (1) the legality of professional negotiation; (2) the subject matter of negotiations; (3) the role of the superintendent of schools; (4) the composition of the negotiating unit and its implications for the role of administrative-supervisory personnel; (5) exclusive recognition; (6) the relationship of sanctions to professional negotiation; and (7) the relationship of grievance procedures to professional negotiation.

## Legality of Professional Negotiation

It is often stated unequivocally that in the absence of a statute specifically forbidding a board of education to enter into a negotiating relationship with representatives of its professional staff, it is perfectly legal to do so. This is a moot question. But there is a considerable body of evidence that boards, as a general rule, could exercise broad discretionary authority in this regard (see Chapter 2). Such authority would appear to be vested in boards in the general discretionary powers granted to them for establishing reasonable rules and regulations governing the efficient operation of the schools. To maintain, as some boards have done, that entering into such agreements constitutes an illegal delegation of authority, is a questionable interpretation of the law as it applies to the public schools.

Moreover, it would appear that there is no legal barrier to the adoption of an agreement which calls for mediation or fact-finding in the event of an impasse in negotiations, so long as any recommendations resulting from such mediation or fact-finding are advisory in nature. One authority on the subject of school law has gone so far as to maintain that, on any specific matter, a board of education may agree beforehand to be bound by the recommendations made by an impartial third party. Reutter has said that:

> There seems to be no legal bar to mediation should an impasse occur between teachers and school boards. Some states have passed statutes related to mediation in certain cases involving public employees. In any state, however, since mediation does not involve any element of compulsion on the parties to follow the suggestions of the mediator, this observer sees no legal problem in voluntary mediation and no basic legal problem in compulsory mediation.
>
> Legal aspects of arbitration as a means of settling teacher-board impasses are not clear. An arbitration decision is considered binding on the parties. A frequently expressed view is that a board could not submit to arbitration *any* matter because this would involve an abdication of its discretion. This, however, is not correct. It depends on the issues. . . .[1]

It seems clear, then, that attempts to avoid entering into negotiation agreements on legal grounds have little basis in fact. Indeed, the inference might be drawn that the citing of legal obstacles by boards of education often is a convenient rationalization for their failure to enter into formal relationships with representatives of their staff. Once the legal obfuscations are overcome, boards of education and teacher groups are free to discuss the issues strictly

[1] E. Edmund Reutter, Jr., *Teacher-Administrator-Board Relationships* (Special Report), New York: Associated Public School Systems, Institute of Administrative Research, Teachers College, Columbia University, 1963, pp. 7–8 (mimeographed).

on their merits, in terms of what is best for the educational program, rather than seeking ways to avoid the inevitable. The relationship of the law to professional negotiation is discussed in detail in Chapter 2.

## What Is Negotiable?

Professional associations seek to negotiate on all matters affecting the educational program, not solely on those that might be termed "welfare" or "working conditions." The problem of determining the subject matter of negotiations, even when defined as narrowly as "working conditions" has been well stated by Steffensen as follows:

The term "conditions of work," when used to indicate the matters which are negotiable, becomes highly nebulous as one discusses it with staff members. First, it is nebulous within the welfare area, including salaries. . . . An even more important extension of "conditions of work" may be found in the curricular offering. There are few program adaptations which do not in some way affect the working conditions of the teacher, whether it be a change in the pupil/staff ratio, the use of TV instruction, the extension of the school day, or the addition of an elementary librarian. The decision to implement each of these practices has undoubtedly been reached after consideration of certain alternatives which would also affect the teacher's conditions of work. On this basis, to what extent do such non-economic factors as the curricular program and organization become negotiable items between the board and the teachers?[2]

The broad scope of subjects which are contemplated under professional negotiation procedures bears no relationship to the industrial relations delineation between management prerogatives and negotiable matters. The philosophy inherent in professional negotiation is that teachers, in common with other professional practitioners, have a deep and transcendent interest in all matters which may bear upon the standards of their practice. Any other position is in direct conflict with the spirit and purpose of the process.

[2] James P. Steffensen, *Teachers Negotiate With Their School Boards,* Bulletin 1964, No. 40, Washington, D. C.: U. S. Office of Education, 1964, pp. 27–38.

It is nonsense to proclaim, on Teacher Recognition Day, that teachers are dedicated professionals who strive tirelessly to improve the quality of the educational program, while attempting to deny them, on the other hand, the right to negotiate on matters other than "bread and butter." If professionalism in education means anything, it means that teachers have a legitimate interest in every decision that affects their pupil clientele and the effectiveness of their work. As pointed out earlier, most negotiation agreements recognize the interest of teachers in negotiating educational matters. One might go so far as to say that teachers, through their professional associations, are in unique positions to offer maximum assistance in assigning educational priorities and making difficult judgments with respect to budgetary allocation. It is precisely at these points that their professional expertise and competence may be brought most fruitfully to bear. The subject matter of negotiation, then, should be as broadly defined as the educational program itself. This is the reason that in so many school districts negotiation is looked upon as a year-round process, rather than one which comes into play at budget-making time.

## Role of the Superintendent of Schools

Conflicting definitions of the superintendent's role have led to a good deal of confusion with respect to this important aspect of professional negotiation. Chapter 5 deals with this subject in depth; therefore, only brief attention will be given to it here.

The basic contention of those who hold that the superintendent must align himself with one faction or another in the negotiation process is that he cannot "serve two masters," that he cannot remain neutral if there is a conflict of opinion between teachers and board. This contention is valid only if the superintendent's role is narrowly perceived as being analogous to that of the manager of a corporate enterprise.

Another line of reasoning holds that the superintendent is being bypassed in the negotiation process, that teachers seek to go *around* the superintendent in their dealings with the board of education. While it is true that teachers *do* seek to deal directly with the board of education, this is so because meaningful negotiations over many aspects of the educational program can be conducted only with persons who have policy-making authority. This becomes even more crucial when negotiating on matters having fiscal implications. To deny teachers access to boards of education is to indulge in the grossest form of paternalism; moreover such action connotes a serious lack of security on the parts of administrators who engage in it. Superintendents in hundreds of districts throughout the nation have for years encouraged boards of education and teacher organizations to come together for the purpose of discussing mutual problems and matters of educational policy with no discernible loss at all in their prestige or authority. In fact, such practice fosters desirable working relationships and a high degree of staff morale in school districts which actually *enhances* the position of the chief school administrator rather than detracting from it.

The contention of those who believe in professional negotiation as a rational process for solving educational problems is that the superintendent can and should play a role which aligns him with neither the school board nor the teachers' organization. Rather, he should function as an active participant in the negotiations, favoring neither side but giving both the benefit of his knowledge, experience, and educational statesmanship.

A recent edition of *Educator's Dispatch,* a national publication geared to the interests and needs of school administrators, referred to the proliferation of written agreements between teachers' organizations and boards of education. The following advice was offered to school superintendents:

These agreements are a step forward. They are expressions of the willingness of boards, administrators, and teachers to put their heads together to come up with the best education possible for students.

These agreements, however, create a problem for the superintendent. They place him smack in the middle between the board and the teachers' organization. So long as their relations are amicable, the superintendent will have little difficulty mediating between them. But if relations deteriorate and teachers and board clash, the middleman may come under fire from both sides. And, if the battle gets heated enough, he may be the major casualty.

If you face this unpleasant possibility, forestall it by working to keep teachers and board on friendly terms and willing to negotiate in good faith. Then when negotiations do start, act, as much as you can, as an independent third party who eyes every proposal in light of its effects on students and who makes his own recommendations to both parties in an attempt to bring them to an agreement. And above all, build a reputation as a man who sides not with the board or the teachers but with the good of the students.[3]

## Composition of the Negotiating Unit

The question of the appropriateness of various forms of unit composition in the negotiation process has been a thorny one. Specifically, controversy centers about representation for administrative and supervisory personnel. At the heart of this question lies a more basic one: the structure and organization of teachers organizations.

One of the purported differences between local NEA affiliates and those of the American Federation of Teachers is the admission to membership of administrative and supervisory personnel. It is generally assumed that administrators and supervisors are specifically banned from membership in the AFT. Likewise, it is assumed that all local affiliates of the NEA are "all-inclusive," i.e., that they accept all professional personnel into membership. Both assumptions are false.

In actuality, the constitution of the American Federation of Teachers clearly leaves the question of administrative-supervisory membership squarely in the hands of local affiliates. Article III, "Membership," of the *Constitution of the American Federation of Teachers* contains the following sections:[4]

*Section 1.* This organization shall consist of federations of public and private school teachers, or educational workers organized in conformity with the provisions of this constitution. *Other school employees may be members of any local whose constitution so permits* [emphasis supplied].

*Section 2.* The Executive Council may admit to membership organizations of public school principals, assistants to principals, heads of departments or other supervising officers, except superintendents, pro-

---

[3] *Educator's Dispatch, The Letter for Administrators,* New London, Connecticut: Croft Educational Services, Vol. 20, No. 21, July 15, 1965, p. 4.

[4] *Constitution of the American Federation of Teachers,* Chicago: American Federation of Teachers, 1964, pp. 3–4.

vided that the existing local or locals shall recommend granting of a charter to those applying under this section.

*Section 3.* Classroom teachers with supervisory authority may be admitted to membership by any local whose constitution so permits.

\*    \*    \*

*Section 6.* Locals which have been organized for at least one year may admit to membership principals or other supervisory officers, excepting superintendents, college deans, or college presidents.

Clearly, insofar as public elementary and secondary schools are concerned, the only personnel barred from membership in AFT locals by the national constitution are superintendents of schools. No information is available relative to the number of AFT locals which by local constitutional provision actually bar supervisory-administrative personnel from membership or from holding office. Significantly, Charles Cogen, former president of the United Federation of Teachers local AFT affiliate in New York City, was prevented from voting in the collective bargaining election held in that city in 1961 because of the fact that at the time he held a supervisory position in the New York City public schools.

Similarly, the National Education Association places no restrictions upon local organizations seeking to affiliate. As is the case with the American Federation of Teachers, local affiliates of the NEA are free to organize in any manner deemed most suitable to their purposes. Article X, "Affiliated Associations" of the NEA Bylaws contains the following section:[5]

LOCAL AFFILIATES

*Section 4.* Any local professional education association located within a city, county, or other local school administrative unit of any state, commonwealth, or the District of Columbia shall be eligible for application with the Association and shall be designated as a local affiliate. In addition any association recognized as a local unit by a state affiliate shall be eligible for application. A local professional education association shall be interpreted to mean any local organization of educators whether its membership is open to all professional educators, or all classroom teachers, or all administrators within the

[5] *NEA Handbook for Local, State, and National Associations, 1964–65,* Washington, D. C.: National Education Association, 1964, p. 44.

jurisdictional boundaries of the organization, or to all members of a university or college staff.

A 1960 study by the Research Division of NEA indicated that, for the school year 1958–59, 13 per cent of the samples of both city and county affiliates of the NEA were restricted to classroom teacher-only membership.[6]

Although precise figures are not available, it may be assumed that the number of classroom teacher-only organizations currently working under the provisions of written professional negotiation agreements is at least in proportion to the percentage of classroom teacher-only affiliates of the NEA.

It would appear from the foregoing that the only substantive difference between NEA and AFT positions in regard to the question of unit composition is in the exclusion of the superintendent from membership. And in view of the superintendent's role in professional negotiation, as outlined in NEA literature, his membership or nonmembership in the local association is of little significance with respect to the negotiation process itself.

Significantly, of the six "educators-only" negotiation statutes passed in 1965, three call for secret ballot elections to determine the negotiation representative (Connecticut, Oregon, and Washington). In all three instances the laws call for participation of *all* professional personnel below the rank of superintendent in the elections. The five statutes pertaining to all public employees show considerable variation. The Massachusetts statute permits elections to include all professional personnel. The Wisconsin statute is silent on the matter; however, the Wisconsin Employment Relations Board does not permit supervisory personnel to participate in elections which it conducts. Although the Michigan statute prohibits supervisory employees from participating in elections, it permits the state labor mediation board to recognize units which previously had been recognized by the employer or identified by certifications, contract, or past practice as a unit for bargaining purposes. Presumably such units could include those all-inclusive units which

---

[6] *Local Associations—Organization, Practices, and Programs, 1958–59,* Washington, D. C.: Research Division, National Education Association, 1960, p. 6.

had been recognized *before* passage of the statute in 1965. The statutes in Alaska and New Hampshire do not mention unit composition, and there have been no labor board rulings in these states which shed light on the question.

The Connecticut statute is unique in that it provides for local determination of the negotiation unit. Prior to voting for the negotiating representative, a vote is held to ascertain whether the staff wishes to negotiate through a single all-inclusive organization or through separate units composed of classroom teachers on the one hand and administrative-supervisory personnel on the other. This approach is a very desirable one, since it recognizes that local preferences should control the plan to be followed in negotiations. On the other hand, a recent ruling by the Attorney General of the state of Washington held that, in order for an organization to be certified as negotiating agent under provisions of the law, it *cannot* be restricted to classroom teachers only, but must be all-inclusive in its composition.

As was pointed out in Chapter 3, "Elements of Professional Negotiation Agreements," administrative-supervisory personnel are represented in negotiations in three ways: (1) through all-inclusive organizations, (2) through separate organizations, or (3) not at all. Since most negotiable items pertain to all professional personnel, there is no inherent conflict of interest in all-inclusive organizations. Even in the case of salary schedules, there is a strong tendency to include all personnel in a single structure, relating administrative-supervisory positions to the teachers' schedule by means of ratios or percentages. The situation here is analogous to that obtaining in the federal government, where all-inclusive employee unions are frequently to be found.

According to Hart:

> This [composition of the unit] is one area in which there are significant differences between industry and government. The dividing line between labor and management or between workers and supervisors is much more clearly drawn in industry than in government. Civil service laws, rules, and regulations generally apply, without differentiation, to both workers and supervisors. Both are covered by the same leave systems, the same pay systems, the same pension plans, and the same operating rules.

Industry is more likely to accentuate the dividing line between the two categories of personnel by subjecting them to different company rules. Perhaps as a result of the different relationship which exists in government, government employee unions have not generally followed the normal trade-union practice of restricting eligibility for membership to non-supervisory workers. The only eligibility requirement laid down by most government employee unions is that the member or applicant for membership must be on the federal payroll. Presumably even the President of the United States could qualify. While no presidents have ever joined, there have been instances where high-ranking presidential appointees, including the heads of independent agencies, have become government employee union members.[7]

Naturally, any differences or disagreements among various segments of all-inclusive organizations should be aired and reconciled before negotiations take place. What frequently occurs in all-inclusive associations is that administrative-supervisory employees are free to join, but are ineligible to assume positions of leadership. If the all-inclusive membership concept does not or cannot operate satisfactorily in specific instances, then different arrangements are worked out. Future patterns may call for administrative-supervisory employees to be included in the memberships of local associations with respect to all matters of broad professional concern, but *excluded* from the unit for purposes of contract negotiation. Again, local preferences should control the pattern of negotiations and unit composition to be employed.

Another question frequently raised relates to the grievance process. How, it is asked, can an organization process a member's grievance when the object of the complaint may be a supervisor who is a member of the same organization? Obviously, a party of interest to a grievance cannot serve on any association committee charged with processing or hearing the grievance. Good judgment, and adequate policies, will provide for such contingencies.

Pertinent here is a memorandum prepared by Professor Sterling D. Spero in 1962 at the request of Labor Lodge 12 of the American Federation of Government Employees. The point at issue was the propriety of union representation of an aggrieved employee

[7] Wilson R. Hart, *Collective Bargaining in the Federal Civil Service,* New York: Harper & Brothers, 1961, pp. 184–85.

if the management official who is the object of the complaint is also an official of the same union as the person lodging the complaint. The report based on Spero's memorandum states:

> Professor Spero suggests that any conflict of interest that might arise can be avoided through carefully drawn procedures. He lays special stress on the fact that the employee in the classified service wears several hats. He is both supervisor and supervised, manager and managed. Supervisors as such have no defined role in grievance procedures. Such procedures actually operate on an ad hoc basis so that the role of the supervisor in the procedure is determined by the circumstances of the particular case. He may be a witness for or against the employee or testify to clarify the circumstances as neither side's witness. Where a higher rated employee who may be a union member is a party in a grievance procedure involving those who work with him in a lower rated capacity, such higher rated employee obviously could not function in the grievance procedure as a unionist. *The union as an organization represents employees as employees and can under no circumstances function in behalf of management. The application of this principle in specific cases under carefully drawn collective agreements governing the grievance procedure should indicate the direction for the solution of this problem on a common sense basis* [emphasis added].[8]

The composition of the negotiation unit (that is, inclusion or noninclusion of administrative-supervisory personnel) presents no obstacles to effective negotiations that cannot be surmounted by carefully drawn procedural safeguards and a modicum of common sense displayed by all parties. While the NEA has no official preference for one type of local affiliate organization over another, it holds very firmly that the all-inclusive approach to negotiations can be made to operate successfully so long as all parties *desire* to make it operate successfully, so long as individual segments of the organization are able to arrive at important policy decisions free of domination by other segments, and so long as diverse needs and interests can be reconciled satisfactorily before reaching the negotiating table. The future development of local NEA affiliates may well tend toward: (1) exclusion of the superintendent of schools from the negotiation unit and (2) the creation of exclu-

[8] *Government Employee Relations Report,* Number 88, Washington, D. C.: Bureau of National Affairs, Inc., May 17, 1965, p. A-8.

sively classroom teacher associations or the creation of such units as specialized departments of the all-inclusive local associations, thus assuring uninhibited discussion and action on problems of classroom teachers. In the final analysis, determination of the negotiation unit should be left to local preference, based upon what is most desirable practice in view of unique local circumstances—*not* mandated by state legislation designed to regulate traditional labor-management relationships which have little or no applicability to education.

## Exclusive Recognition

An essential ingredient of the professional negotiation process is that the organization of staff members receiving majority support should be recognized by the board of education as exclusive negotiating agent for the staff. According to the NEA:

The desired result of the negotiation process is agreement. Several organizations can present proposals or participate in discussions, but experience has made it clear that only one organization can participate in negotiations which lead to agreement. Members-only representation by several teacher organizations is impracticable because several agreements are impracticable.... This difficulty cannot be overcome by having a negotiating committee consisting of equal or proportionate membership from several competing organizations. The evidence is that such organizations are often torn with interorganizational rivalries and that it is difficult to place responsibility for good-faith negotiation on any of the organizations represented.[9]

The concept of exclusive recognition is well grounded in laws and regulations governing private employment relations, and has become so in public employment also. As pointed out in Chapter 2, Executive Order 10988, promulgated by President Kennedy in 1962,[10] governs the relationship between federal government agencies and their employee organizations. It recognizes a legitimate distinction between employee organizations on the basis of their relative membership strengths. The Order places such or-

[9] *Guidelines for Professional Negotiation,* Rev. ed., Washington, D. C.: Office of Professional Development and Welfare, National Education Association, 1965.
[10] Executive Order 10988, 27 Fed. Reg. 551 (1962).

ganizations into three categories: (1) those entitled to informal recognition, (2) those entitled to formal recognition, and (3) those entitled to exclusive recognition. Exclusive recognition in any federal agency is reserved for the employee organization that enjoys majority support, and only the organization accorded exclusive recognition has the right to negotiate in an effort to reach agreements with the employing agency on the formulation of policies.

The following excerpt from the Report of the President's Task Force on Employee-Management Relations in the Federal Service, which led to the adoption of Executive Order 10988, is directly related to this point:

> Under this system, if an employee organization is chosen by the majority of the employees in an appropriate unit it becomes the *only* formal recognized representative for the unit. In its dealings with management officials it is considered to speak for *all* of the employees of the unit, a responsibility which it must, of course, meet.
>
> It should be emphasized that exclusive recognition in the form proposed by the Task Force would not prevent any individual employee from bringing matters of personal concern to the attention of management officials, nor, for example, from choosing his own representative in a grievance action. Similarly, under a system of exclusive recognition other organizations of limited membership continue to receive informal recognition, and may from time to time merely present their views to management. However, only one voice may speak for all the employees in the appropriate unit, and management may negotiate and reach agreement only with it. Representatives of the organization with ex-clusive recognition normally have the right to be present at any discussion of personnel policy matters between management and other employees or employee representatives. . . .
>
> *Wherever exclusive recognition is now practiced in the Federal Government it has proved successful, and the Federal officials concerned have unanimously recommended its adoption elsewhere in the Government* [emphasis supplied].[11]

The concept of exclusive recognition has been slower to be recognized in public education than in other jurisdictions of em-

---

[11] *A Policy for Employee-Management Cooperation in the Federal Service,* Report of the President's Task Force on Employee-Management Relations in the Federal Service, Washington, D. C.: The Task Force, November 30, 1961, pp. 25–26.

ployment. That there are no legal barriers, in the absence of a statute to the contrary, to a board of education voluntarily recognizing a single organization for the purpose of negotiating, is attested to by the fact that hundreds of teachers organizations throughout the country currently are recognized as exclusive negotiating agents. The legal basis for the adoption of such a policy is the power of a board of education to promulgate those policies which, in its considered judgment, are in the best interest of the school system, its pupils and teachers, and are calculated to result in the efficient and harmonious operation of the system. Of course, as pointed out in Chapter 2, a board cannot be *forced* to grant exclusive recognition in the absence of a statute compelling it to do so.

In reply to questions put to him by the state superintendent of public instruction with respect to a proposed teacher referendum in Detroit, the Michigan Attorney General published Opinion No. 4306, dated March 18, 1964. The opinion clearly upheld the right of the Detroit Board of Education to recognize for the purposes of negotiation the organization receiving majority support from the staff. In part, the opinion read as follows:

It must be concluded that in the absence of statute providing to the contrary, a board of education can limit representation of employees in resolving differences involving salary, working conditions, personal welfare or other related problems to the teacher association receiving a majority of the teachers' votes at the representation election. At the same time the right of the individual teacher to handle his own dispute individually and without representation with the said board of educaton is preserved. . . .

Because the board of education of the school district of the City of Detroit has statutory power to determine terms and conditions of employment of teachers, it must follow that it is authorized in its discretion to recognize as the exclusive negotiating representative for the purpose of carrying out the procedures outlined by the board that association of teachers which receives a majority of the teachers' votes at a representation election.

Since the legislative discretion to determine the terms and conditions of services to be performed by teachers rests *finally* in the board of education of the school district, a decision of the board of education to recognize a teacher association as the exclusive negotiating representative for the purpose of carrying out the procedures as outlined by the above board does not constitute a surrender of such discretion to the teacher association. See the special concurring opinion of Mr. Justice Pringle in *Fellows* v. *LaTronica,* 377 P. (2d) 547 (Colorado 1962).

In the event the board of education of the school district of the City of Detroit chooses to recognize the teacher association which receives the majority of the teachers' vote at a representation election as the exclusive negotiating representative for the purpose of resolving differences in terms and conditions of employment, and as a result of such negotiations would have to be available to teachers of the school district without discrimination as to membership or lack of membership in such teacher association. The board of education is without authority to require membership in such teacher association as a condition precedent to receipt of the benefits of such negotiations. *Benson* v. *School District No. 1 of Silver Bow County,* 344 P. (2d) 117 (Montana 1959).

Therefore, it is my opinion that a board of education of a school district is empowered, *in its discretion,* to recognize as the exclusive representative an association of teachers which receives a majority of the teachers' votes at a representation election for the purpose of negotiating differences concerning salary, status, working conditions, personal welfare or other related problems.[12]

It would appear to follow that the granting of exclusive negotiating rights to a majority staff organization is perfectly legal so long as two conditions are met: (a) the rights of individuals and minority groups to present their views to the governing board are protected, and (b) the policies developed in the joint negotiation process shall apply to all staff members regardless of membership or nonmembership in the majority organization, or *any* organization.

While secret ballot election is a commonly accepted method of determining majority status, it is by no means the only method currently in use. Other means include: (a) verified membership lists, (b) authorization or designation cards signed by a majority of the staff, and (c) signed petitions requesting representation by one organization.

However the majority representative is determined, it is essential, if negotiations in good faith are to take place, that one organiza-

[12] *Michigan A.G.O. No. 4306,* March 18, 1964.

tion be empowered to speak for the professional staff. The vast majority of professional negotiation agreements on file at the NEA provide for negotiations with a single, majority organization.

Following are the advantages of granting exclusive negotiation rights to the majority staff organization:[13]

1. *It is simple, clear cut, and direct.* One organization selects its representatives, and these representatives are the only ones with whom the board of education must deal. Arrangements for meetings can be made easily, and there is just one group through which to seek agreement.

2. *It provides a single, clear cut line of organizational authority.* The entire negotiating committee is fully responsible to the organization it represents, and the organization is able to hold all of the representatives on the committee to account. The board of education knows that the entire committee is authorized to speak for the majority concerned.

3. *It provides for negotiation by a unified group, selected by and working on behalf of a majority of those being represented.* If the negotiating committee were to include representatives of a minority group rejected by the majority of teachers, the majority representatives on the committee would be subject to harrassment and undermining by the minority even while seeking to negotiate. Since majority decision must ultimately determine acceptance of any agreement, the majority's position must be that which is presented in negotiations.

4. *It provides for testimony rights for individuals and minority groups who may not wish to be represented by the majority organization.* Under procedures which could be drawn up the board of education would simply arrange for an occasion, either at the start of negotiations or at some other time before reaching a final decision, when opportunity would be provided, not for discussion or negotiation, but for any individual or minority group to be heard and to present its views so that these could be subject to appropriate consideration as part of negotiations with the majority organization.

[13] Adapted from *Teacher Representation in Towns Having More Than One Teachers' Organization,* Hartford: Connecticut Education Association, 1963, pp. 4–5 (mimeographed).

5. *It is in keeping with the majority rule principle of democracy whereby the representative chosen by the majority speaks for all until replaced.* Under this principle, members of a minority group have the opportunity either to join the majority group and seek to influence its decisions, or to transform the minority into a majority group which could then assume the position of representing all.

6. *It makes possible the responsible use of parent organization resources.* Experience in negotiations has demonstrated the value to all parties concerned of the prompt availability of research data, field service, legal counsel, and conciliation through state organization representatives. Such assistance is less likely to be used, and more difficult to use effectively, where teachers with conflicting organizational alignments are involved in negotiations.

7. *It is in harmony with the concept of free choice among alternatives, which lies at the heart of the democratic process.* Only if teachers have the opportunity to make a choice which makes a difference—to select one alternative over another—can their determination be genuine. A joint committee of teacher representatives from two or more organizations nullifies the principle of meaningful selection. Exclusive representation by one organization selected by majority decision makes possible the exercise of bona fide choice. With the assumption that the possibility always exists of changing the choice, and selecting a different organization to be represented by at a future date, the democratic principle of significant alternatives will have constructive effect.

So long as exclusive representation for the purpose of negotiating does not preclude the right of any individual or group to be heard by the board, so long as negotiated policies are made applicable to all members of the staff, and in the absence of a statute to the contrary, it would appear to be perfectly legal for a board of education, if it so desires, to enter into an exclusive negotiating relationship with representatives of the staff organization determined to constitute a majority of the professional staff. Any arrangement short of this makes the negotiation process far less than satisfactory.

## The Relationship of Sanctions to Professional Negotiation

The subject of professional sanctions was discussed in Chapter 6. The purpose of this brief section is to place sanctions in their proper perspective vis-à-vis the negotiation process. The assumption that the relationship between sanctions and professional negotiation is identical to the relationship between strikes and collective bargaining is erroneous. Likewise, the fear on the part of some boards of education and administrators that sanctions are a natural concomitant of professional negotiation is ungrounded.

Sanctions may indeed be applied in cases of persistent refusal to listen, to discuss, and to negotiate. Although not officially endorsing sanctions, and though reference is never made to the process by name, the American Association of School Administrators has furnished justification for this type of action:

> We believe that in those exceedingly rare situations where the professional staff believes that the school board or some other legal fiscal control body has denied reasonable requests for conferences, for study, and for presentation of welfare proposals, or has demonstrated flagrant unwillingness to provide reasonable salary contracts or other welfare provisions, the professional staff has the right to present all the facts to the public and to their professional associates in other school districts. On the other hand, where the staff obstinately holds to an unreasonable position which disrupts or seriously impairs the operation of the schools, the school board has comparable rights and responsibilities.[14]

Moreover the revised edition of NEA's *Guidelines for Professional Negotiation* suggests the possibility of sanctions in cases in which ". . . the board of education refuses to meet with association leaders to discuss the request [for professional negotiation], if a decision on the matter is unreasonably delayed, if the proposal is rejected out of hand. . . ."[15]

---

[14] *Roles, Responsibilities, Relationships of the School Board, Superintendent, and Staff*, Washington, D. C.: American Association of School Administrators, 1963, p. 14.

[15] *Guidelines, op. cit.*, p. 11.

Sanctions could, then, be used *in the absence* of a professional negotiation agreement, either to rectify alleged intolerable teaching conditions or to protest the failure of a school board to discuss the joint development of a negotiation agreement. In *no* case, however, have sanctions been invoked where mediation provisions of professional negotiation agreements exist and have been used.

While it cannot be categorically maintained that local or state associations will *never* apply forms of sanctions where negotiation agreements exist, it would appear reasonable to assume that those boards of education willing to enter into such agreements and to negotiate in good faith will not be those which will be sanctioned. On the other hand, those boards which continue to refuse to enter into agreements and refuse to negotiate in good faith lay themselves open to the possibility of punitive action, and with some justification.

The key to the situation lies in the inclusion of mediation and appeal procedures in negotiation agreements. Such procedures, if adhered to, should preclude arbitrary action on the part of either the board or the association. The success of professional negotiation, then, depends upon the good faith of those negotiating and the good offices of an impartial third party in the event that agreement cannot be reached. Once an agreement is adopted, it does *not* depend for its success upon a display of raw power on either side. So long as a Level III agreement is in effect, there should be no need for accompanying weapons of any sort.

## The Relationship of Grievance Procedures to Professional Negotiation

Confusion sometimes exists concerning the relationship of grievance procedures to professional negotiation. A grievance may be defined as a claim based upon an event or condition under which an employee works, allegedly caused by misinterpretation or inequitable application of an established policy. Professional negotiation is the process by which such policy is formulated and established. A grievance policy, then, is a most necessary concomitant of any negotiation procedure, since it provides for the democratic adjudication of any questions of alleged injustice to an individual or group arising from the interpretation and application of policy or from the day-by-day management of school affairs. Significantly, even in the absence of negotiation laws many states have enacted specific statutes pertaining to the processing of employee grievances (see Table 2-1 in Chapter 2).

The NEA Commission on Professional Rights and Responsibilities has published a document containing a recommended grievance procedure which includes organizational channels for processing grievances in addition to the traditional administrative channels.[16]

The New Rochelle, New York, professional negotiation agreement, reproduced in Appendix C, contains a grievance procedure (see Article XI, page 227) which may be considered one of the more advanced of the employed procedural approaches. With the following modifications, it could serve as a model of this type of procedure:

- Under "Level Two" of the grievance policy, the Ad Hoc Committee should not have the authority to make final judgment concerning the merit of a teacher's grievance or the decision of the local association to support or not to support processing of the grievance but, rather, should make recommendations to the Professional Rights and Responsibilities Panel. This Panel should make a formal judgment on the merits, based upon the Ad Hoc Committee's recommendations.

- Similarly, it should be the P. R. and R. Panel, rather than the Ad Hoc Committee, which meets with the superintendent's committee and the Board's Review Committee.

Another issue to be considered is the advisability of binding, as opposed to advisory, arbitration as the final step in the grievance process. Few, if any, grievance procedures in public education contain this feature, although it is almost universal in private employment. Since the disposition of grievance actions generally hinges upon the dispassionate interpretation of written policies, it would appear desirable to leave the final judgment on such matters to the good offices of an experienced, impartial arbitrator rather

---

[16] *Implementing the Code of Ethics of the Education Program and Strengthening Professional Rights,* Washington, D. C.: Commission on Professional Rights and Responsibilities, National Education Association, June 1964, pp. 20–22.

than to an individual or group which was a party to the development and adoption of the policy in question. In the absence of a statute to the contrary, there would be no legal impediment to a board of education agreeing beforehand to abide by the judgment of an impartial, educationally oriented arbitrator with respect to a specific fact situation. It is emphasized that such binding arbitration is suggested as the final step in a grievance procedure and not for the negotiation process itself. Determinations, then, would be made concerning already-established policy. While such a proposal is not likely to be greeted warmly by all parties, its use should merit serious consideration in the interests of efficient school operation and improved employee morale.

# Chapter 8. The Need for a New Public Policy

In the light of events and developments since 1960, it is evident that the need for the derivation of a vastly changed policy regarding employer-employee relationships in the public schools is compelling. Indeed, the emergence of a new policy is already well under way, is clearly visible. The new policy for public school teachers will parallel closely that for public employees in general, in terms both of the timing of emergence and the general provisions. For teachers, because of the unique relationships which should exist in the public schools, there will probably be some different connotations, some unique procedures. But the liberalization of past and existing policy will come into being for teachers as public employees and, alongside that, for other public employees.

## Rights of Public Employees

The drive for collective action by public employee groups has emerged, so to speak, almost overnight, virtually within the last decade. This is attributable to a number of factors, some of which will be discussed below. The suddenness of this development, however, is worthy of separate treatment.

Change, of course, in one degree or another of rapidity, has been a companion of society throughout history. In some eras, it has been so slow as to be imperceptible, the results only noticeable in succeeding generations. In other eras, change has been perceptible but gradual. Throughout this century, the pace has been marked by a steady acceleration. In the United States since World

War II, that pace has reached the proportions of a runaway. The changes in every aspect of American life (and, of course, this is also true of some other areas of the world) have been massive and, to some extent, overwhelming.

The unprecedented rapidity of the flow of events since World War II has conditioned the American people to the tolerance, if not enthusiastic acceptance, of new mores. Thus, demands for more considerate treatment of public employees have found an increasingly receptive climate. Whereas, a generation ago, any suggestion that such employees should be consulted or given any part in determining the conditions and policies under which they worked and were employed would have been a radical one. Any implication that such employees should have the right to strike would have been interpreted widely as bordering on the subversive. The aphorism of Calvin Coolidge, uttered in 1919 as Governor of Massachusetts, in reference to a threatened strike of Boston policemen for higher pay, fixed itself in the public mind as political, economic, and social gospel. He said: "There is no right at any time or place for public employees to strike against the government."

This mind-set prevailed in absolute terms for a generation. But the stirrings of dissatisfaction among public employees, of the cities, the states, and of the Federal Government, in the 1950's, had their impacts in influencing governmental agencies to reexamine the traditions of employer-employee relationships. Civil Service had long since been instituted in many of these agencies—and long since employees had begun in an informal way to influence improved conditions of work and welfare considerations. President Kennedy's Executive Order 10988 and Little Wagner Acts in Philadelphia and New York City were indications of the groping for liberalized and democratic procedures.

But perhaps the major influence in the evolution of employee rights was a changed climate of public opinion resulting from a new image of public employees engendered by the nature of services society was demanding of such employees, and the increased degree of competence demanded. In past generations, the public employee was almost universally regarded as the holder of a political sinecure, as without competence to do anything else.

As such, he was viewed as a sort of parasite on society, as a tax eater, and as a useless burden on the taxpayer.

With the growing complexity of society, however, governmental services had to multiply. Moreover, the services increasingly became highly skilled types—technical, scientific, and professional in nature. Economists, physicians, sociologists, engineers, scientists, mathematicians, tax experts, skilled planners, and many other professional groups, were required by governments and were enticed in such employment by matching government pay and working conditions with private employment.

Too, the increase in the number of public employees, as complexity of society demanded more and more services, reached unprecedented proportions. In 1947 the total number of public employees was 5,474,000, as contrasted with a total of 9,502,000 in 1964. Public employees now comprise one sixth of the total working force of the nation. The number of federal employees, as of May 1965, was 2,337,000. But the great increases in public employees in recent years have been at state and local levels. Since 1947, nine workers have been added by state and local governments for every one added by the federal government. The greatest increase in the number employed has been in public school teachers. In 1947 there were 887,130 employed in the instructional staffs of the public schools; and in 1964 the total was 1,788,805.

Another shift in the employment figures which has had a profound influence upon the climate concerning the rights of public workers is the drastic decline in the number of farm jobs. In a decade and a half, farm workers declined from 14 per cent to about 7 per cent of the total work force. This shift, accompanied by rapid urbanization of the nation, has made the city population, rather than the rural one, the dominant group. As a consequence, political representation has drastically changed. This change will be accelerated by the reapportionment of state legislatures ordered by the U. S. Supreme Court. In effect, these shifts mean that the climate of public opinion is shifting from a predominantly rural and highly conservative posture to a highly liberal urban one. There is a new, liberalized concept about the rights of public employees.

The upgrading of the nature of the services of governments

mandated a similar upgrading in the caliber and preparation of employees. Where once the typical government employee was a political hack who needed only the rudiments of learning, a facile tongue, and the appearance of being about the people's business, the new order demanded professional people with broad backgrounds of college and university training. Such professionals have depth and breadth of knowledge and rare skills to sell in the open market. Government could only compete successfully for their services by matching the considerate treatment which these professionals could receive elsewhere. Thus, the scared hired hand or lackey image of the public employee rapidly became an image of one worthy of, and demanding public respect.

## Rights of Teachers

Somewhat the same evolutionary steps have affected the status of teachers. Although both the improved image and considerate treatment of teachers emerged more slowly than those of most other public employees, the trends in these directions are now gathering unmistakable momentum. Perhaps it is more accurate to say that legal recognition of teachers' rights to representative negotiation with their employers evolved more slowly than for most other public employees.

In many other respects, teachers have been in the forefront as objects of enlightened legislation. Such provisions as tenure, retirement, and minimum salary, for examples, have been in existence in most states for a generation. Of course, these provisions are not universal but they do exist in most states; and some provisions, such as retirement, exist in all states and apply to all teachers.

Rights to bargain regarding conditions of work, salary provisions, and fringe benefits, plus rights to participate in policy-making, have emerged only in recent years. It may be surmised that the protective legislation referred to above actually lessened the demand at the local level for greater rights; at least these legislative provisions delayed such demands.

Aside from the impacts of what was happening in other areas of public employment, and the steady evolution of the concept of human rights, the greatest single factor in the public's relatively new and vastly improved respect for teachers has been the teachers' increasing professional competence. Only a little more than a decade ago, the average preparation of teachers was dismally low. As late as 1946, about two thirds of the states did not require a degree for beginning elementary teachers; and the requirements ranged downward to less than high school graduation and the passing of an examination based upon elementary school content in some states. It may be assumed that the generally low opinion of the public of teachers and of teaching reflected these low requirements. Only a decade ago, at least one fourth of the nation's public school teachers had not completed a college degree. In 1965, fewer than 10 per cent of public school staffs (about 1,800,000) had not completed the bachelor's or higher degrees; about one fourth had completed the master's degree. Moreover the great gap that existed a decade ago between the preparation of elementary and high school teachers has been largely closed. Thus the teacher now typically appears to the public somewhat the same as the professional government service employee. He appears, by virtue of his preparation, the complex demands upon his skills, the indispensable nature of his services to society, as an employee of undoubted quality, and worthy of respect and the dignity accorded all professional people.

## What Public Policy for Teachers?

For about a generation now, workers in the United States have had national legislation spelling out their right to organize and bargain with their employers regarding working conditions, salaries and other welfare matters. It is now evident that public opinion is growing that these rights accorded by law to workers in private industry should be applied to public employees. But the right of public employees to strike—a legal weapon in the private sector— does not as yet have wide public acceptance.

The National Labor Relations Act excluded public employees from its provisions. This exclusion would, of course, apply to teachers. Thus, collective action by teachers is only just demanding a clearly spelled out public policy in law.

This demand can be met in two ways—(1) By action of school boards in entering into professional negotiation agreements (or collective bargaining contracts); or (2) By state legislation mandating these rights. Since education is a state responsibility, the legislation must necessarily be at the state level. In only eleven states now (1965–66 school year) are there any provisions in the law to compel or permit school boards to recognize teacher groups for collective negotiating or bargaining.

Representation elections have been held often in the absence of any legislation specifically authorizing such action or prohibiting it. In view of this legal vacuum, teachers organizations frequently have no option but to improvise on the basis of local conditions. Formal state legislation has been late in coming, but it is interesting to note that the eleven statutes presently in existence cover approximately 30 per cent of the instructional staffs in the public schools of the United States. In the absence of statute, it is necessary for teachers to strike out on their own.

It seems obvious that the time has come to establish collective rights of teachers as a matter of public policy and by law. This premise immediately raises the question of the kind of legislation. Should it be of the labor relations type now existing for employees in private industry? Or, should it be another approach based upon the uniqueness of the teacher's work and working conditions? The position taken herein, the reasons for which have been set forth elsewhere in this volume, is the latter. Of course, whatever kind of state legislation emerges will borrow heavily from precedents and experiences of labor legislation. Also such legislation will draw heavily upon provisions now in existence for federal employees and legislation concerning public employees in states and municipalities.

State legislation, as proposed herein, should be of two types. First, statutes which will vest in the teaching profession certain responsibilities for setting and enforcing standards of preparation, licensure, and practices, including adherence to the code of ethics. Presently, six states (California, Florida, Kentucky, North Dakota, Oklahoma, and Oregon) have enacted professional practices laws. Second, statutes which require school boards to participate in professional negotiation procedures at the request of their local professional organizations.

President Kennedy's Executive Order 10988, of 1962 (see Appendix I for full text) is indicative of the trend to derive a set of procedures apart from the labor laws. The phrase "collective bargaining" is not used in the Order. Both labor organizations and other types of employee organizations, including professional associations, may be recognized. Organizations are excluded that (1) assert the right to strike against the federal government or any of its agencies; (2) advocate the overthrowing of the constitutional form of government; (3) discriminate in their membership because of race, color, creed, or national origin.

The President's Task Force Report, upon which the Order was based stated: ". . . There are fundamental differences between public and private employment . . . The obvious dissimilarities are such that it would be neither desirable nor possible to fashion a federal system of employee-management relationships directly upon the system that has grown up in the private economy." Three types of recognition for employee organizations are authorized by the Order: (1) exclusive, (2) formal, (3) informal.

### State Legislation on Professional Negotiation

It has been previously pointed out that the states of California, Connecticut, Florida, New Jersey, Oregon, and Washington passed legislation in the spring of 1965 providing for professional negotiation arrangements for public school employees. In addition, five statutes apply to all public employees, including teachers.

The laws' provisions are compared in Table 8-1, and are briefly summarized below.

*Alaska—Public Employees*

1. The state or a political subdivision, including independent school districts, may but is not required to enter into collective bargaining contracts with labor organizations of employees.

2. Labor organizations include an organization constituted wholly or in part to bargain collectively or deal with employers, including the state or political subdivision.

3. Negotiation subjects are grievances, terms or conditions of employment, or other mutual aid or protection in connection with employees.

### California—School Employees

1. Teachers are removed from "Public Employees Formal Representation Act" and negotiation provisions are placed in the Education Code.

2. Educational matters are negotiable as well as working conditions.

3. Membership verification is required. A negotiating council is required if there are more than two employee organizations, and representation on it is proportional according to the numbers of members in each organization.

4. Public school employees have the right to form, join, and participate in the activities of employee organizations of their own choosing for the purpose of representation on all matters of employer-employee relations. Employees also have the right to refuse to join such organizations and have the right to represent themselves with the employer.

### Connecticut—School Employees

1. Classroom teachers and administrators in any town may negotiate through one all-inclusive organization, *or* through separate representatives as determined by majority vote in a secret ballot election.

2. An election to select an organization for representation purposes must be held on petition of twenty per cent or more of certificated professional employees.

3. The organization selected is the exclusive representative of all the employees in the unit for purposes of negotiation.

4. Local boards of education and representative organizations must negotiate in good faith concerning salaries and other conditions of employment, and the negotiations must include meetings appropriately related to the budget-making process.

5. A written contract incorporating any agreement reached must be executed if either party requests it.

6. Certificated professional employees are prohibited from

striking to effect a settlement of any salary disagreement with a board of education.

7. Disagreements as to terms and conditions of employment must be submitted to the state commissioner of education for mediation.

8. If mediation fails, either party may submit unresolved issues to an impartial board of three arbitrators (one member named by each party, and the third by the two selected) for an advisory decision.

*Florida—School Employees*

1. Boards of education may appoint committees or recognize existing committees of the teaching profession in arriving at a determination of policy affecting certificated personnel.

2. The committee membership shall include all levels of instructional and administrative personnel.

3. The committees may be involved in the consideration of policies for resolving problems or reaching agreements affecting certificated personnel.

*Massachusetts—Public Employees*

1. Boards of education are included among the municipal employers who must bargain collectively with their employees.

2. Representation controversies are submitted to the state labor commission, and it shall direct a secret ballot election or use any other suitable method to determine which employee organization is to be the exclusive bargaining representative. The labor commission shall determine the composition of the unit and who is eligible to vote. No unit shall include both professional and nonprofessional employees, unless approved by a majority vote of the professional employees.

3. Boards of education and the exclusive representative of employees must bargain collectively in good faith.

4. Negotiable subjects are wages, hours, and other conditions of employment.

5. A written contract incorporating any agreement reached must be executed.

6. Negotiation disputes, or lack of agreement 60 days prior to

final budget date, may be submitted to the state board of conciliation and arbitration for fact-finding. Fact-finders may mediate the dispute and must submit written findings and recommendations to the parties within 60 days of appointment, unless the conciliation and arbitration boards extends the time. The board may also conciliate grievances or disputes over the terms of a written agreement.

7. Municipal employees, including school employees, are prohibited from engaging in, inducing, or encouraging any strike, work stoppage, slowdown, or withholding of services.

### Michigan—Public Employees

1. Public employers, including school boards, shall bargain collectively with the exclusive representative of their employees.

2. Representation questions may be referred to the state labor mediation board by employers or employee groups or unions. After determining that a representation question exists, or if both parties consent, the board shall direct a secret ballot election. The state labor mediation board determines the appropriate unit and who is eligible to vote.

3. Public employers, including boards of education, and exclusive bargaining representatives shall bargain collectively in good faith.

4. Negotiable subjects are rates of pay, wages, hours, and other terms and conditions of employment.

5. A written contract, ordinance, or resolution incorporating any agreements reached shall be executed if requested by either party.

6. Unfair labor practices may be investigated by the state labor mediation board, and it may mediate grievances at the request of the employer, a majority of employees, or the collective bargaining representative.

7. Public employees, including school employees, are prohibited from striking.

### New Hampshire—Public Employees

1. Towns may recognize unions of employees and enter into collective bargaining contracts with such unions.

*New Jersey—School Employees**

1. Boards of education are required to make rules and regulations establishing reasonable grievance procedures and procedures for discussion of matters of mutual concern with employees or their recognized organizational representatives.

2. In the event of impasse both sides may agree to request the commissioner of education to appoint a mediator agreeable to both sides from a list of 10 disinterested persons. The mediator, who must be appointed within five days of a request, may make public any data or recommendations. Mediation costs are shared by the parties.

3. If the mediator cannot effect a settlement (or there is disagreement on the choice of a mediator) within 30 days, an *ad hoc* board of review must be created. Each party names one member and these two name the third member, who is the chairman. If the first two named cannot agree on a chairman in five days the commissioner of education designates the chairman. If the parties do not reach agreement within 60 days, the board of review shall make its findings and recommendations public. Costs of the board of review are shared by both parties.

*Oregon—School Employees*

1. Teaching is recognized as a profession, and certificated school personnel are removed from the collective bargaining law.

2. Individual employees or their elected representatives have the right to confer, consult, and discuss with the board of education matters of salaries and related economic policy affecting professional services.

3. The school board is required to establish the election procedures to select a committee to represent its certificated employees.

4. In the event of impasse either party can request the appointment of consultants. One consultant is appointed by each party and a third is chosen by the first two. The consultants may recommend a reasonable basis for settlement, but neither group must abide by the recommendations.

* This legislation was vetoed by the governor of New Jersey.

*Washington—School Employees*

1. An employee organization which desires to represent certificated employees, except the chief administrator, and which wins a majority of votes in a secret ballot representation election has the right to meet, confer, and negotiate with the board prior to final adoption of proposed school policies.

2. Negotiable subjects relate to, but are not limited to, curriculum, textbook selection, inservice training, student teaching programs, personnel, hiring and assignment practices, leaves of absence, salaries, and salary schedules and noninstructional duties.

3. The same rights are accorded community college (junior college) organizations.

4. Individuals are permitted to appear before governing boards in their own behalf.

5. In the event of impasse either party may request the appointment of a committee composed of educators and school directors by the state superintendent. The committee must make a written advisory report to both parties within 15 days after a request.

6. Boards of education and administrative officers may not discriminate against certificated personnel exercising their rights under the law.

7. Boards of education must adopt reasonable rules and regulations for the administration of employer-employee relations under the law.

8. Existing agreements between representatives of school employees and school districts are not annulled or modified by the law.

*Wisconsin—Public Employees*

1. Municipal employees, including school employees, have the right of self-organization, affiliation with labor organizations and representation by labor organizations in conferences and negotiations with their employers.

2. Representation questions are submitted to the state employment relations board, and either the employer or union may request the board to conduct a representation election among the employees. The organization receiving the majority of votes is

certified as the bargaining representative. The employment relations board also determines the bargaining unit and who is eligible to vote.

3. Employers and unions must meet and negotiate in good faith.

4. Negotiable subjects are wages, hours, and conditions of employment.

5. A written agreement, ordinance, or resolution incorporating any settlements reached shall be executed.

6. The employment relations board may initiate fact-finding at deadlocked negotiations or if the parties refuse to meet. On request of both parties the board may mediate disputes. The employment relations board shall not initiate fact-finding when an employer has established procedures substantially in compliance with those in the statute.

7. Municipal employees, including school employees, are prohibited from striking.

## Projected Impact of State Legislation

New public policy regarding employer-employee relationships in the public schools will come into being faster under state legislation establishing and defining it than any other way. School district by school district adoption of professional negotiation agreements, in absence of state legislation, cannot move as fast or be as effective in causing change. Thus state legislation establishing professional negotiation is needed.

But what kind of legislation will it be? What kind should it be? These questions can be answered in part by an analysis of the statutes now in effect which govern negotiation in public school districts. In 1965, at least eleven state legislatures considered negotiation legislation applicable only to school employees; six statutes were enacted. (Another was passed in Minnesota, but was vetoed by the Governor.) These six statutes, passed in one year, are the first professional negotiation laws.

Negotiation or collective bargaining legislation applicable to all public employees, including school employees, was also considered by many state legislatures in 1965. Two statutes were enacted in 1965, bringing the number of statutes of this type to five: those of

Massachusetts and Michigan, enacted in 1965, of Wisconsin, enacted in 1959 and amended in 1962, and of Alaska, enacted in 1959, and the New Hampshire provision, added in 1955. The impetus for the 1965 legislation in Massachusetts and Michigan originally came from the state AFL-CIO organizations. But, significantly, the state professional education associations were instrumental in both states in securing amendments to make the laws more acceptable to teachers. These amendments enabled the state education associations to lend their support to securing passage of the laws.

The provisions of the eleven negotiation statutes now in effect will be studied with care in other states where such legislation is contemplated. Table 8-1 contains an analysis of the statutes by comparing the provisions of each with the elements of professional negotiation discussed in detail in Chapter 3, and other pertinent provisions. Thus, it is possible to see not only how the provisions compare among the eleven states, but how they compare with the elements of professional negotiation considered basic.

## Negotiation, Recognition, and Mediation

Most of the statutes have fairly specific provisions on negotiation. The New Jersey legislation is less specific, concentrating instead on establishing procedures to be used in the event of impasse, and authorizing boards of education to establish rules and regulations to handle employer-employee relations. A similar provision, authorizing boards to establish such rules, is also found in several other statutes. Under these statutory provisions, boards of education and employee organizations retain freedom and flexibility to develop procedures which suit them best. The statute is a catalyst getting the parties started, establishing ground rules without restricting unnecessarily the development of procedures peculiar to the local situation.

The value of a flexible statute, in addition to that just mentioned —permitting joint procedural development at the local level—is that it encourages experimentation. After experience with provisions of the statute is gained, amendments can be made if needed. And the statute can be improved, or made more specific, if its major possible drawback becomes reality in practice: that too much leeway is left at the local level, permiting avoidance of statutory intent.

The Connecticut statute, the most specific of the six statutes applicable only to school employees, is based on years of Connecticut experience in the negotiation field in absence of statute. This experience includes state policy developed by the "Committee of Nine," a group of classroom teachers, administrators, and board of education members created in 1951 by the state education commissioner. Its first report was issued in 1952 and subsequent reports on working relations of boards of education and teachers' organizations were issued thereafter.[1] The 1965 Connecticut statute, therefore, rests on the base of long experience.

Future statutes should provide that exclusive negotiation rights and exclusive recognition be accorded the organization supported by the majority of the certificated personnel. There is much to support this concept. An exclusive representative will have the full responsibility for negotiations. Such a representative will not be able to blame another organization for its failures, or lose credit undeservedly to another group when it succeeds. Teachers and the board will know who has the authority to negotiate.

Exclusive negotiation rights accorded one organization will also promote efficiency in negotiations and will encourage the representative to be fully prepared. And the recalcitrant boards of education will not be able to play one organization against another, which situation promotes not only bad negotiating but staff turmoil.

That exclusive recognition and negotiation rights are procedures which will come is illustrated by the fact that they are provided in six of the eleven statutes: in Connecticut, Massachusetts, Michigan, Oregon, Washington, and Wisconsin. And, in the New Jersey statute, exclusive recognition is strongly implied by the use of the term "recognized organizational representative."

The concept of third party fact-finding, mediation, and appeal in educational channels must be included in future legislation. There is little doubt that this kind of procedure is what the profession wants most, next to negotiating with boards of education itself. Four of the six 1965 negotiation statutes applicable only to

[1] See Chapter 4 for a discussion of the "Committee of Nine" report.

**T A B L E  8 - 1 .  Comparison of Negotiation Statutes**

| A. PROFESSIONAL NEGOTIATION BASIC ELEMENTS | 1 ALASKA STATUTE | 2 CALIFORNIA STATUTE | 3 CONNECTICUT STATUTE |
|---|---|---|---|
| *Recognition:* The board of education recognizes the local association as the representative of the professional staff. | *Permitted:* The state and its political subdivisions, including school districts, may enter into collective bargaining contracts with a labor organization of employees. | *Required in part:* Boards of education must meet and confer with organizations representing their members and with a proportionately representative negotiating council, if there is more than one employee organization. | *Required:* Boards of education must negotiate with the exclusive representative of the employees. |
| *Channels:* The local association uses professional (administrative) channels in preliminary discussion of matters under negotiation. | *Not provided nor prohibited.* | *Provided:* A designated administrative officer may meet and confer with representative organizations before the organization requests to meet and confer with the board of education. | *Not provided nor prohibited.** |
| *Negotiation:* Representatives of the local association and the board of education meet and negotiate in good faith. | *Permitted:* The state and its political subdivisions, including school districts, may bargain collectively with a labor organization of their employees. | *Required in part:* At the request of an employee organization or negotiation council, the board of education must meet and confer with their representatives. | *Required:* Boards of education shall negotiate, meet, and confer in good faith with the exclusive representative of the employees. |
| *Agreement:* A written document containing the matters agreed to is signed by the local association and the board of education at the conclusion of negotiations. | *Permitted:* The state and its political subdivisions, including school districts, may, but are not required to, enter into collective-bargaining contracts with a labor or-organization of employees. | *Not provided nor prohibited.** | *Provided:* If requested by either party, a written contract incorporating any agreement reached shall be executed. |
| *Impasse:* Educational channels for mediation, fact-finding, and appeal are established. Recommendations are advisory. | *Not provided nor prohibited.* | *Not provided nor prohibited.** | *Provided:* Disagreements are submitted for meditation to the secretary of the state board of education. If mediation fails, either party may cause a board of arbitrators to be established, one |

\* The statute provides that boards of education are authorized to adopt rules and regulations to implement it.

188

| 4 FLORIDA STATUTE | 5 MASSACHUSETTS STATUTE | 6 MICHIGAN STATUTE |
|---|---|---|
| *Permitted:* The board of education may appoint or recognize existing committees of the teaching profession in arriving at a determination of policy. | *Required:* Municipal employers, including boards of education, must bargain collectively with the exclusive bargaining agent of the employees. | *Required:* Public employers including boards of education, must recognize as the exclusive bargaining representative the organization designated or selected by the majority of employees. |
| *Not provided nor prohibited.* | *Not provided nor prohibited.* | *Not provided nor prohibited.* |
| *Permitted:* Committees of the teaching profession may be involved in the consideration of policies for resolving problems or reaching agreement. | *Required:* Municipal employers, including boards of education, must bargain collectively in good faith with the exclusive bargaining agent of the employees. | *Required:* Public employers, including boards of education, must bargain collectively in good faith with the exclusive bargaining representative. |
| *Not provided nor prohibited.* | *Provided:* Written contracts incorporating any agreement reached shall be executed. | *Provided:* If requested by either party, a written contract, ordinance, or resolution incorporating any agreements reached shall be executed. |
| *Not provided nor prohibited.* | *Provided in labor channels:* Representation questions are submitted to state labor commission and it may require an election to determine the exclusive bargaining agent; it determines unit composition. Fact-finding in negotiation | *Provided in labor channels:* Representation questions are referred to the state labor mediation board by employers, employee groups, or unions. If a representation question exists, or if both parties consent, the board shall direct an election to |

**TABLE 8-1.** Comparison of Negotiation Statutes (*Continued*)

| A. PROFESSIONAL NEGOTIATION BASIC ELEMENTS (*Cont.*) | *1* ALASKA STATUTE | *2* CALIFORNIA STATUTE | *3* CONNECTICUT STATUTE |
|---|---|---|---|
| | | | member selected by each party, and those two selecting a third. Recommendations of the state secretary or the board of arbitrators are advisory. |
| *Subjects of negotiation:* Included, but not limited to setting standards in employing professional personnel, community support for schools, in-service training of personnel, class size, teacher turnover, personnel policies, salaries, working conditions, and communications within the school system. | *Provided in part:* Subjects are grievances, terms or conditions of employment, or other mutual aid or protection in connection with employees. | *Provided:* Subjects are all matters relating to employment conditions and employer-employee relations, including but not limited to wages, hours, and other terms and conditions of employment. | *Provided:* Subjects are salaries and all other conditions of employment. |

B. OTHER PERTINENT PROVISIONS

| *Procedures for selecting employee representatives.* | *No provision.* | Rules and regulations adopted by the board shall include provisions to verify the number of certificated employees in an employee organization or organizations. Membership lists may be used for verification. | Exclusive representative may be designated or selected by a majority of all employees below the rank of superintendent, or by a majority of employees in separate units of all certificated teachers, of certificated administrative and supervisory personnel. If 20 percent or more of all certificated personnel below the rank of superintendent or of either separate unit petition the secretary of the state board of education for a representation election, one shall be held. |

| 4<br>FLORIDA<br>STATUTE | 5<br>MASSACHUSETTS<br>STATUTE | 6<br>MICHIGAN<br>STATUTE |
|---|---|---|
| | disputes, or when agreement is not reached prior to 60 days before final budget date, may be initiated by state board of mediation and conciliation and arbitration on request of parties. This board may conciliate grievances and contract disputes and disputes over contract terms interpretation. | determine the exclusive bargaining representative. The labor mediation board determines the appropriate bargaining unit.<br><br>The board may initiate fact-finding to investigate unfair labor practices. It may also mediate grievances at the request of the collective bargaining representative, or, if none, a majority of employees or an employer. |
| *Provided:* Subjects are matters affecting all certificated personnel. | *Provided in part:* Subjects are wages, hours, and other conditions of employment. | *Provided in part:* Subjects are rates of pay, wages, hours, and other terms and conditions of employment. |
| Existing committees of the teaching profession or committees appointed by the board of education may be recognized. If the matters under joint consideration affect certificated personnel, the committee membership shall include all levels of instructional and administrative personnel. | On petition of employer or employee organization, and after investigation to determine that a representation question exists, the state labor commission determines whether a representation controversy exists. If one does, the commission shall direct a secret-ballot election, or use another suitable method, to select the organization to be the exclusive bargaining agent. The commission determines the appropriate unit in each case. | A public employee, group, or labor organization alleging that 30% or more of the employees in the appropriate unit wish collective bargaining representation and alleging that the employer will not recognize their representative, or a public employer alleging recognition claims have been presented, may petition the labor mediation board.<br><br>The board shall direct an election if a representation question exists, or if the parties consent, and shall certify the organization receiving a majority of the votes. The board determines the appropriate unit. |

TABLE 8-1. Comparison of Negotiation Statutes (*Continued*)

| B. OTHER PERTINENT PROVISIONS (*Cont.*) | *1* ALASKA STATUTE | *2* CALIFORNIA STATUTE | *3* CONNECTICUT STATUTE |
|---|---|---|---|
| *Rights of individuals.* | *No provision.* | Individual school employees have the right to appear before the board of education on their own behalf in their employment relations with the school district. | Any certificated employee or group shall have the right to present grievances to those designated for that purpose by the board at any time. |
| *Rights to join employee organizations.* | Implied in collective bargaining provision and in the definition of a labor organization which is one constituted wholly or in part to bargain collectively or deal with employers, including school districts. | School employees have the right to form, join, and participate in the activities of employee organizations of their own choosing for the purpose of representation on all matters of employer-employee relations. They also have the right not to do so.<br><br>Public school employers and employee organizations shall not interfere with, initimidate, restrain, coerce, or discriminate against public-school employees because of their exercise of their rights under this statute. | *No provision.* [Another statute provides that members of the teaching profession have the right to join or refuse to join any organization for professional or economic improvement. *Connecticut Statues Annotated,* Title 10, sec. 10-153a.] |
| *Right to strike.* | *No provision.* | *No provision.* | Certificated employees are prohibited, in an effort to effect a settlement of any salary dispute, to engage in any strike or concerted refusal to render services. |

|  4 | 5 | 6 |
| :---: | :---: | :---: |
| FLORIDA<br>STATUTE | MASSACHUSETTS<br>STATUTE | MICHIGAN<br>STATUTE |

*No provision.*

*No Provision.*

Individual employees may present grievances to their employers and have them adjusted, without intervention of the bargaining representative, if the adjustment is not inconsistent with the collective-bargaining contract. The bargaining representative has the opportunity to be present at the adjustment.

*No provision.* [Another statute provides that public employees have the right to organize and to present proposals relating to wages and conditions of employment. *Florida Statutes Annotated,* Chapter 839, sec. 839.221.]

Employees have the right to self-organization, to form, join, or assist any employee organization, to bargain collectively free from actual interference, restraint, or coercion.

It is lawful for public employees, including school employees, to organize together or to form, join, or assist in labor organizations, to engage in lawful concerted activities for the purpose of collective negotiation or bargaining or other mutual aid or protection, or to negotiate or bargain collectively with their employers through representatives of their own free choice.

It is unlawful for public employers, including boards of education, to interfere with, restrain, or coerce employees in the exercise of their rights under the statute.

*No provision.* [Public employees are prohibited from striking under another statute. *Florida Statutes Annotated,* Chapter 839, sec. 839.221.]

Employees are prohibited from engaging in, inducing, or encouraging any strike, work stoppage, slowdown, or withholding of services.

Public employees are prohibited from striking for the purpose of inducing, influencing, or coercing a change in the conditions, compensation, rights, privileges, or obligations of employment.

| A. PROFESSIONAL NEGOTIATION BASIC ELEMENTS | 7 NEW HAMPSHIRE STATUTE | 8 NEW JERSEY STATUTE** |
|---|---|---|
| *Recognition:* The board of education recognizes the local association as the representative of the professional staff. | *Permitted:* Towns may recognize unions of employees. Educational employees are not specifically mentioned. | *Required:* Boards of education must discuss matters of mutual concern with employees or recognized organizational representative. |
| *Channels:* The local association uses professional (administrative) channels in preliminary discussion of matters under negotiation. | *Not provided nor prohibited.* | *Not provided nor prohibited.** |
| *Negotiation:* Representatives of the local association and the board of education meet and negotiate in good faith. | *Permitted:* Towns may bargain collectively with unions of employees. | *Required in part:* Boards must establish procedures to discuss matters of mutual concern with recognized organizational representatives. |
| *Agreement:* A written document containing the matters agreed to is signed by the local association and the board of education at the conclusion of negotiations. | *Permitted:* Towns may enter into collective bargaining contracts with unions of employees. | *Not provided nor prohibited.** |
| *Impasse:* Educational channels for mediation, factfinding, and appeal are established. Recommendations are advisory. | *Not provided nor prohibited.* | *Provided:* On mutual agreement, recognized organizational representative and board of education may request state commissioner of education to appoint a mediator.  The mediator shall be selected from a list of 10 persons experienced with the problems of public education.  If mediation fails, or if the parties cannot agree on a person to mediate, either may cause ad hoc board of review to be established. One member is appointed by |

* The statute provides that boards of education are authorized to adopt rules and regulations to implement it.

** This legislation was vetoed by the governor of New Jersey.

| 9 OREGON STATUTE | 10 WASHINGTON STATUTE | 11 WISCONSIN STATUTE |
|---|---|---|
| *Required in part:* Boards of education must meet and discuss matters with a representative or committee elected by the certificated employees, but an organization need not be the representative. | *Required:* Boards of education must meet, confer, and negotiate with the organization elected by a majority of the certificated employees as their representative. | *Required:* Municipal employers, including boards of education, must negotiate with the labor organization representing the majority of the employees in the bargaining unit. |
| *Not provided nor prohibited.** | *Provided:* The representatives of the organization elected use established administrative channels prior to conferring and negotiating with the board of education. | *Not provided nor prohibited.* |
| *Required in part:* Elected representaitves of the certificated employees have the right to confer, consult, and discuss matters in good faith with the board of education or a committee thereof. | *Required:* Representatives of the elected organization have the right to meet, confer, and negotiate with the board of education or a committee thereof. | *Required:* Municipal employers, including boards of education, must meet and negotiate in good faith with the certified representatives of the employees in the bargaining unit. |
| *Not provided nor prohibited.** | *Not provided nor prohibited:** The statute shall not be construed to modify or preclude the renewal or continuation of any existing agreements. | *Provided:* Written agreements, ordinances, or resolutions incorporating any settlements reached shall be executed. |
| *Provided:* Either party may cause consultants to be appointed, one member selected by each party, and the third by those two. Recommendations are advisory. | *Provided:* Either party may cause a committee of educators and board members to be appointed by the state superintendent of public instruction. Recommendations are advisory. | *Provided in labor channels:* Fact-finding may be initiated by the employment relations board at deadlocked negotiations or if either party refuses to meet. The board may mediate disputes on request of both parties. Either party may petition the board to determine the bargaining unit. Recommendations of the fact-finder are advisory. The employment relations board shall not initiate fact-finding proceedings when an employer has established procedures substantially in |

* The statute provides that boards of education are authorized to adopt rules and regulations to implement it.

**TABLE 8-1.** Comparison of Negotiation Statutes *(Continued)*

| A. PROFESSIONAL NEGOTIATION BASIC ELEMENTS *(Cont.)* | 7 NEW HAMPSHIRE STATUTE | 8 NEW JERSEY STATUTE |
|---|---|---|
| | | each party and these two select a third, who is chairman.<br><br>Recommendations of the mediator or the board of review are adisory. |
| *Subjects of negotiation:* Included, but not limited to setting standards in employing professional personnel, community support for schools, in-service training of personnel, class size, teacher turnover, personnel policies, salaries, working conditions, and communications within the school system. | *No provision.* | *Provided:* Subjects are grievances and matters of mutual concern. |
| **B. OTHER PERTINENT PROVISIONS** *(Cont.)* | | |
| *Procedures for selecting employee representatives.* | *Not provided nor prohibited.* | *No provision.** |
| *Rights of individual.* | *No provision.* | *No provision.** |

* The statute provides that boards of education are authorized to adopt rules and regulations to implement it.

196

9
OREGON
STATUTE

10
WASHINGTON
STATUTE

11
WISCONSIN
STATUTE

compliance with those in the statute.

*Provided in part:* Subjects are matters of salaries and related economic policies affecting professional services.

*Provided:* Subjects are policies relating to, but not limited to, curriculum, textbook selection, in-service training, student teaching programs, personnel, hiring and assignment practices, leaves of absence, salaries and salary schedules, and noninstructional duties.

*Provided in part:* Subjects are wages, hours, and conditions of employment.

A committee of certificated personnel may represent all certificated personnel if elected by majority vote of certificated personnel below the rank of superintendent.

Boards of education shall establish election procedures and shall certify the committee elected by the certificated school personnel.

Individual certificated employees have the right to confer, consult, and discuss matters with the board of education.

Employee organization which has been elected by a majority of the certificated employees below the rank of superintendent shall represent all certificated employees.

Similar provisions apply to organizations of certificated employees of community colleges.

Individual certificated employees have the right to appear on their own behalf before the board on matters relating to their employment relations with the school district.

Either party may request the employment relations board to conduct an election if representation questions arise.

*No provision.*

| B. OTHER PERTINENT PROVISIONS (*Cont.*) | 7 NEW HAMPSHIRE STATUTE | 8 NEW JERSEY STATUTE |
|---|---|---|
| *Rights to join employee organizations.* | Implied in recognition provision. | *No provision.* [The New Jersey Constitution, Art. I, sec. 19, provides that public employees have the right to organize.] |
| *Right to strike.* | *No provision.* | *No provision.* |

198

| | | |
|---|---|---|
| *No provision.* | Boards of education and administrative officers shall not discriminate against certificated employees because of their exercise of rights under the statute. | Municipal employees, including school employees, have the right to affiliate with labor organizations of their own choice and to be represented by such organizations.<br><br>Municipal employers, including boards of education, may not encourage or discourage membership in any labor organization, employee agency, committee, association, or representation plan by discrimination in regard to hiring, tenure, or other terms or conditions of employment. |
| *No provision.* [Public employees prohibited from striking under another statute. *Oregon Revised Statutes,* Chapter 243, sec. 243.760.] | *No provision.* | Municipal employees, including school employees, are prohibited from striking. |

school employees have this kind of provision (Connecticut, New Jersey, Oregon, and Washington), and it is not prohibited in California. The Florida law, weakest of these six laws, does not provide mediation. Three of the five laws applicable to all public employees, including school employees, provide mediation or fact-finding through state labor channels rather than educational channels.

Teachers simply are not willing to go through a negotiating process only to get what seems an arbitrary "no" from a board. The third party concept undoubtedly bothers board members more than almost any other. The use of educational channels and the fact that resulting recommendations should be advisory will make the third party concept more acceptable to many board members. It is important for board members to remember that recommendations could be in their favor as well as in favor of the profession. The "safety valve" aspect of third party help is probably the best reason for boards as well as teachers to support it. Acceptance of another's position or terms is often easier when recommended by a disinterested party.

*Compulsory Membership and Strikes*

Two issues with which the teaching profession must deal directly are those of compulsory membership of some type and the right to strike. As shown in Table 8-1, the statutory provisions on these issues, where they exist, are prohibitory. These prohibitions seem to exist more because of tradition than because the profession, after careful consideration, requested the legislatures to include them in the statutes. Nevertheless, it is true that many members of the profession do not look with favor on compulsory membership provisions or on the right of teachers to strike. What is required is a more systematic study and airing of the issues. At present, opposition often is more an automatic response than one based on study and reflection.

Canadian teachers in 10 provinces are required by law to belong to the independent teachers' organizations in those provinces. This means that the organizations can be freed from expending energy and funds on membership campaigns and promotions and instead work on all the problems facing the profession as well as negotiate. It is the belief of many that compulsory membership makes for a more responsible organization, one not forced, in order to gain attention and membership, to make exorbitant and irresponsible demands.

If professional organizations fulfill their stated roles, not only to promote welfare, but also to elevate the professional standards of members and to improve education, then it can be reasonably assumed that membership in such an organization should improve the individual, and that it is a mark of the profession to belong. To repeat the statement of the Missouri Court quoted more fully in Chapter 2:

> Membership in professional organizations is no guaranty of professional excellence, but active participation in such organizations . . . [is] reasonably related to the development of higher professional attainments and qualifications.

Proper safeguards are necessary concomitants to some form of compulsory membership. Any statutory provision on the subject should be permissive, not mandatory. That way, the local organization members will decide. Among the safeguards which could be provided at the local level are these:

- The employees involved must make the decision on compulsory membership.
- The provision for compulsory membership, if agreed to by the employees, would be a subject for negotiation with the board of education.
- Provision could be made to require membership only after a certain period of service up to a maximum of the full probationary period.
- The compulsory membership provision could be made subject to review after a reasonable trial period of at least three years.
- Provision could be made for the payment of a fee in lieu of dues for those who have a pressing reason not to belong to the organization.

Other safeguards could be listed, but the above are sufficient to suggest that although "compulsory" is a word not favored by members of the teaching profession, it could be made less offensive if the profession comes to believe compulsory membership to be in its best interest.

Whether or not strikes are effective in the public school setting, there will continue to be pressure to give school employees the right to strike. Pressure may be most severe to obtain the right for other types of public employees, but teachers will be included in the group, unless there is contrasting pressure to exclude them.

There are those members of the teaching profession who believe teachers should not be denied the right to strike. Lieberman has held this view for some time, although he has recognized strikes used by school employees may not *always* be as effective as when used by private employees.[2] The American Federation of Teachers, which long had a specific no-strike policy, changed it in 1963 to a policy of support of locals which strike.[3] The National Education Association which for most of its existence made no specific reference to strikes by members of the teaching profession in its resolutions, mentioned strikes first in a 1947 resolution.[4] The resolution expressed the belief that the strike was an unsatisfactory method of solving professional problems. In 1948, 1949, and 1950 NEA resolutions stated that conditions which cause dissatisfaction should be improved so that strikes would be unnecessary.[5] Not until 1961 were strikes mentioned again in an NEA resolution. It stated that strikes would not be necessary if teachers had the right to participate with boards of education in determining policies of common concern.[6] Similar views were contained in professional negotiation resolutions of 1962, 1963 and 1964.[7] However, the word "strike" was eliminated from the 1965 professional negotiation resolution.[8]

Although strikes have received relatively little attention in NEA resolutions, it seems clear that the NEA has had a policy on the

[2] Myron Lieberman, "Teachers Strikes: An Analysis of the Issues," *Harvard Educational Review*, Vol. 26, No. 1, Winter 1956, pp. 39–69.

[3] *Convention Proceedings, 1963* (abridged), Chicago: The American Federation of Teachers.

[4] *Addresses and Proceedings, 1947,* Washington, D. C.: National Education Association, pp. 129–32.

[5] *Addresses and Proceedings, 1948,* p. 188; *Addresses and Proceedings, 1949,* pp. 160–61; *Addresses and Proceedings, 1950,* pp. 153–56, Washington, D. C.: National Education Association.

[6] *Addresses and Proceedings, 1961,* pp. 216–18, Washington, D. C.: National Education Association.

[7] *Addresses and Proceedings, 1962,* pp. 174–183, 191, 397–98; *Addresses and Proceedings, 1963,* pp. 198–99, 236–37, 464–65; *Addresses and Proceedings, 1964,* pp. 190–91, 446, Washington, D.C.: National Education Association.

[8] *Addresses and Proceedings, 1965,* pp. 415–16, Washington, D. C.: National Education Association.

subject for many years. This is evidenced by statements in NEA's Codes of Ethics.

Dating back to 1929, successive revisions of the NEA Code of Ethics have included a declaration similar to that in the 1963 Code (Code of Ethics of the Education Profession, which Code has been adopted by all NEA affiliated state education associations), which reads as follows:

Adhere to the conditions of a contract or to the terms of an appointment until either has been terminated legally or by mutual consent (Principle IV, Section 4).

There has been some pressure from outside the profession to give teachers the right to strike. For example, a 1963 policy statement of the American Civil Liberties Union contained these words:

Like other occupational groups in an industrial society, ever concerned with the maintenance of living standards, teachers should be free to join unions of their own choosing, whether locally organized or part of a nation-wide federation. The right to participate in union activity should include the right to strike. A teachers' strike cannot ordinarily be interpreted as endangering the public health, safety or welfare. Where laws forbidding strikes by teachers exist, teachers and their organizations are justified in taking all steps necessary to test their constitutionality and to work for their repeal.

The ACLU statement asserted that to ban the right to strike:

... invades the freedom of employees to decide what working conditions they believe should govern their employment. This decision represents the employees' opinion which is expressed through their association with other persons in a union. Therefore, prohibitions on the right to strike do weaken the First Amendment guarantees.

The policy on a teacher's right to strike, the civil liberties group said, was an amplification of the ACLU's 1959 policy upholding the civil rights of government employees.

There is evidence that strikes, even in the private sector, are becoming less effective and that they are of limited value in the school setting. However, those who favor giving teachers the right to strike disagree and believe that the right to strike must accompany negotiation procedures. In any event, the strike issue should be faced squarely in the development of future public policy and in drafting professional negotiation legislation.

## Summary of Need to Enact State Legislation

It is clear from the condition of the law on negotiation by boards of education and school employees, that properly conceived state legislation would clear up gray areas. Although in almost all jurisdictions professional negotiation, including most of its component procedures, is legally permissible, legal questions are often raised which a statute would obviate.

A new public policy must be achieved, in part, through state legislation. The *kind* of statute required is not only thoroughly discussed here, but is touched on in other chapters. Here it is sufficient to list the reasons, from a legal standpoint, to press for enactment of state laws for professional negotiation. Of course, the need is based on the assumption that really is basic in this volume: Professional negotiation is a process needed in public education. Here are a few reasons for enacting state legislation:

- The argument that professional negotiation is beyond the board of education's power, whether based on the law in a particular jurisdiction or not, will be eliminated by authorizing legislation.

- Legislation can provide for exclusive negotiation rights and protect the rights of minorities. Thus it will bring both efficiency to the negotiation process by providing for only one negotiator, clearly placing responsibility there, and dispel the fear that the minority will somehow be mistreated.

- Legislation can require that rules and regulations to implement professional negotiation be promulgated. Thus the parties will be required to determine the ground rules by which they will operate, before plunging into negotiations on the merits.

- Legislation can prevent the automatic exclusion of any part of the profession such as supervisory personnel, not only from voting in representation elections, when required, but also from membership in the organization, or its affiliates, seeking to represent the profession in these elections. It can provide flexibility in determining who may vote, on the basis of local practice, past custom, and the views of the staff involved.

- Legislation can provide guidelines for, or require that reasonable rules be established for representation elections in the state. In the absence of statutory or state standards, rules are established which permit an organization very much in the minority to force an election. Also, without rules, there are other problems in the election process, such as where to vote and when, permitted and prohibited campaign practices, and the like. Legislation can require rules to be promulgated and thus eliminate setting them just before a heated election.

- Legislation can establish mediation and appeal procedures through educational channels. Under such legislation, boards of education will be authorized to participate in the procedures and all parties will be assured that precedent set will be oriented to education.

- Legislation will accelerate the pace of professional negotiation agreements. Although there are several hundred agreements in about 35 states, adoption is slower in some states than in others. With legislation, boards and employee organizations can spend their time on the substantive issues, rather than spending it arguing whether the process is legal or not.

### Conclusion

In reviewing educational developments which have taken place since 1960, one cannot but be struck by the rapidity with which changes have been taking place in the relationships between school staffs and boards of education. Twenty years of history have been compressed into five. There are those who continue to debate the desirability of such change and some who bemoan its speed. But the change is here, and its pace will quicken rather than slacken in the years just ahead. Teachers, administrators, and school board members—those directly concerned with public education in this country—should, if they have not already done so, begin now to devise negotiation policies and procedures. They and their leaders are the ones who must develop and set the new public policy which will establish effective and satisfactory negotiation relationships among them. This job must not go by default to others.

A basic premise of professional negotiation is that these groups *can* solve together the problems they face. State legislation is proposed as the most satisfactory means of doing this, but the absence of state legislation should not prevent the cooperative development and adoption of professional negotiation agreements on a district-by-district basis throughout the nation. Most teachers, administrators, and school boards will establish meaningful negotiation relationships, as evidenced by the number of negotiation agreements in existence.

The phenomenal progress that has been made in establishing formal negotiation procedures reflects not only the fact that the procedures are long overdue in public education, but also that teacher demand for an equal role in the development of educational policy is mounting.

# *Appendix A.* NEA Resolutions Concerning Professional Negotiation

### Resolution No. 18[1]

The teaching profession has the ultimate aim of providing the best possible education for all the people. It is a professional calling and a public trust. Boards of education have the same aim and share this trust.

The National Education Association calls upon boards of education in all school districts to recognize their identity of interest with the teaching profession.

The National Education Association insists on the right of professional associations, through democratically selected representatives using professional channels, to participate with boards of education in the determination of policies of common concern, including salary and other conditions of professional service.

Recognizing both the legal authority of boards of education and the educational competencies of the teaching profession, the two groups should view the consideration of matters of mutual concern as a joint responsibility.

The seeking of consensus and mutual agreement on a professional basis should preclude the arbitrary exercise of unilateral authority by boards of education and the use of the strike by teachers.

The Association believes that procedures should be established which provide an orderly method for professional education associations and boards of education to reach mutually satisfactory agreements. These procedures should include provisions for appeal through designated educational channels when agreement cannot be reached.

Under no circumstances should the resolution of differences between

---

[1] Adopted by the Denver Convention, 1962.

professional associations and boards of education be sought through channels set up for handling industrial disputes. The teacher's situation is completely unlike that of an industrial employee. A board of education is not a private employer, and a teacher is not a private employee. Both are public servants. Both are committed to serve the common, indivisible interest of all persons and groups in the community in the best possible education for their children. Teachers and boards of education can perform their indispensable functions only if they act in terms of their identity of purpose in carrying out this commitment. Industrial-disputes conciliation machinery, which assumes a conflict of interest and a diversity of purpose between persons and groups, is not appropriate to professional negotiations in public education.

The National Education Association calls upon its members and upon boards of education to seek state legislation and local board action which clearly and firmly establishes these rights for the teaching profession.

## Resolution No. 15[2]

The teaching profession has the ultimate aim of providing the best possible education for all the people. It is a professional calling and a public trust. Boards of education have the same aim and share this trust.

The National Education Association calls upon boards of education in all school districts to recognize their identity of interest with the teaching profession.

The National Education Association insists on the right of professional associations, through democratically selected representatives using professional channels, to participate with boards of education in the formulation of policies of common concern, including salary and other conditions of professional service.

Recognizing the legal authority of the board of education, the administrative function of the superintendent, and the professional competencies of teachers, the National Education Association believes that matters of mutual concern should be viewed as a joint responsibility. The cooperative development of policies is a professional approach which recognizes that the superintendent has a major responsibility to both the teaching staff and school board. It further recognizes that the

[2] The Denver Resolution, as amended in the Seattle and New York Conventions, 1964 and 1965.

school board, the superintendent or administration, and the teaching staff have significantly different contributions to make in the development of educational policies and procedures.

The seeking of consensus and mutual agreement on a professional basis should preclude the arbitrary exercise of unilateral action by boards of education, administrators, or teachers.

The Association believes that procedures should be established which provide for an orderly method of reaching mutually satisfactory agreements and that these procedures should include provisions for appeal through designated educational channels when agreement cannot be reached.

The Association commends the many school boards, school superintendents, and professional education associations which have already initiated and entered into written negotiation agreements and urges greater effort to improve existing procedures and to effect more widespread adoption of written agreements.

The National Education Association calls upon its members and affiliates and upon boards of education to seek state legislation and local board action which clearly and firmly establish these rights for the teaching profession.

# *Appendix B.* NEA Resolution Concerning Professional Sanctions

## Resolution No. 16[1]

The National Education Association believes that, when other means for preventing unethical or arbitrary policies or practices that have a deleterious effect on the welfare of the schools have been exhausted, professional sanctions should be invoked. Guidelines which define, organize, and definitely specify procedural steps for invoking sanctions by the teaching profession have been devised. Similar procedural guidelines should now be devised for the lifting of sanctions. State and local affiliates and their members should familiarize themselves with these guidelines and with the circumstances in which they are applicable. The National Education Association calls upon its officers, commissions, committees, staff, and affiliated state associations to apply these guidelines where appropriate and, through the experience of use, continuously to improve them.

Further, a violation of sanctions by a member of the profession is a violation of the Code of Ethics of the Education Profession. Therefore, the offering or accepting of employment in areas where sanctions are in effect should be evaluated in terms of the Code, and local, state, and national associations should begin developing procedures for disciplining members who violate sanctions.

[1] As amended at the 1965 Annual NEA Convention.

# *Appendix C.* Example of a Professional Negotiation Agreement

**Principles Governing Relationships Between the Board of Education of the City School District of New Rochelle and New Rochelle Teachers Association**

### PREAMBLE

The Board of Education of the City of New Rochelle and New Rochelle Teachers Association recognize that the development and operation of educational programs of the highest quality, for the benefit of the students and the community of New Rochelle, is a common responsibility which requires, for its effective discharge, consultation among the Board, the Superintendent and administrative staff, and members of the teaching staff speaking through their elected representative. Since these groups have the same ultimate aim of providing the best possible educational opportunity for all pupils enrolled in the schools consistent with community resources, relationships must be established and maintained which are based upon this common interest and the concept of education as a public trust and as a professional calling.

The Board of Education, the Superintendent and the administrative staff, and the members of the teaching staff can best attain their common objectives and discharge their common responsibilities if each utilizes the ability, experience and judgment of the other in formulating policies and making decisions that involve matters of mutual concern and which affect the quality of New Rochelle's educational program. It is the purpose of this Agreement to set forth the policies and standards governing such matters of mutual concern to the parties.

THIS AGREEMENT IS MADE AND ENTERED INTO on this —————— day of ——————, 1964 by and between the BOARD OF EDUCATION OF

THE CITY SCHOOL DISTRICT OF NEW ROCHELLE (hereinafter referred to as the "Board") and the NEW ROCHELLE TEACHERS ASSOCIATION (hereinafter referred to as the "Association").

## RECOGNITION

It is recognized that teaching is a profession requiring specialized educational qualifications and that the quality of the educational programs conducted in the public schools of New Rochelle depends primarily upon the quality of the teaching service. It is recognized that the professional preparation of teachers qualifies them to make significant contributions to the conduct of educational affairs of the district and to the determination of policy and program.

The Association, as the organizational representative of the members of the teaching staff, recognizes the paramount responsibility of the Board for the operation of the New Rochelle public schools.

The Board recognizes the responsibilities of the Association for maintaining and improving standards of professional practice.

The Board and the Association recognize their responsibilities toward each other and the community for negotiating in good faith and seeking agreement on matters of mutual concern. Neither will demean the process, and both recognize that the controlling determinant of policy development and implementation is the quality of the educational program and the welfare of the children.

The Board recognizes the Association as the exclusive representative of all professional personnel, certified by the State Department of Education, on tenure, on probation, and on interim but no per diem appointment, including teachers, guidance counsellors, psychologists, social case workers and attendance officers, but excluding administrative and supervisory employees whose function is to evaluate the performance of professional personnel for the purpose of discipline, tenure or promotion, or effectively to recommend discipline, tenure or promotion, the Superintendent, Assistant Superintendents, Administrative Assistant to the Superintendent of Schools, Principals, Assistant Principals, Teachers assigned to the Principal's Office, Department Chairmen, Unit Chairmen, Directors, Coordinators, Curriculum Librarian, Senior Psychologist and Medical Supervisor. All personnel represented by the Association shall, unless otherwise indicated, hereinafter be referred to as "teachers."

## NEGOTIATION PROCEDURE

The parties hereto recognize that the Board of Education is legally charged with the responsibility of enacting policies governing the operations of the School District but that the parties are jointly concerned with the formulation of basic educational policies and other long-range educational goals. To foster mutual participation in the discussion of such policies, and to make available to the Board of Education the views and the professional expertise of the teaching staff, a Professional Negotiation Committee shall be established.

The purpose of this Committee shall be to negotiate on appropriate matters which affect the collective interests of the members of the unit described hereinabove.

The Committee shall consist of representatives designated by the Association on the one hand and the Board on the other. One of the representatives of the Association shall be its President, and one of the representatives of the Board shall be the Superintendent.

The Board and the Superintendent agree to furnish to the Association's members of the Professional Negotiation Committee, in accordance with their reasonable requests, all available information concerning financial resources of the District, tentative budgetary requirements and allocations, and such other information as will assist the Association in developing intelligent, accurate, and constructive programs on behalf of the teachers and their students.

If both parties concur, the Committee may, at its discretion, appoint subcommittees for the purpose of studying matters of mutual concern, such as the financial resources of the district, tentative budgetary requirements and allocations, trends in salary schedules and fringe benefits, and other pertinent matters which affect the quality of New Rochelle's educational program. The Board shall provide and make available to such subcommittees reasonable clerical assistance necessary to the performance of their duties.

The Committee, or any group represented thereon, may call upon competent professional and/or lay representatives to assist it in considering matters under discussion. The services of educational consultants may also be utilized during deliberations.

Teacher members of the Committee shall be released in reasonable number and at reasonable times from school duties without loss of salary when negotiation meetings are scheduled during the school day.

Negotiations for a new agreement between the parties shall be commenced within four months of the date of expiration of this Agreement. It is the intention of the parties that the policies and regulations set forth in this agreement shall govern their relations during the term hereof, but nothing herein contained shall be construed to prevent either of the parties prior to the expiration of this

Agreement from requesting the opportunity to discuss and negotiate with the other on matters of substance arising during the term hereof.

## AGREEMENT

When the Committee has arrived at a consensus with regard to any matter, it shall frame its agreement in the form of a written recommendation to be submitted to the Board and the governing body of the Association. Upon acceptance of the Committee's recommendation by both, its recommendation shall be publicly announced and put into effect as official policy, and shall constitute a modification of the articles of this Agreement.

## RESOLVING DISAGREEMENT

Recognizing, as they do, their respective responsibilities for the education of the children of the community, the parties accept their obligation to assure the uninterrupted operations of the school system.

To this end the parties pledge themselves to negotiate in good faith such matters as may appropriately be included in an agreement between them, and, in the event of failure to reach agreement, to utilize in good faith such mediatory facilities as may usefully contribute to arriving at agreement between them. In this connection the parties recognize that, in the event that they call upon any third party to assist them in arriving at agreement, such person shall be qualified by general background in the educational field and special understanding of the issue at hand. The report of such person shall be advisory only and shall not be binding on the parties. Although the parties include the provisions of this paragraph for the purpose of indicating their pledge to the community to prevent the interruption of the operation of the school system, they nevertheless reiterate that each of them will make every effort to reach agreement at the local level where important details of the needs of the school system can most clearly and thoroughly be understood.

## COSTS

Any costs and expenses which may be incurred in securing and utilizing the services of any person or persons in a mediatory capacity shall be shared equally by the Board and the Association.

## SALARIES AND WORKING CONDITIONS

The salary schedule and policy statements, attached hereto in the form of Articles, are hereby made a part of this agreement and shall be negotiated in conformance with the dates listed in the next section and with the procedures outlined above.

## DURATION

The provisions of each article attached hereto shall be effective as of July 1, 1964 and shall continue in full force and effect until June 30, 1965.

Negotiations for a subsequent agreement may be commenced at any time on or after March 1, 1965 upon two weeks notice given in writing by any party to the Agreement.

IN WITNESS WHEREOF, the parties have hereunto set their hands and seals this _____ day of _____, 1964.

BOARD OF EDUCATION OF THE CITY SCHOOL DISTRICT OF NEW ROCHELLE

By _____

NEW ROCHELLE TEACHERS ASSOCIATION

By _____

## Article I

### SALARIES

The salaries of teachers covered by this Agreement are set forth in Appendix A which is attached hereto and made a part of this Agreement.

## Article II

### TEACHING CONDITIONS

The parties recognize that the availability of satisfactory school facilities for both student and teacher is necessary to insure the high quality of education that is the goal of both teacher and the Board. In addition, it is recognized that the primary duty and responsibility of the teacher is to teach and that the organization of the school and the school day should be directed at insuring that the energy of the teacher is primarily utilized to this end.

### 1. Class Size

The parties recognize that the pupil-teacher ratio is an important aspect of an effective educational program. Therefore they agree that the class sizes set forth below are desirable as maxima under normal conditions and where economically feasible:

| (a) | Elementary School | 29 pupils per teacher; |
| | Secondary School | 30 pupils per teacher. |
| (b) | Kindergartens | 25 pupils per teacher for each ½ day session |
| (c) | Special classes for handicapped pupils | 15 pupils per teacher. |

Departure from these norms may be authorized by the Superintendent when he deems it necessary and in the best interest of the educational process. At the request of the Association, the Superintendent of Schools will advise the Association of any such departures and the reasons for such change. If the reasonableness of the Superintendent's determination is questioned, the Association shall have the right to discuss with the Board (or, at the option of the Board, a committee thereof) an appropriate class size for the case in question.

*2. Teaching Hours*

a. The teacher's school day in the secondary schools shall be as follows:[1]

| | | NRHS | ALJHS | IEYJHS |
|---|---|---|---|---|
| (1) | Teachers check in no later than | 8:10 A.M. | 8:25 A.M. | 8:10 A.M. |
| (2) | Teachers at assigned place of duty not later than | 8:15 A.M. | 8:30 A.M. | 8:15 A.M. |
| (3) | Unless permission is granted by the principal, teachers shall leave the school no earlier than | 3:30 P.M. | 3:45 P.M. | 3:30 P.M. |

b. The teacher's school day in the elementary schools shall be as follows:[2]

(1) Teachers shall be at their assigned place of duty no later than 8:15 A.M.

(2) Teachers are to return to their classrooms after noon dismissal by 12:45 P.M.

(3) Unless permission is granted by the principal, teachers shall leave the school no earlier than 3:30 P.M.

[1] The teaching hours stated may be adjusted, earlier or later, by the Superintendent of Schools, but the total hours shall remain the same.
[2] The teaching hours stated may be adjusted, earlier or later, by the Superintendent of Schools, but the total hours shall remain the same.

c. All teachers shall be entitled to a duty-free lunch period of forty-five minutes in the junior and senior high schools, and a minimum of one hour in the elementary schools, except where required to supervise student lunchtime activities and then with minimum of one-half hour.

d. The normal weekly load in the senior high school will be 25 teaching periods and 5 supervised study periods and 5 unassigned preparation periods per week. Exceptions to the foregoing include among others, teachers of vocational education subjects, music teachers, special teachers, and teachers of physical education. Departures from these norms may be authorized by the principal when he deems it necessary and in the best interests of the educational process. If the reasonableness of the principal's determination is questioned, the matter shall be referred to the Superintendent of Schools. If the reasonableness of the Superintendent of School's determination is questioned, the Association shall have the right to discuss with the Board (or, at the option of the Board, a Committee thereof) an appropriate load for the case in question.

e. The normal weekly load in the junior high schools will be 25 teaching periods and 5 supervised study or activity periods and 5 unassigned preparation periods per week. Departures from these norms may be authorized by the principal when he deems it necessary and in the best interests of the educational process. If the reasonableness of the principal's determination is questioned, the matter shall be referred to the Superintendent of Schools. If the reasonableness of the Superintendent of School's determination is questioned, the Association shall have the right to discuss with the Board (or, at the option of the Board, a Committee thereof) an appropriate load for the case in question.

f. Participation in extra curricular activities for which no additional compensation is paid shall be voluntary. At the same time, the teachers recognize that their responsibility to their students and their profession requires the performance of duties that involve the expenditure of time beyond that of the normal school day.

g. Teachers in the elementary schools may be permitted to schedule conferences with parents or other teachers during periods when a class is being taught by a special teacher.

### 3. Teacher Facilities

The Board shall make available in each school one room which shall be reserved for use as a faculty lounge.

### 4. Special Teachers

The Board shall employ special teachers in the elementary schools whose major duties shall consist of speech therapy and the teaching of creative art, music, physical education, and remedial reading. In addition, all librarians and nurses shall be certified teachers.

Special teachers may not be assigned nonteaching duties in excess of those performed by regular teachers. Consideration will be given to the fact that the load of a particular special teacher may exceed the normal load of a regular teacher before any nonteaching assignments are made. Solely for the purpose of nonteaching assignments, special teachers teaching in more than one school shall be assigned to one school by the Central Office.

### 5. Central Register

The Administration has agreed to the desirability of making arrangements for central register keeping in the elementary and secondary schools. The Association and the Administration will establish a Joint Study Committee to study the best means of accomplishing the above and to estimate the cost thereof. This Committee will issue a timely report to the Board.

## Article III

### TEACHER ASSIGNMENTS

1. Teachers shall not be assigned, except temporarily and for good cause, outside the scope of their teaching certificates or their major or minor field of study.

2. Teacher(s) who will be affected by change of grade assignment in the elementary school grades will be notified and consulted by their principals as soon as practicable and under normal circumstances before the end of the school year. Such changes will be voluntary as far as practicable. Probationary elementary school teachers, whenever practicable, should not be reassigned grades.

3. Teacher(s) who will be affected by changes of subject assignment in the secondary school grades will be notified and consulted by their principals as soon as practicable and under normal circumstances before the end of the school year. Such changes will be voluntary as far as possible.

## Article IV

### TRANSFERS

The Board recognizes the frequent transfer of teachers from one school to another is disruptive of the educational process and interferes with optimum teacher performance. Although the Association also recognizes that some flexibility in regard to teacher transfers must remain with the Administration, a substantial degree of stability must be provided for all teachers, but especially with respect to new teachers. Therefore, it is agreed as follows:

1. Probationary teachers, whenever practicable, should serve their probationary period in one school.

2. When a reduction in the number of teachers in a school is necessary, to the extent possible all volunteers shall first be transferred, after which transfer will be made on the basis of years of service in the school building, those lowest in service being transferred first. Notice of all transfers will be given to the teachers concerned as soon as practicable, and under normal circumstances before the end of the school year.

3. When involuntary transfers are necessary, lists of positions in other schools shall be made available to all teachers being transferred. In filling such positions, preference shall be given to presently employed teachers, over newly appointed teachers, and shall be based on length of service in the New Rochelle school system.

4. Exceptions to the procedure set forth in sections 1, 2 and 3 of this Article may be made when the Superintendent of Schools believes it is in the best interests of the teacher or school(s) affected. The Association shall be notified of every instance in which the Superintendent of Schools shall determine that such an exception should be made and the Association's representative will meet with the Superintendent of Schools to discuss the transfer. A disagreement over whether the circumstances justify such an exception shall be subject to the procedure set forth in Article XI which shall be initiated at Level Three thereof.

## Article V

### PROMOTIONS

It is the desire and policy of the Board of Education to reward competent and faithful employees by promotion from within the ranks wherever it is practicable, educationally desirable and consistent with the educational needs of the community. All openings for promotional and/or new positions and positions paying salary differentials shall be adequately publicized in every school and all qualified teachers shall be given adequate opportunity to make application for such positions.

## Article VI

### SUMMER SCHOOL

1. No position shall be filled by a teacher not employed by the New Rochelle school system if there is a qualified applicant for such a position who is employed by the New Rochelle school system.

2. A teacher who has filled a summer school position and has performed satisfactorily shall be appointed to the same position in the following year, if the position is needed.

3. All openings for summer school positions shall be posted in the Superintendent's Bulletin as soon as possible, so all interested teachers might apply.

4. When applicants for summer school positions exceed the positions available, the best qualified applicant shall be selected. In making such selections, the administration shall consider the teacher's area of competence, major or minor field of study, quality of teaching performance, record of attendance, years of service in New Rochelle, and frequency of prior applications for summer school positions.

5. Summer school teachers may be granted a leave of absence from summer school after four consecutive years of service or when in conjunction with a sabbatical leave, for one year, upon written request and approval of the Superintendent. Teachers on leave of absence from summer school shall not forfeit thereby their right to a position in summer school for the year following such a leave. Teachers assigned to summer school positions as replacements for teachers on leave shall be so informed at the time of their assignment.

6. New Rochelle summer school salary schedules are attached hereto and made a part of this Agreement.

## Article VII

### PROTECTION OF TEACHERS

*1. Assistance in Assault Cases*

a. Principals and teachers shall be required to report, in writing, all cases of physical assault suffered by teachers in connection with their employment to the Superintendent of Schools. The Superintendent of Schools shall acknowledge receipt of such written statements.

b. The School Counsel shall inform the teacher immediately of his rights under the law and shall provide such information in a written document.

c. The School Counsel shall notify the teacher of his readiness to assist the teacher as follows:

(1) by obtaining from police and/or from the principal relevant information concerning the culprits;

(2) by accompanying the teacher in court appearances; and

(3) by acting in other appropriate ways as liaison between teacher, police and the courts.

## 2. *Legal Counsel*

The Board agrees to provide legal counsel to defend any teahcer in any action arising out of an assault on a teacher or any disciplinary action taken against a student by a teacher.

## 3. *Compensation for Lost Time*

If the physical assault on a teacher results in loss of time, the teacher shall be paid in full for a period not to exceed one month and such paid absence shall not be deducted from any sick leave to which such teacher is entitled under this Agreement. Any Workmen's Compensation benefits due to a teacher during this period shall be paid to the School District. In the event the absence due to an assault exceeds one month, payments thereafter shall be covered by Article VIII, Section 1.d of this Agreement.

## Article VIII

### LEAVE PAY

1. (a) All regularly employed teachers absent from duty on account of personal illness or any other approved reason who have been in the employ of the Board for less than five years shall be allowed full pay for a total of fifteen days absence and half pay for an additional fifteen days absence in any school year. All regularly employed teachers absent from duty on account of personal illness or any other approved reason who have been in the employ of the Board for five years or more shall be allowed full pay for a total of twenty-five days absence and half pay for an additional twenty-five days absence in any school year.

(b) Application for such pay by reason of personal illness or death in the immediate family must be made in writing on forms provided to the Superintendent of Schools through the principal or director at the end of the month during which such absence occurs and must be approved in writing by the Superintendent. In cases of absence for personal illness, application must be accompanied by the attending physician's certificate. If such absence does not exceed 3 consecutive days, the physician's certificate may be waived by the Superintendent of Schools.

(c) Absence for any reason other than personal illness or death in the immediate family must be applied for in writing in advance of such absence, if time permits, and approved either in writing or verbally. Such application must contain the signature of the principal of the school or schools concerned on the day of the anticipated absence. Teachers in special subject areas also should procure the signature of the director. If, because of lack of time in an emergency situation, permission is sought and granted orally, such permission must be confirmed by a letter of request countersigned by the principal or director.

(d) When a teacher sustains injury or illness arising out of and in the course of his employment, and is entitled to the benefits provided under the Workmen's Compensation Law of the State of New York for his disability, he may elect in writing to receive in lieu thereof the sick leave benefits provided in this Article, not to exceed the period of this accumulated unused sick leave time.

If the teacher's absence due to injuries or illness arising out of and in the course of his employment and for which he is entitled to benefits under the Workmen's Compensation Law exceeds the time of his accumulated unused absence leave under Board regulations, the teacher may, at the time his accumulated unused absence leave expires then receive Workmen's Compensation Law benefits.

The matter of payment of medical expenses under Workmen's Compensation is separate and distinct from sick leave benefits and each case will be reviewed and passed on by the Workmen's Compensation Board in the light of the facts of the specific case. The election of an option to receive sick leave benefits in lieu of workmen's compensation does not affect the teacher's right to any workmen's compensation medical benefits which may be due him.

During the period of time a teacher is receiving his accumulated sick leave benefit from the Board, the compensation benefits due him under the Workmen's Compensation Law shall be paid to the School District.

2. Each teacher shall be entitled to an accumulation for the unused portion of each year's leave to a maximum of 150 days at full salary. The parties agree that the present Section 2 of Article VIII—Leave Pay is superseded by Section 3505-b of the Education Laws of the State of New York, effective July 1, 1965.

3. Notwithstanding the provisions of Section 1 of this Article, absences which are chargeable against the allowance under that section for reasons other than personal illness or death in the immediate family shall not exceed six days in any one school year.

4. When a teacher has served twenty-five continuous years in the School District, the Board may, upon recommendation of the Superintendent of Schools, waive the time limitation beyond said teacher's accumulated leave under Section 2 of this Article and pay leave benefits for such period as it may deem appropriate.

## Article IX

### LEAVES OF ABSENCE

*1. Sick Leave*

a. Any teacher whose personal illness extends beyond the period compensated under Article VIII, upon written request shall be granted a leave of absence without pay for one full school year after the expiration of the above period. Leave may be extended for an additional year upon application therefor.

*2. Leaves of Absence with Pay Chargeable to Teacher's Allowance*

Leaves of absence with pay chargeable against the teacher's allowance under Article VIII, Section 1, and subject to the provisions of Article VIII, Section 3, shall be granted for the following reasons:

(a) A maximum of five days per school year for a critical illness or death in the immediate family.

(b) One day when necessary in the case of an emergency illness in a family to enable a teacher to make arrangements for necessary medical or nursing care.

(c) Attendance at a ceremony awarding a degree to a staff member for such portion of the day as is necessary.

(d) One day, except when travel requires additional time, for attendance at the college graduation of a son, daughter, husband or wife.

(e) Time necessary for the conduct of personal affairs which cannot normally be handled outside school hours, performance of religious obligations, medical and dental appointments when such appointments cannot be made at any other time.

### 3. Leaves of Absence with Pay Not chargeable to Teacher's Allowance

Leaves of absence with pay and not chargeable against the teacher's allowance under Article VIII, Section 1 or subject to the provisions of Article VIII, Section 3, shall be granted for the following reasons:

(a) Time necessary for attendance at the funeral service in New Rochelle of a person whose relationship to the teacher warrants such attendance.

(b) Required when a teacher is summoned for jury service.

(c) Court appearances as a witness in any case connected with the teacher's employment or the school.

(d) Approved visitation at other schools.

### 4. Absences Prior to or After Holidays

Leave of absence with pay shall not be granted under Sections 2 and 3 of this Article for the day immediately preceding or immediately following a holiday period except for personal illness or death in the immediate family.

### 5. Maternity Leave

a. Leave of absence without pay shall be granted for married women teachers on permanent tenure. Such absence is required for at least three months before and three months after the birth of a child. Leave will be granted for one full school year in addition to the six months absence required by the Board and may be extended for an additional year upon application therefor. Whenever possible, maternity leaves should begin on September 1 or February 1.

b. All non-tenure teachers who become pregnant shall resign their position at least three months prior to the birth of the child. Resignations should be submitted effective September 1, except when a non-tenure teacher becomes aware of pregnancy between September 1 and February 1 such resignation shall be effective on February 1.

### 6. Exchange Teacher Leave

a. Upon recommendation of the Superintendent of Schools, leave for exchange teacher positions under either national or international programs may be granted by the Board to teachers who have successfully completed their required three year probationary period in the School District and who have completed at least an additional two years of competent service.

b. The Board shall compensate any teacher granted exchange teacher leave on the basis of said teacher's regular salary status. Any period served as an exchange teacher shall be applied to the salary schedule set forth in Appendix A of the Agreement as if such period has been served by the teacher in the New Rochelle School District.

### 7. Peace Corps Leave

a. Leave of absence will be granted of up to two years to any teacher who joins the Peace Corps as a full-time participant in such program.

b. Compensation for such service shall be paid by the United States Government, except that any period so served shall be applied to the salary schedule set forth in Appendix A of this Agreement as if such period had been served by the teacher in the New Rochelle School District.

### 8. Sabbatical Leave

Upon recommendation by the Superintendent of Schools, sabbatical leaves may be granted to a member of the pedagogic staff by the Board of Education subject to the following conditions:

(a) Such requests must be received by the Superintendent of Schools in writing in such form as may be required by the Superintendent of Schools no later than December 31 of the fiscal year preceding the fiscal year in which the sabbatical leave is requested.

(b) Provision for such sabbatical leave is included in the final budget for the fiscal year in which the sabbatical leave is granted.

(c) The teacher has completed at least seven consecutive full school years of service in the New Rochelle schools. Sabbatical Leave may be granted on the following bases:
   (1) One-half the annual salary rate for a semester's leave or one-quarter the annual salary rate for a full year's leave for study or travel; or
   (2) Where such sabbatical leave is granted for the purpose of taking a full course of study leading to a doctoral degree at a university recognized by the State Education Department of New York as authorized to grant such Degree, such sabbatical leave shall be granted at full annual salary rate for a semester's leave and one-half the annual salary rate for a full year's leave upon proof of matriculation.

(d) The teacher shall agree to return to employment in New Rochelle Public Schools for:

(1) One full school year if the teacher is granted a leave under Section (c) 1 above, or

(2) Two full school years if the teacher is granted a leave under Section (c) 2 above.

## 9. Convention Leave

a. When it is evident that convention or conference attendance will contribute to the effectiveness of the instructional program, the Superintendent of Schools, with reasonable limitations as to time and number of individuals involved, may grant convention or conference leave.

b. Expenses of attendance at conventions or conferences will be paid by the Board within the limitations of the amounts budgeted for such expenses. Expenses which will be reimbursed are limited to those allowed by State law and noted on Request for Travel form. Teachers interested in convention or conference attendance should estimate the expenses thereof, secure the approval of their principal or director, and file their requests with the Superintendent of Schools well in advance.

c. Teachers attending conventions or conferences will be required to submit a short report highlighting the meetings attended so that the benefits thereof may be shared with other staff members.

## 10. Return After Leave of Absence

a. Teachers who have been granted leaves of absence shall notify the Superintendent of Schools in writing on or before the first day of December or April preceding the opening of the semester following the expiration of leave of their intention to resume work at the beginning of the ensuing school semester.

b. To the extent possible, all teachers returning from leaves of absence granted under this Article shall be restored to the same position they held at the time leave was granted.

## Article X

### GENERAL

1. There shall be no reprisals of any kind taken against any teacher on account of membership in the Association or participation in the activities of the Association.

2. Each teacher shall have the right upon request to review the contents of his own personal file as maintained by building principal, supervisor, or director.

3. No restriction, other than that of good judgment, is placed upon the freedom of teachers to use their own time for gainful employment insofar as it does not interfere with satisfactory performance.

4. When it is necessary for officers of the Association to engage in Association activities directly relating to the Association's duties as representative of the teachers, they shall be given such free time, without loss of pay, as is necessary to perform any such activities. The Association, and its officers, recognize and agree that this privilege should not be abused.

5. The Board and the Association affirm their continued support of a policy of no discrimination on account of race, color, creed, nationality, sex, marital status, or age.

## Article XI

PROCEDURE FOR HANDLING GRIEVANCES

### 1. Definitions

a. A grievance is a claim based upon an event or condition which affects the conditions or circumstances under which a teacher works, allegedly caused by misinterpretation or inequitable application of established policy or the terms of this Agreement. *Provided:* No claim or cause for which there is another procedure, settlement, or adjudication established by law or rule or regulation having the force of law shall constitute a grievance.

b. The term "teacher" may include a group of teachers who are similarly affected by a grievance.

c. A "party in interest" is the person making the claim and any person who might be required to take action or against whom action might be taken in order to resolve the problem.

d. The term "days" when used in this Article shall, except where otherwise indicated, mean working school days.

### 2. Purpose

The primary purpose of the procedure set forth in this Article is to secure, at the lowest level possible, equitable solutions to the problems of the parties. Except as is necessary for the purpose of implementing this Article, both parties agree that these proceedings shall be kept as informal and confidential as may be appropriate at any level of such procedure. Nothing contained herein shall be construed as limiting the right of any teacher having a grievance to discuss the matter informally with any appropriate member of the administration.

### 3. Structure

a. There shall be a School Representative for each school building chosen by the Executive Committee of the Association.

b. The Association shall establish a Professional Rights and Responsibilities Panel (hereinafter referred to as the PR&R Panel).

In the event that any member of the Panel is a party in interest to any grievance brought before it, he shall disqualify himself from considering such grievance and shall be replaced by his alternate.

c. The PR&R Panel shall constitute an advisory group of teachers who shall be broadly representative of teacher classifications and representative of the various elements of the School District.

From time to time the chairman of the PR&R Panel shall appoint from the PR&R Panel Ad Hoc—three man advisory groups to determine, in accordance with the procedure hereinafter set forth, whether in the opinion of any such committee a particular grievance brought to it by a School Representative or a teacher is or is not meritorious.

The Association will provide the Superintendent with the names of members of the PR&R Panel at the beginning of the school year.

d. The Board shall establish the "Board's Review Committee." Such Committee shall consist of as many Board members as the Board shall determine.

### 4. Procedure

It is important that grievances be processed as rapidly as possible. The number of days indicated at each level should be considered as maximum and every effort should be made to expedite the process. However, when mutually agreed upon, the time limits given below may be extended.

In the event a grievance is filed on or after the 1st of June which, if left unresolved until the beginning of the following school term, could result in irreparable harm to the teacher or group of teachers concerned, the time limits set forth herein shall be appropriately reduced.

a. *Level One.* The teacher with a grievance shall first discuss the matter with his immediate supervisor or principal, whichever has the authority to deal most effectively with the grievance, either directly or through his School Representative, with the objective of resolving the matter informally. In the event the grievance is first discussed with anyone other than the principal, the principal shall be apprised of such meeting.

b. *Level Two.* (i) In the event that the teacher is not satisfied with the disposition of his grievance at Level One, he shall file the grievance in writing with the appropriate Ad Hoc Committee within five (5) days after the decision at Level One, for the purpose of review by such Committee. The Ad Hoc Committee shall within ten (10) days make a judgment on the merits. If the Ad Hoc Committee decides either that the grievance lacks merit or that the decision at Level One is in the best interests of the educational system, it shall so notify the teacher and the School Representative. If the Ad Hoc Committee decides that, in its opinion, the grievance has merit, it shall refer such grievance in writing to the Superintendent of Schools.

(ii) The Superintendent of Schools shall designate two persons, who may include himself, to represent the administration in working with the Ad Hoc Committee to arrive at an equitable solution of such grievance. Within ten (10) days after receipt of the written grievance by the Superintendent of Schools, he and/or his representatives shall meet with the Ad Hoc Committee to consider the problem and to resolve it. The Superintendent and/or his representative shall prepare a written report, including any agreement reached, of the meeting with the Ad Hoc Committee.

c. *Level Three.* If the grievance is not resolved by the Superintendent or his representatives and the Ad Hoc Committee within five (5) days of its consideration by them, it shall be referred for consideration to the Board's Review Committee. After such referral, the Ad Hoc Committee and the Board's Review Committee shall meet for the purpose of discussing the matter and disposing of it in a mutually satisfactory manner. The Superintendent and/or the Board's Review Committee shall prepare a written report, including any agreement reached, of the meeting with the Ad Hoc Committee.

d. *Level Four.* (i) If the Board's Review Committee and the Ad Hoc Committee are unable to agree on a disposition of the grievance, either party may submit such matter to advisory arbitration in accordance with the procedure hereinafter set forth. The arbitration shall be commenced by either party within ten (10) days after such failure to agree, filing with the other party and with the President of Teachers College, Columbia University, a notice of intention to submit the grievance to an arbitrator for an advisory decision.

(ii) The parties will attempt to select an arbitrator by mutual agreement. If they are unable to agree on an arbitrator within ten (10) days after notice of arbitration has been received, then the arbitrator shall be selected by the President of Teachers College, Columbia University. The arbitrator shall be an experienced, impartial and disinterested person of recognized competence in the field of public education.

(iii) The arbitrator shall issue his decision not later than twenty (20) calendar days from the date of the closing of the hearings or, if oral hearings have been waived, then from the date of transmitting the final statements and proofs to the arbitrator. The decision shall be in writing and shall set forth the arbitrator's opinion and conclusions on the issues submitted. The parties recognize that the Board is legally charged with the responsibility of operating the school system. The sole power of the arbitrator shall be to determine whether established policy or the terms of this Agreement have been misinterpreted or inequitably applied in such a manner as to affect the condition or circumstances under which a particular teacher or group of teachers works; and the arbitrator shall have no power or authority to make any decision which modifies, alters or amends any then established policy or term of this Agreement, or which requires the commission of an act prohibited by law or which is violative of the terms of this Agreement. The arbitrator shall not substitute his judgment for that of the Board where the Board's action is not unreasonable. The decision of the arbitrator shall be rendered to the Board and to the Association and shall be advisory only, and no judgment may be entered thereon.

(iv) The expenses of the arbitration will be borne equally by the Association and the Board.

(v) In the event that, in the judgment of the PR&R Panel, a grievance affects a group or class of teachers, the PR&R Panel may submit such grievance in writing to the Superintendent of Schools directly, and such grievance shall be disposed of in accordance with the procedure set forth commencing at Level b(ii) above.

## 5. Rights of Teachers to Representation

a. Any party in interest may be represented at all meetings and hearings at all steps and stages of the grievance and arbitration procedure by another teacher or by another person. *Provided, however:* That the party in interest may in no event be represented by an officer, agent or other representative of any teacher organization other than the New Rochelle Teachers Association. *Provided, further:* When a teacher is not represented by the Association, the Association shall have the right to be present and to state its views at all stages of grievance processing, except where the grievance involves only questions of fact peculiar to the individual grievant.

b. There shall be no reprisals of any kind by supervisory or administrative personnel taken against any party in interest or his School Representative, any member of the PR&R Panel or of the Ad Hoc Committees, or any other participant in the procedure set forth herein by reason of such participation.

c. All documents, communications and records dealing with the processing of a grievance shall be filed separately from the personnel files of the participants.

d. Copies of a written grievance and all written answers will be given to all parties in interest and to the Ad Hoc Committee.

## Article XII

### PROCEDURES INVOLVING QUESTIONS OF ETHICAL CONDUCT

The Board of Education understands that the Code of Ethics of the Education Profession is considered by the Association and its membership as the guide line for acceptable professional behavior. The Board further understands that as to its membership the Association shall deal with ethical problems arising under the Code of Ethics of the Education Profession, in accordance with the terms thereof, through procedures developed locally and with emphasis upon raising professional standards through counseling.

## Article XIII

### DUES DEDUCTION

a. The Board agrees to deduct from the salaries of teachers who are members of the New Rochelle Teachers Association the dues of that Association as said teachers individually and voluntarily authorize the Board to deduct, and to transmit the monies promptly to said Association. Teacher authorizations shall be in writing in the form set forth as follows:

*Dues Authorization Card*

Name _____

School or

Department _____

I hereby request the Board of Education of the City School District of the City of New Rochelle, N.Y., to deduct $10.00 from my earnings to be paid to the New Rochelle Teachers Association, during such time as it shall be recognized as the duly authorized representative of teachers, as payment of the current rate of membership dues.

This authorization shall continue until revoked by me in writing. I understand that such revocation must be received by the Business Office, Board of Education, 515 North Avenue, New Rochelle, N.Y., no later than June 30 of any year preceding the school year in which I wish such revocation to take effect.

Date _____   Signature _____

*Note:* For the school year 1965-1966, this Dues Authorization Card must be received by the Business Office no later than November 1, 1965. Dues will be deducted from monthly salary check commencing January, 1966 through June, 1966 at a rate of $1.67 per month. Thereafter dues deduction on the basis of this authorization will be at the rate of $1.00 per month.

b. The Association named in Section a. of this Article shall certify to the Board the current rate of membership dues.

## Article XIV

### MATTERS NOT COVERED

The parties agree to meet periodically during the term of this Agreement to discuss matters of mutual concern, and the Board (or a committee of the Board, or the Superintendent of Schools) will bring to the attention of the Association at such meetings any contemplated changes which are of mutual interest and concern.

IN WITNESS WHEREOF, the parties have hereunto set their hands and seals this 24th day of November, 1964.

BOARD OF EDUCATION OF THE CITY SCHOOL DISTRICT OF NEW ROCHELLE

By _____

NEW ROCHELLE TEACHERS ASSOCIATION

By _____

APPENDIX A

**Teachers' Salary Schedules**

(*Effective September 1, 1965*)

|  | I | II | III | IV | V | VI | VII |
|---|---|---|---|---|---|---|---|
| STEP | BA | BA+15 | BA+30 | MA | BA+60 | MA+30 | DR |
| 1 | $5600 | $5750 | $ 6050 | $ 6150 | $ 6450 | $ 6650 | $ 7350 |
| 2 | 5900 | 6050 | 6350 | 6450 | 6750 | 6950 | 7650 |
| 3 | 6200 | 6350 | 6650 | 6750 | 7050 | 7250 | 7950 |
| 4 | 6600 | 6750 | 7050 | 7150 | 7450 | 7650 | 8350 |
| 5 | 7000 | 7150 | 7450 | 7550 | 7850 | 8050 | 8750 |
| 6 | 7260 | 7410 | 7730 | 7830 | 8140 | 8340 | 9050 |
| 7 | 7520 | 7670 | 8010 | 8110 | 8430 | 8630 | 9350 |
| 8 | 7780 | 7930 | 8290 | 8390 | 8720 | 8920 | 9650 |
| 9 | 8040 | 8190 | 8570 | 8670 | 9010 | 9210 | 9950 |
| 10 | 8300 | 8450 | 8850 | 8950 | 9300 | 9500 | 10250 |
| 11 | 8560 | 8710 | 9130 | 9230 | 9590 | 9790 | 10550 |
| 12 | 8820 | 8970 | 9410 | 9510 | 9880 | 10080 | 10850 |
| 13 | 9100 | 9300 | 9850 | 10000 | 10400 | 10500 | 11150 |
| 14 | 9400 | 9600 | 10150 | 10350 | 10700 | 10850 | 11450 |
| 15 | 9700 | 9900 | 10450 | 10700 | 11000 | 11200 | 11750 |
| 16 |  |  | 10750 | 11050 | 11300 | 11550 | 12050 |

SALARY SCHEDULE CONDITIONS FOR TEACHERS

## I. Salary Placement

a. The salary placement on the new schedules as of September 1, 1965 of all teachers who have been serving under regular appointment in the New Rochelle Public Schools in the 1964–65 school year through June 30, 1965 and who continue to serve under regular appointment on September 1, 1965 shall be on the same step of the new schedules that they would have been placed on the present schedules had the present schedules remained in effect, except that teachers who meet the conditions noted under Salary Schedule Condition Number IV shall be placed on the next higher step.

b. The salary placement of teachers specifically appointed to take the place of teachers who have been granted leaves of absence by the Board of Education shall be as set forth on the Salary Schedules for Teachers, with credit for prior service as set forth in Section II and III herein except, however, that no such interim teachers may be appointed beyond Step 6 of the appropriate Salary Schedule.

## II. Prior Service Credit

Credit for experience outside the New Rochelle Public Schools shall be evaluated by the Superintendent of Schools. For the school year 1965–66, full credit shall be given for the first eight years of experience and on a two-for-one basis for the ninth through tenth year. Such credit shall be given only when the prior service is rated by former school systems as satisfactory. No credit shall be permitted for a fractional part of a school year.

### III. *Military Service Credit*

Teachers shall be advanced one step on the salary schedule for between one and three years of active military service, and two steps for active military service in excess of three years.

### IV. *Double Increment*

All teachers employed by the New Rochelle Public Schools on a probationary or permanent status on March 26, 1963, shall, upon the completion of five full school years of continuous service in the New Rochelle Public Schools, be entitled to a double increment upon recmmendation of the Superintendent of Schools. Leaves of Absence shall not be considered as an interruption of continuous service except that school years in which Leaves of Absence without pay occur, regardless of the length of Leave without pay, shall not constitute a full school year of service.

### V. *Other Regulations*

a. Increments become effective September 1 of each year. Teachers entitled to such consideration shall be granted specified increments as per salary schedule and assigned to the next higher step.

b. Advancement from step to step each September 1 shall be automatic for such steps as are specified in the State Education Law. Beyond this point one or more further increments for any teacher may be withheld for valid reasons by the Board upon recommendation by the Superintendent of Schools.

c. Advancement from one schedule to another shall be made to the same step on the higher schedule that the teacher would be entitled to on the lower schedule if the teacher had continued service on the lower schedule after evidence of completion of the required study has been presented and has been approved by the Superintendent of Schools.

d. Advancement from one schedule to another shall be effected as of September 1 or February 1, following the completion of the required academic and professional courses.

e. A teacher entering the employ of the City School District on a probationary basis shall begin at such step in the schedule applicable to him as the Board, upon the recommendation of the Superintendent, shall approve and determine. Said teacher shall continue on such step from the month appointed until the June 30 following his appointment.

f. All members of the professional staff except teachers of vocational subjects, who possess a Baccalaureate Degree, shall be placed on Schedule I. Teachers of vocational subjects who have the requisite trade experience required by the State of New York and a provisional license (32 hours of teacher training courses) and less than 15 semester hours of approved study shall be placed on Schedule I.

g. All members of the professional staff except teachers of vocational subjects, who have completed at least fifteen semester hours of approved study beyond the Baccalaureate Degree of which not over 8 may be undergraduate credit, shall be placed on Schedule II. Such fifteen semester hours shall be completed subsequent to the completion of the preparation necessary for a Baccalaureate Degree at an institution of higher learning recognized by the State Department of Education of New York as qualified to offer such courses, or in the New Rochelle In-Service Education Program as approved by the Superintendent of Schools and by the State Department of Education of New York for In-Service and Professional Improvement Credit. These credits must be in academic and professional areas in the teacher's general subject field or in the field of education. Teachers of vocational subjects who have the requisite trade experience required by the State of New York and a provisional license (32 hours of teacher training courses) and 15 semester hours of approved study beyond this requirement shall be placed on Schedule II.

h. All members of the professional staff except teachers of vocational subjects, who possess at least 30 semester hours of approved study beyond the Baccalaureate Degree shall be placed on Schedule III. Such 30 semester hours shall be completed subsequent to the completion of the preparation necessary for a Baccalaureate Degree at an institution of higher learning recognized by the State Department of Education of New York as qualified to offer such courses, or in the New Rochelle In-Service Education Program as approved by the Superintendent of Schools and by the State Department of Education of New York for In-Service and Professional Improvement Credit. These credits must be in academic and professional areas in the teacher's general subject field or in the field of education. Teachers of vocational subjects who have the requisite trade experience required by the State of New York and a provisional license (32 hours of teacher training courses) and 30 semester hours of approved study beyond this requirement, shall be placed on Schedule III.

i. All members of the professional staff who possess the following qualifications shall be placed on Schedule IV:

(1) Candidate must possess a Baccalaureate Degree earned at a University recognized by the State Department of Education of New York as authorized to grant such degree; and

(2) Candidate must possess a Master's Degree earned at a University recognized by the State Department of Education of New York as authorized to grant such degree.

j. All members of the professional staff who have completed at least 30 semester hours of approved study beyond the fifth year of preparation of which not over 8 may be undergraduate credit shall be placed on Schedule V. Thirty semester hours shall be completed subsequent to the completion of the preparation necessary for a Baccalaureate Degree from an institution of higher learning recognized by the State Department of Education of New York as qualified to offer such courses, or in the New Rochelle In-Service Education Program as approved by the Superintendent of Schools and by the State Department of Education of New York for In-Service and Professional Improvement Credit. These credits must be in academic and professional areas in the teacher's general subject field or in the field of education.

k. All members of the professional staff who possess the following qualifications shall be placed on Schedule VI:

(1) Candidate must possess a Baccalaureate Degree earned at a University recognized by the State Department of Education of New York as authorized to grant such degree; and

(2) Candidate must possess a Master's Degree earned at a University recognized by the State Department of Education of New York as authorized to grant such degree; and

(3) Candidate must possess at least 30 semester hours of approved graduate study of which not over 8 hours may be in undergraduate courses all of which must be completed subsequent to the completion of the preparation necessary for the Master's Degree from an institution of higher learning recognized by the State Department of Education of New York as qualified to offer such courses, or in the New Rochelle In-Service Education Program as approved by the Superintendent of Schools and by the State Department of Education of New York for In-Service and Professional Improvement Credit. These credits must be in academic and professional areas in the teacher's general subject field or in the field of education.

l. All members of the professional staff who, in addition to all other requirements, hold a Degree of Ph.D., Ed.D., Sc.D., earned at a University recognized by the State Department of Education of New York as authorized to grant such degrees, shall be placed on Schedule VII.

m. Persons appointed by the Board of Education to the positions listed below shall be assigned to the appropriate step on Schedules I, II, III, IV, V, VI or VII, depending upon their academic and professional preparation as indicated in the foregoing conditions, but in addition thereto shall be paid the amount set forth:

| | |
|---|---:|
| Attendance Officer | $ 500 |
| Band and Orchestra Director—New Rochelle H. S. | 500 |
| Department Chairman | 650 |
| Guidance Counselor | 500 |
| Head Teacher | 1,000 |
| Helping Teacher | 200 |
| Social Case Worker | 500 |
| Supervisor | 1,000 |
| Teacher Assigned to Elementary Principal's Office | 500 |
| Treasurer of General Organization—New Rochelle High School | 1,000 |
| Unit Chairman | 650 |
| Visiting Teacher | 500 |
| Coaches: | |

*Senior High School:*

| | |
|---|---:|
| Baseball—Varsity | 650 |
| Baseball—Junior Varsity | 425 |
| Basketball—Varsity | 900 |
| Basketball—Junior Varsity | 600 |
| Bowling—Varsity | 150 |
| Football—Varsity—Head | 1,125 |
| Football—Varsity—Line | 700 |
| Football—Asst. 2nd Vars. | 550 |
| Football—Jr. Vars.—Head | 550 |
| Football—Asst.—Jr. Vars. | 425 |
| Golf—Varsity | 150 |
| Gymnastics—Varsity | 600 |
| Ice Hockey—Varsity | 650 |
| Ice Hockey—Jr. Varsity | 425 |
| Intramural Superv.—Early Winter | 300 |
| Intramural Superv.—Late Winter | 300 |
| Riflery—Varsity | 350 |
| Soccer—Varsity | 625 |
| Soccer—Junior Varsity | 425 |
| Swimming—Varsity | 550 |
| Swimming—Junior Varsity | 300 |
| Tennis—Varsity | 350 |
| Track—Cross Country | 400 |

| | |
|---|---:|
| Track—Indoor | 700 |
| Track—Indoor—Assistant | 450 |
| Track—Outdoor | 700 |
| Track—Outdoor—Assistant | 500 |
| Wrestling—Varsity | 700 |
| Wrestling—Junior Varsity | 425 |

*Junior High School:*

| | |
|---|---:|
| Baseball—Head | 425 |
| Basketball—Head | 425 |
| Football—Head | 425 |
| Football—Assistant | 325 |
| Track—Head | 425 |
| Track—Assistant | 350 |

| | |
|---|---:|
| Teachers in Adult Education and Summer School— | |
| Baccalaureate | $6.00 per hour |
| Baccalaureate + 30 points or Master's | 6.50 per hour |
| Teacher of Home-Bound Students | 7.50 per hour |

# *Appendix D.* Summary of Professional Negotiation Agreements on File[1]

| STATE | LEVEL I | LEVEL II | LEVEL III | TOTAL |
|---|---|---|---|---|
| *Arizona* | | 1 | 2 | 3 |
| *California* | 6 | 28 | 5 | 39 |
| *Colorado* | 2 | 4 | 1 | 7 |
| *Connecticut* | | | 68 | 68 |
| *Delaware* | | | 2 | 2 |
| *Florida* | | 1 | | 1 |
| *Idaho* | 1 | 3 | 1 | 5 |
| *Illinois* | 1 | 6 | 10 | 17 |
| *Indiana* | | 2 | | 2 |
| *Iowa* | 1 | | 1 | 2 |
| *Kansas* | | 2 | 4 | 6 |
| *Kentucky* | | 1 | | 1 |
| *Maryland* | 2 | 1 | 3 | 6 |
| *Massachusetts* | | 4 | 1 | 5 |
| *Michigan* | 2 | 11 | 20 | 33 |
| *Missouri* | 1 | | 1 | 2 |
| *Nebraska* | | 1 | | 1 |
| *Nevada* | 2 | | | 2 |
| *New Hampshire* | | 1 | | 1 |
| *New Jersey* | 6 | 17 | 6 | 29 |
| *New Mexico* | 1 | 1 | | 2 |
| *New York* | 3 | | 4 | 7 |
| *North Dakota* | | 1 | | 1 |
| *Ohio* | 14 | 26 | 10 | 50 |
| *Oklahoma* | | | 2 | 2 |
| *Oregon* | 32 | 1 | 3 | 36 |
| *Pennsylvania* | 2 | 1 | 2 | 5 |
| *Rhode Island* | | 2 | | 2 |
| *South Carolina* | 8 | | | 8 |
| *Texas* | | 1 | | 1 |
| *Utah* | 1 | 3 | | 4 |
| *Washington* | 19 | 4 | 9 | 32 |
| *West Virginia* | 1 | | | 1 |
| *Wisconsin* | | 1 | | 1 |
| *Wyoming* | | | 1 | 1 |
| *Overseas Dependents Schools* | | 1 (all units) | 2 (local units) | 3 |
| Total | 105 | 125 | 158 | 388 |
| *Distribution by Percentage* | 27% | 32% | 41% | |

1 September 20, 1965

**239**

# *Appendix E.* State Laws on Negotiation Pertaining Exclusively to Public School Personnel

## California

SECTION 1. Section 3501 of the Government Code is amended to read:
*3501.* As used in this chapter:

(a) "Employee organization" means any organization which includes employees of a public agency and which has as one of its primary purposes representing such employees in their relations with that public agency.

(b) Except as otherwise provided in this subdivision, "public agency" means the State of California, every governmental subdivision, every district, every public and quasi-public corporation, every public agency and public service corporation and every town, city, county, city and county and municipal corporation, whether incorporated or not and whether chartered or not. As used in this chapter, "public agency" does not mean a school district or a county board of education or a county superintendent of schools or a personnel commission in a school district having a merit system as provided in Chapter 3 (commencing with Section 13580) of Division 10 of the Education Code.

(c) "Public employee" means any person employed by any public agency excepting those persons elected by popular vote or appointed to office by the Governor of this state.

SEC. 2, Article 5 (commencing with Section 13080) is added to Chapter 1 of Division 10 of Part 2 of the Education Code, to read:

*Article 5. Employee Organizations*

*13080.* It is the purpose of this article to promote the improvement of personnel management and employer-employee relations within the public school systems in the State of California by providing a uniform basis for recognizing the right of public school employees to join organizations of their own choice and be represented by such organizations in their professional and employment relationships with public school employers and to afford certificated employees a voice in the formulation of educational policy. Nothing contained herein shall be deemed to supersede other provisions of this code and the rules and regulations of public school employers which establish and regulate tenure or a merit or civil service system or which provide for other methods of administering employer-employee relations. This article is intended, instead, to strengthen tenure, merit, civil service and other methods of administering employer-employee relations through the establishment of uniform and orderly methods of communication between employees and the public school employers by which they are employed.

*13081.* As used in this article:

(a) "Employee organization" means any organization which includes employees of a public school employer and which has as one of its primary purposes representing such employees in their relations with that public school employer.

(b) "Public school employer" means a school district, a county board of education, a county superintendent of schools, or a personnel commission of a school district which has a merit system as provided in chapter 3 of this division.

(c) "Public school employee" means any person employed by any public school employer excepting those persons elected by popular vote or appointed by the Governor of this state.

*13082.* Except as otherwise provided by the Legislature, public school employees shall have the right to form, join and participate in the activities of employee organizations of their own choosing for the purpose of representation on all matters of employer-employee relations. Public school employees shall also have the right to refuse to join or participate in the activities of employee organizations and shall have the right to represent themselves individually in their employment relations with the public school employer.

*13083.* Employee organizations shall have the right to represent their members in their employment relations with public school employers. Employee organizations may establish reasonable restrictions regarding who may join and may make reasonable provisions for the dismissal of individuals from membership. Nothing in this section shall prohibit any employee from appearing in his own behalf in his employment relations with the public school employer.

*13084.* The scope of representation shall include all matters relating to employment conditions and employer-employee relations, including, but not limited to wages, hours and other terms and conditions of employment.

*13085.* A public school employer or the governing board thereof, or such administrative officer as it may designate, shall *meet and confer* with representatives of employee organizations upon request with regard to all matters relating to employment conditions and employer-employee relations, and in addition, shall *meet and confer* with representatives of employee organizations representing certificated employees upon request with regard to all matters relating to the definition of educational objectives, the determination of the content of courses and curricula, the selection of textbooks, and other aspects of the instructional program to the extent such matters are within the discretion of the public school employer or governing board under the law. The designation of an administrative officer as provided herein shall not preclude an employee organization from meeting with, appearing before, or making proposals to the public school employer at a public meeting if the employee organization requests such a public meeting.

Notwithstanding the provisions of Sections 13082 and 13083, in the event there is more than one employee organization representing certificated employees, the public school employer or governing board therefore shall *meet and confer* with the representatives of such employee organizations through a negotiating council with regard to the matters specified in this section, provided that nothing herein shall prohibit any employee from appearing in his own behalf in his employment relations with the public school employer. The negotiating council shall have not more than nine nor less than five members and shall be composed of representatives of those employee organizations who are entitled to representation on the negotiating council. An employee organization representing certificated employees shall be entitled to appoint such number of members of the negotiating council as bears as nearly as practicable the same ratio to the total number of members of the negotiating council as the number of members of the employee organizations bears to the total number of certificated employees of the public school employer who are members of employee organizations representing certificated employees. Each employee organization shall adopt procedures for selecting its proportionate share of members of the negotiating council, provided that such members shall be selected no later than October 31 of each school year. Within 10 days after October 31, the members of the negotiating council shall meet and select a chairman, and thereafter such negotiating council shall be legally constituted to *meet and confer* as provided for by the provisions of this article. Employee organizations shall exercise the rights given by Section 13083 through the negotiating council provided for in this section.

*13086.* Public school employers and employee organizations shall not interefere with, intimidate, restrain, coerce or discriminate against public school employees because of their exercise of their rights under Section 13082.

*13087.* A public school employer shall adopt reasonable rules and regulations for the administration of employer-employee relations under this article.

Such rules and regulations shall include provision for verifying the number of certificated employees of the public school employer who are members in good standing of an employee organization on the date of such verification, and where a negotiating council is required by Section 13085, for the size of the negotiating council. The public school employer may require an employee organization to submit any supplementary information or data considered by the public school employer to be necessary to the verification of the number of members in an employee organization and such information or data shall be submitted by the organization within 10 days after request, provided that membership lists, if requested, shall not be used as a means of violating Section 13086. In addition, such rules may include provisions for (a) verifying the official status of employee organization officers and representatives, (b) access of employee organization officers and representatives to work locations, (c) use of official bulletin boards and other means of communication by employee organizations, (d) furnishing complete and accurate nonconfidential information pertaining to employment relations to employee organizations and (e) such other matters as are necessary to carry out the purposes of this article.

*13088.* The enactment of this article shall not be construed as making the provisions of Section 923 of the Labor Code applicable to public school employees.

### Connecticut

AN ACT CONCERNING THE RIGHT OF TEACHERS' REPRESENTATIVES
TO NEGOTIATE WITH BOARDS OF EDUCATION

*Section 1.* (a) Any organization or organizations of certificated professional employees of a local or regional board of education may be selected for the purpose of representation in negotiations concerning salaries and all other conditions of employment. Representatives may be designated or selected for the purpose of negotiating by the majority of the employees in the entire group of employees of said board of education or school district below the rank of superintendent or by the majority of the employees in separate units as described in subsection (b). (b) All certificated professional personnel below the rank of superintendent, other than temporary substitutes, employed and engaged either (i) in positions requiring a teaching or special services certificate or (ii) in positions requiring an administrative or supervisory certificate, may select a separate representative by a secret ballot decision of a majority of the personnel voting in each of the two said categories. If twenty per cent or more of the certificated professional employees of a local or regional board of education below the rank of superintendent in either the entire group or in the separate units described in (i) or (ii) above file with the secretary of the state board of education a petition requesting that a teacher representation referendum be held to select an organization for the purpose of representation, said secretary shall file notice of such petition with the local or regional board of education. The signatures on such petition shall remain confidential with the secretary of said board. Any organization having an interest in representing teachers in any of the units authorized by this section may intervene within fifteen days by filing with the secretary of the state board of education a petition supported by ten per cent of the employees of such unit. The local or regional board and the petitioning organization and any intervening teacher's organization may agree on an impartial person or agency to conduct such a referendum consistent with the other provisions of this section, provided not more than one such referendum shall be held in any one school year. In the event of a disagreement on the agency to conduct the referendum, the method shall be determined by the board of arbitration selected in accordance with section 2 of this act. An election shall be held to determine the representatives of the appropriate unit or units, as the case may be, within forty-five days after the filing of the petition with the secretary of the state board of education. (c) The representatives designated or selected as provided in subsection (a) of this section shall be the exclusive representatives of all the employees in such unit for the purposes of negotiating with respect to salary schedules and personnel policies relative to employment of certificated professional employees, provided any certificated professional employee or group of employees shall have the right at any time to present any grievance to such persons as the local or regional board of education shall designate for that purpose.

*Section 2.* Any dispute as to the eligibility of personnel to vote in an election, or the agency to conduct the election required by section 1 hereof, shall be submitted to a board of arbitration as provided by section 5 (b) of this act except that, where there are two or more organizations seeking to represent employees, each shall be permitted to name an arbitrator and such arbitrators, together with an equal number designated by the board of education, shall select an additional impartial member thereof. The agency selected to conduct the election shall decide on matters relating thereto.

*Section 3.* The local or regional board of education and the organization designated as exclusive representatives for the appropriate unit, through designated officials or their representatives, shall have the duty to negotiate with respect to salaries and other conditions of employment, and such duty shall include the obligation of such board of education to meet at reasonable times, including meetings appropriately related to the budget-making process, and confer in good faith with respect to salaries and other conditions of employment, or the negotiation of an agreement, or any question arising thereunder and the execution of a written contract incorporating any agreement reached if requested by either party, but such obligation shall not compel either party to agree to a proposal or require the making of a concession. The local or regional board of education, and its representatives, agents and superintendents shall not interfere, restrain or coerce employees in the rights guaranteed by this act, and in the absence of any certification as the exclusive representative as provided by section 1, all organizations seeking to represent members of the teaching profession shall be accorded equal treatment with respect to access to teachers, principals, members of the board of education, records and participation in discussions with respect to salaries and other conditions of employment.

*Section 4.* No certificated professional employee shall, in an effort to effect a settlement of any salary disagreement with his employing board of education, engage in any strike or concerted refusal to render services.

*Section 5.* (a) In the event of any disagreement as to the terms and conditions of employment between the board of education of any town or regional school district and the organization or organizations of certificated professional employees of said board, selected for the purpose of representation, the disagreement shall be submitted to the secretary of the state board of education for mediation. The parties shall meet with him or his agents and provide such information as he may require. The secretary may recommend a basis for settlement but such recommendations shall not be binding upon the parties. (b) In the event mediation by the secretary of the state board of education provided by subsection (a) of this section fails to resolve the disagreement, either party may submit the unresolved issue or issues to an impartial board of three arbitrators. Each party to the dispute shall designate one member of the board and the arbitrators so selected shall select the third. The decision of such board, after hearing all the issues, shall be advisory and shall not be binding upon the parties to the dispute. If the parties are unable to agree upon a third arbitrator, either party may petition the superior court or, if the court is not in session, a judge thereof, to designate the third arbitrator in the manner provided by section 52-411 of the general statutes or, if either party refuses to arbitrate, an action to compel arbitration may be instituted in the manner provided by section 52-410 of the general statutes.

*Section 6.* This act shall take effect from its passage.

## Florida

SECTION 230.23. POWERS AND DUTIES OF COUNTY BOARD. The county board, after considering recommendation submitted by the county superintendent, shall exercise the following general powers:

1. *Determine Policies.* The county board shall determine and adopt such policies as are deemed necessary by it for the efficient operation and general improvement of the county school system. In arriving at a determination of policies affecting certificated personnel, the county board may appoint or recognize existing committees composed of members of the teaching profession, as defined in the professional teaching practices act, sections 231.54–59, Florida Statutes. When such committees are involved in the consideration of policies for resolving problems or reaching agreements affecting certificated personnel the committee membership shall include certificated personnel representing all work levels of such instructional and administrative personnel as defined in the school code.

## New Jersey[1]

An Act to provide procedures for the presentation, discussion and solution of grievances and matters of mutual concern by and between boards of education and their employees and supplementing Title 18 of the Revised Statutes.

BE IT ENACTED by the Senate and General Assembly of the State of New Jersey:

1. A board of education shall make rules and regulations establishing reasonable and orderly procedures for the presentation of grievances by and the discussion of matters of mutual concern with its employees or their recognized organizational representative.

2. Should any controversy over the formulation or modification of policy develop and the solution thereof not be reached under such procedures established by a board of education, the employees' recognized organizational representative and the board of education may, if they agree, request the Commissioner of Education to appoint a mediator for the purpose of assisting the parties in reconciling their differences and resolving the controversy on terms which are mutually acceptable. The commissioner shall maintain a list of at least 10 disinterested persons with experience in dealing with problems of public education who are willing to serve as mediators. The commissioner shall, within 5 days after the receipt of such requests, appoint a mediator who is acceptable to both parties from those persons on the list. The mediator so appointed shall meet with the parties or their representatives, or both, forthwith, either jointly or separately, and shall take such other steps as he may deem appropriate in order to remove causes of friction, promote good feeling, restore confidence and persuade the parties to resolve their differences and effect a mutually acceptable agreement. The mediator may make public any data or recommendations that he deems advisable. The cost of the services of the mediator shall be shared equally by the parties.

3. If the mediator is unable to effect a settlement of the controversy within 30 days after his appointment, or if the parties are unable to agree upon the appointment of a mediator, either party may, by written notification to the other, cause an *ad hoc* board of review to be convened for the purpose of meeting with the parties, making such inquiries and investigations, holding such hearings, and taking such other steps as it deems appropriate, for the purpose of making

[1] This legislation was vetoed by the governor of New Jersey.

findings of fact and advisory recommendations upon the basis of which the controversy may be settled. The members of the *ad hoc* board of review shall be selected as follows: each party shall submit to the other, within 5 days after receipt of the aforesaid written notification, the name of one member. Within 5 days of the naming of the respective members, the 2 persons so selected shall select a third person to serve as chairman of the board. If they are unable to agree on a chairman within 5 days after their selection, the 2 board members shall request the Commissioner of Education to designate a chairman. The commissioner shall make such designation within 5 days after receipt of such request. The board of review shall, within 10 days after its establishment, meet with each party and shall thereafter make inquiries and investigations, hold hearings, or take such other steps as it deems appropriate, and shall, if the parties have not reached agreement within 60 days after the board of review's first meeting with the parties, make findings of fact and recommend terms of settlement; the board of review may, in its discretion, make such findings and recommendations public. The costs for the services of the board of review, including per diem expenses, if any, and actual and necessary travel and subsistence expenses, shall be shared equally by the board of education and the employees' recognized organizational representative.

4. The Commissioner of Education with the approval of the State Board of Education, shall promulgate such rules and regulations and shall make such recommendations as he shall deem necessary in order to implement the provisions of this act.

5. This act shall take effect immediately.

---

STATEMENT

This bill provides orderly and reasonable procedures for boards of education and their employees to present, discuss and solve matters of mutual concern such as salaries, fringe benefits, personnel policies and working conditions.

While the bill requires each board to adopt rules and regulations for establishing procedures on the presentation of grievances and matters of mutual concern, it grants each local board full freedom to develop its own personnel policies to meet local needs and conditions.

Two procedures are provided should a controversy develop between a board of education and its employees and is not resolved under the procedures established by the board of education:

1. The board and the representative of its employees may jointly

request the Commissioner of Education to appoint a mediator from a list acceptable to each party to assist in resolving the controversy;

2. If no mediator is appointed, or if he fails to effect a settlement within 30 days, either party may then cause an *ad hoc* board of review of 3 to be convened. Each party names one member of the board of review and these 2 select a third person who acts as chairman. In the event there is no agreement on the selection of the chairman, the Commissioner of Education shall make the selection. The board of review would have power to hold hearings, make investigations and, if the controversy is not resolved within 60 days, to make findings of fact and to recommend terms of settlement. These recommendations may be made public. The recommendations are not binding upon either party.

Boards of education in New Jersey need legal machinery to peaceably settle differences that arise on occasion with their employees. The procedures needed are found in this bill.

## Oregon

Relating to working relations between boards of education and the teaching profession.

BE IT ENACTED by the People of the State of Oregon:

*Section 1.* The Legislative Assembly, recognizing that teaching is a profession, declares that in matters arising between district school boards and certificated school personnel with reference to professional services rendered or to be rendered by such personnel, it is in the best interest of public education in this state to establish a procedure for the orderly, equitable, and expeditious resolution of such matters.

*Section 2.* Certificated school personnel, individually or by a committee of such personnel elected for the purpose of representing other such personnel by the vote of a majority of the certificated school personnel below the rank of superintendent in a school district, shall have the right to confer, consult, and discuss matters in good faith with the district school board by which they are employed, or a committee thereof, on matters of salaries and related economic policies affecting professional services. However, nothing in this section is intended to affect the powers and duties of the district school board over matters of salaries and economic policies affecting professional services.

*Section 3.* The district school board shall establish election procedures and shall certify the committee which has been elected by the certificated school personnel under section 2 of this Act.

*Section 4.* Whenever it appears to the district school board or the certificated school employees meeting with the board under section 2 of this Act that a persistent disagreement over a matter of salaries or economic policies affecting professional services exists between the board and the employees, the board or the employees may request the appointment of consultants. The consultants shall consist of one member appointed by the board, one member appointed by the employees and one member chosen by the other two members. The consultants may determine a reasonable basis for settlement of the disagreement and may recommend such basis to the board and to the employees.

*Section 5.* ORS 243.710 through 243.750 shall not apply to certificated public school personnel. (This section removes certificated school personnel from collective bargaining law.)

## Washington

An Act relating to education; recognizing the right of employee organizations to represent certificated employees in their relations with school districts.

BE IT ENACTED by the Legislature of the State of Washington:

*Section 1.* It is the purpose of this act to strengthen methods of administering employer-employee relations through the establishment of orderly methods of communication between certificated employees and the school districts by which they are employed.

*Section 2.* As used in this act:

"Employee organization" means any organization which includes as members certificated employees of a school district and which has as one of its purposes the representation of the employees in their employment relations with the school district.

"Certificated employee" means any employee holding a regular teaching certificate of the state and who is employed by any school district with the exception of the chief administrative officer of each local district.

*Section 3.* Representatives of an employee organization, which organization shall by secret ballot have won a majority in an election to represent the certificated employees within its school district, shall have the right, after using established administrative channels, to meet, confer and negotiate with the board of directors of the school district or a committee thereof to communicate the considered professional judgment of the certificated staff prior to the final adoption by the board of proposed school policies relating to, but not limited to, curriculum, textbook selection, in-service training, student teaching programs, personnel, hiring and assignment practices, leaves of absence, salaries and salary schedules and noninstructional duties.

*Section 4.* If in any school district there is a separate employee organization of certificated employees of a community college which organization shall, by secret ballot, have won a majority in an election to represent the certificated employees of the community college, as determined by a secret election, the representatives of the separate aggregation shall have the right, after using established administrative channels, to meet, confer, and negotiate with the board of directors of the school district or a committee thereof to communicate the considered professional judgment of the certificated staff prior to the final adoption by the board of proposed school policies related to, but not limited to, curriculum, textbook selection, in-service training, student teaching programs, personnel, hiring and assignment practices, leaves of absence, salaries and salary schedules, and noninstructional duties.

*Section 5.* Nothing in this act shall prohibit any certificated employee from appearing in his own behalf on matters relating to his employment relations with the school district.

*Section 6.* In the event that any matter being jointly considered by the employee organization and the board of directors of the school district is not settled by the means provided in this act, either party may request the assistance and advice of a committee composed of educators and school directors appointed by the state superintendent of public instruction. This committee shall make a written report with recommendations to both parties within fifteen days of receipt of the request for assistance. Any recommendations of the committee shall be advisory only and not binding upon the board of directors or the employee organization.

*Section 7.* Boards of directors of school districts or any administrative officer thereof shall not discriminate against certificated employees because of their exercise of rights under this act.

*Section 8.* Boards of directors of school districts shall adopt reasonable rules and regulations for the administration of employer-employee relations under this act.

*Section 9.* Nothing in this law shall be construed to annul or modify, or to preclude the renewal or continuation of, any lawful agreement heretofore entered into between any school district and any representative of its employees.

# *Appendix F.* State Laws on Negotiation Pertaining to All Public Employees Including Public School Personnel

## Alaska

23.40. LABOR ORGANIZATIONS

*Section 23.40.010.* Union contracts with state and political subdivisions. (a) The state or a political subdivision of the state, including but not limited to an organized borough, municipal corporation, independent school district, and public utility district, may enter into a contract with a labor organization whose members furnish services to the state or the political subdivision.

(b) Nothing contained in this chapter requires the state or political subdivision of the state to enter into a union contract.

*Section 23.40.020.* Enforcement of certain contracts only if union registers. No labor contract executed in this state by a labor organization which has no local in this state or which contract is not to be executed by one or more of its locals in this state may be enforced in the courts of this state unless the labor organization has registered with the department [of labor] and complied with all regulations made by it.

*Section 23.40.030.* Definition of labor organization. For the purpose of this chapter "labor organization" includes an organization constituted wholly or partly to bargain collectively or deal with employers, including the state and its political subdivisions, concerning grievances, terms, or conditions of employment or other mutual aid or protection in connection with employees.

## Massachusetts

CHAPTER 149 of the General Laws is hereby amended by inserting after section 178F the following eight sections:—

*Section 178G.* When used in this section and in sections 178H–178N, inclusive, the following words shall, unless the context requires otherwise, have the following meanings:

"Municipal employer," any county, city, town, or district, and any person designated by the municipal employer to act in its interest in dealing with municipal employees.

"Employee," any employee of a municipal employer, whether or not in the classified service of the municipal employer, except elected officials, board and commission members, police, and the executive officers of any municipal employer.

"Employee organization," any lawful association, organization, federation or council having as a primary purpose the improvement of wages, hours and other conditions of employment.

"Professional employee," any employee engaged in work which is predominantly intellectual and varied in character as opposed to routine mental, manual, mechanical or physical work, which involves the consistent exercise of discretion and judgment in its performance, of such a character that the output produced or the result accomplished cannot be standardized in relation to a given time period, and which requires knowledge of an advanced type in a field of science or learning customarily acquired by a prolonged course of specialized intellectual instruction and study in an institution of higher learning or a hospital, as distinguished from a general academic education or from an apprenticeship or from training in the performance of routine mental, manual or physical processes.

*Section 178H.* (1) Employees shall have, and be protected in the exercise of, the right to self-organization, to form, join or assist any employee organization, to bargain collectively through representatives of their own choosing on questions of wages, hours and other conditions of employment and to engage in other concerted activities for the purpose of collective bargaining or other mutual aid or protection, free from actual interference, restraint or coercion; provided, however, that an employee organization recognized by a municipal employer or designated as the representative of the majority of the employees in an appropriate unit, shall be the exclusive bargaining agent for all employees of such unit, and shall act, negotiate agreements and bargain collectively for all employees in the unit, and shall be responsible for representing the interests of all such employees without discrimination and without regard to employee organization membership.

(2) Whenever, in accordance with such regulations as may be prescribed by the state labor relations commission, a petition is filed with said commission by a municipal employer alleging that one or more employee organizations have presented a claim to be recognized as the representative of a majority of employees in a specified unit, or by an employee or group of employees or an employee organization alleging that a substantial number of employees wish to be represented for collective bargaining by an employee organization as exclusive representative, or that the employee organization currently certified or recognized by the municipal employer as the bargaining representative does not currently represent a majority of the employees in the unit, said commission shall investigate such petition and, if it has reasonable cause to believe that a question of representation exists, shall provide for an appropriate hearing upon due notice.

(3) If, after hearing, the commission finds that there is a controversy concerning the representation of employees, it shall direct an election by secret ballot or shall use any other suitable method to determine whether and by which employee organization the employees desire to be represented and shall certify the results thereof. No election shall be directed in any bargaining unit or any subdivision thereof within which in the preceding twelve-month period a valid election has been held. No election shall be directed during the term of a collective bargaining agreement; except that for good cause shown the commission may direct such an election. An employee organization which receives a majority of votes cast in an election shall be designated by the commission as exclusive representative of the employees in the unit. In any election where none of the choices on the ballot receives a majority, a run off shall be conducted, the ballot providing for a selection between the two choices receiving the largest and the second largest number of valid votes cast in the election.

(4) The commission shall decide in each case whether the appropriate unit for purposes of collective bargaining shall be the municipal employer unit or any other unit thereof; provided, uniformed employees of the fire department shall be in a separate unit; and provided, further, that no unit shall include both professional and nonprofessional employees unless a majority of such professional employees vote for inclusion in such unit.

*Section 1781.* The municipal employer and the employee organization recognized or designated as exclusive representative of employees in an appropriate unit shall have the duty to bargain collectively. In such bargaining other than with an employee organization for school employees, the municipal employer shall be represented by the chief executive officer, whether elected or appointed, or his designated representative or representatives. In such bargaining with an employee organization for school employees, the municipal employer shall be represented by the school committee or its designated representative or representatives.

For the purposes of collective bargaining, the representative of the municipal employer and the representative of the employees shall meet at reasonable times, including meetings appropriately related to the budget making process, and shall confer in good faith with respect to wages, hours and other conditions of employment, or the negotiation of an agreement, or any question arising thereunder, and shall execute a written contract incorporating any agreement reached, but neither party shall be compelled to agree to a proposal or to make a concession. In the event that any part or provision of any such agreement is in conflict with any law, ordinance or by-law, such law, ordinance or by-law shall prevail so long as such conflict remains. If funds are necessary to implement such written agreement, a request for the necessary appropriation shall be submitted to the legislative body. If such request is rejected, the matter shall be returned to the parties for further bargaining. The preceding two sentences shall not apply to agreements reached by school committees in cities and towns in which the provisions of section thirty-four of chapter seventy-one are operative.

*Section 178J.* (a) If, after a reasonable period of negotiation over the terms of an agreement, a dispute exists between a municipal employer and an employee organization, or if no agreement has been reached sixty days prior to the final date for setting the municipal budget, either party or the parties jointly may petition the state board of conciliation and arbitration to initiate fact finding.

(b) Upon receipt of such petition the board of conciliation and arbitration shall make an investigation to determine if the conditions set forth in paragraph (a) exist. If the board finds that such conditions do exist, it shall initiate fact finding. Prior to such fact finding, or prior to fact finding ordered by the state labor relations commission in accordance with the provisions of section 178L, the board of conciliation and arbitration shall submit to the parties a panel of three qualified disinterested persons from which list the parties shall select one person to serve as the fact finder and shall notify the board of conciliation and arbitration of their choice. If the parties fail to select the fact finder within five calendar days of receipt of the list, the board of conciliation and arbitration shall appoint the person who shall serve as fact finder.

(c) The person selected or appointed as fact finder may establish dates and place of hearings which shall be where feasible in the locality of the municipality involved. Any such hearings shall be conducted in accordance with rules established by the board of conciliation and arbitration. Upon request, the board of conciliation and arbitration shall issue subpoenas for hearings conducted by the fact finder. The fact finder may administer oaths. Upon completion of the hearings and within 60 days from the date of appointment, unless extended by the board of conciliation and arbitration for good cause shown, the fact finder shall make written findings of fact and recommendations for resolution of the dispute and shall cause the same to be served on the municipal employer and the employee organization involved.

(d) Only employee organizations which are designated or recognized as the exclusive representative under section 178H shall be proper parties in initiating fact finding proceedings.

(e) The cost of fact finding proceedings under this section shall be divided equally between the municipal employer and said employee organization. Compensation for the fact finder shall be in accordance with a schedule of payment established by the board of conciliation and arbitration.

(f) Nothing in this section shall be construed to prohibit the fact finder from endeavoring to mediate the dispute in which he has been selected or appointed as fact finder.

*Section 178K.* The services of the state board of conciliation and arbitration shall also be available to municipal employers and employee organizations for purposes of conciliation of grievances or contract disputes and for purposes of arbitration of disputes over the interpretation or application of the terms of a written agreement. Nothing in this section shall prevent the use of other arbitration tribunals in the resolution of disputes over the interpretation or application of the terms or written agreements between municipal employers and employee organizations.

*Section 178L.* Municipal employers or their representatives or agents are prohibited from: (1) interfering with, restraining or coercing employees in the exercise of the rights guaranteed in section 178H; (2) dominating or interfering with the formation, existence or administration of any employee organization; (3) discharging or otherwise discriminating against an employee because he has signed or filed any affidavit, petition or complaint or given any information or testimony under this section; (4) refusing to bargain collectively in good faith with an employee organization which has been recognized or designated as the exclusive representative of employees in an appropriate unit; and (5) refusing to discuss grievances with the representatives of an employee organization recognized or designated as the exclusive representative in an appropriate unit.

Employee organizations or their agents are prohibited from: (1) restraining or coercing a municipal employer in the selection of its representative for purposes of collective bargaining or the adjustment of grievances; and (2) if recognized or designated as the exclusive representative of employees in an appropriate unit, refusing to bargain collectively in good faith with a municipal employer.

When a complaint is made to the labor relations commission that a practice prohibited by this section has been committed, the commission may issue an order dismissing the complaint or may order a further investigation or a hearing thereon. If a hearing is ordered, the commission shall set the time and place for the hearing, which time and place may be changed by the commission at the request of one of the parties for cause shown. Any complaint may be amended with the permission of the commission. The municipal employer, the employee organization or the person so complained of shall have the right to file an answer to the original or amended complaint within five days after the service of such complaint or within such other time as the commission may limit. Such municipal employer, such employee organization or such person shall have the right to appear in person or otherwise to defend against such complaint. In the discretion of the commission any person may be allowed to intervene in such proceedings. In any hearing the commission shall not be bound by the technical rules of evidence prevailing in the courts. A transcript of the testimony taken at any hearing before the commission shall be filed with the commission.

If, upon all the testimony, the commission determines that a prohibited practice has been committed, it shall state its findings of fact and shall issue and cause to be served on the party committing the prohibited practice an order requiring it or him to cease and desist from such prohibited practice, and shall take such further affirmative action as will comply with the provisions of this section, including but not limited to the withdrawal of certification of an employee organization established by or assisted in its establishment by any such prohibited practice. If it is alleged that either party has refused to bargain collectively, the state labor relations commission shall order fact finding and direct the party at fault to pay the full costs thereof. It shall order the reinstatement with or without back pay of an employee discharged or discriminated against in violation of the first paragraph of this section. If, upon all of the testimony, the commission determines that a prohibitive practice has not been or is not being committed, it shall state its finding of fact and shall issue an order dismissing the complaint.

*Section 178M.* It shall be unlawful for any employee to engage in, induce, or encourage any strike, work stoppage, slowdown or withholding of services by such employees.

*Section 178N.* Nothing in sections 178F–178M, inclusive, shall diminish the authority and power of the civil service commission, or any retirement board or personnel board established by law, nor shall anything in said sections constitute a grant of the right to strike to employees of any municipal employer.

Section 9R of chapter 23 of the General Laws, as appearing in section 1 of chapter 345 of the acts of 1938, is hereby amended by inserting after the word "inclusive," in line 4, the words:    , of this chapter, sections 178H and 178L of chapter 149.

*Approved November 17, 1965*

## Michigan
### (*Public Act 379, 1965*)

An act to prohibit strikes by certain public employees; to provide review from disciplinary action with respect thereto; to provide for the mediation of grievances and the holding of elections; to declare and protect the rights and privileges of public employees; and to prescribe means of enforcement and penalties for the violation of the provisions of this act.

*Section 1.* As used in this act the word "strike" shall mean the concerted, failure to report for duty, the wilful absence from one's position, the stoppage of work, or the abstinence in whole or in part from the full, faithful and proper performance of the duties of employment, for the purpose of inducing, influencing or coercing a change in the conditions, or compensation, or the rights, privileges or obligations of employment. Nothing contained in this act shall be construed to limit, impair or affect the right of any public employee to the expression or communication of a view, grievance, complaint or opinion on any matter related to the conditions or compensation of public employment or their betterment, so long as the same is not designed to and does not interfere with the full, faithful and proper performance of the duties of employment.

*Section 3.* No person exercising any authority, supervision or direction over any public employee shall have the power to authorize, approve or consent to a strike by public employees, and such person shall not authorize, approve or consent to such strike, nor shall any such person discharge or cause any public employee to be discharged or separated from his or her employment because of participation in the submission of a grievance in accordance with the provisions of section 7.

*Section 6.* Notwithstanding the provisions of any other law, any person holding such a position who, by concerted action with others, and without the lawful approval of his superior, wilfully absents himself from his position, or abstains in whole or in part from the full, faithful and proper performance of his duties for the purpose of inducing, influencing or coercing a change in the conditions or compensation, or the rights, privileges or obligations of employment shall be deemed to be on strike but the person, upon request, shall be entitled to a determination as to whether he did violate the provisions of this act. The request shall be filed in writing, with the officer or body having power to remove or discipline such employee, within 10 days after regular compensation of such employee has ceased or other discipline has been imposed. In the event of such request the officer or body shall within 10 days commence a proceeding for the determination of whether the provisions of this act have been violated by the public employee, in accordance with the law and regulations appropriate to a proceeding to remove the public employee. The proceedings shall be undertaken without unnecessary delay. The decision of the proceeding shall be made within 10 days. If the employee involved is held to have violated this law and his employment terminated or other discipline imposed, he shall have the right of review to the circuit court having jurisdiction of the parties, within 30 days from such decision, for determination whether such decision is supported by competent, material and substantial evidence on the whole record.

*Section 7.* Upon the request of the collective bargaining representative defined in section 11, or if no representative has been designated or selected, upon the request of a majority of any given group of public employees evidenced by a petition signed by said majority and delivered to the labor mediation board, or upon request of any public employer of such employees, it shall be the duty of the labor mediation board to forthwith mediate the grievances set forth in said petition or notice, and for the purposes of mediating such grievances, the labor mediation board shall exercise the powers and authority conferred upon said board by sections 10 and 11 of Act No. 176 of the Public Acts of 1939.

*Section 9.* It shall be lawful for public employees to organize together or to form, join or assist in labor organizations, to engage in lawful concerted activities for the purpose of collective negotiation or bargaining or other mutual aid and protection, or to negotiate or bargain collectively with their public employers through representatives of their own free choice.

*Section 10.* It shall be unlawful for a public employer or an officer or agent of a public employer (a) to interfere with, restrain or coerce public employees in the exercise of their rights guaranteed in section 9; (b) to initiate, create, dominate, contribute to or interfere with the formation or administration of any labor organization: Provided, That a public employer shall not be prohibited from permitting employees to confer with it during working hours without loss of time or pay; (c) to discriminate in regard to hire, terms or other conditions of employment in order to encourage or discourage membership in a labor organization; (d) to discriminate against a public employee because he has given testimony or instituted proceedings under this act; or (e) to refuse to bargain collectively with the representatives of its public employees, subject to the provisions of section 11.

*Section 11.* Representatives designated or selected for purposes of collective bargaining by the majority of the public employees in a unit appropriate for such purposes, shall be the exclusive representatives of all the public employees in such unit for the purposes of collective bargaining in respect to rates of pay, wages, hours of employment or other conditions of employment, and shall be so recognized by the public employer: Provided, That any individual employee at any time may present grievances to his employer and have the grievances adjusted, without intervention of the bargaining representative, if the adjustment is not inconsistent with the terms of a collective bargaining contract or agreement then in effect, provided that the bargaining representative has been given opportunity to be present at such adjustment.

*Section 12.* Whenever a petition shall have been filed, in accordance with such regulations as may be prescribed by the board:

(a) By a public employee or group of public employees, or an individual or labor organization acting in their behalf, alleging that 30% or more of the public employees within a unit claimed to be appropriate for such purpose wish to be represented for collective bargaining and that their public employer declines to recognize their representative as the representative defined in section 11, or assert that the individual or labor organization, which has been certified or is being currently recognized by their public employer as the bargaining representative, is no longer a representative as defined in section 11; or

(b) By a public employer or his representative alleging that 1 or more individuals or labor organizations have presented to him a claim to be recognized as the representative defined in section 11; the board shall investigate the petition and, if it has reasonable cause to believe that a question of representation exists, shall provide an appropriate hearing after due notice. If the board finds upon the record of the hearing that such a question of representation exists, it shall direct an election by secret ballot and shall certify the results thereof. Nothing in this section shall be construed to prohibit the waiving of hearings by stipulation for the purpose of a consent election in conformity with the rules and regulations of the board.

*Section 13.* The board shall decide in each case, in order to insure public employees the full benefit of their right to self-organization, to collective bargaining and otherwise to effectuate the policies of this act, the unit appropriate for the purposes of collective bargaining as provided in section 9e of Act No. 176 of the Public Acts of 1939: Provided, That in any fire department, or any department in whole or part engaged in, or having the responsibiilty of, fire fighting, no person subordinate to a fire commission, fire commissioner, safety director, or other similar administrative agency or administrator, shall be deemed to be a supervisor.

*Section 14.* An election shall not be directed in any baragining unit or any subdivision within which, in the preceding 12-month period, a valid election has been held. The board shall determine who is eligible to vote in the election and shall establish rules governing the election. In an election involving more than 2 choices, where none of the choices on the ballot receives a majority vote, a runoff election shall be conducted between the 2 choices receiving the 2 largest numbers of valid votes cast in the election. No election shall be directed in any bargaining unit or subdivision thereof where there is in force and effect a valid collective bargaining agreement which was not prematurely extended and which is of fixed duration: Provided, however, No collective bargaining agreement shall bar an election upon the petition of persons not parties thereto where more than 3 years have elapsed since the agreement's execution or last timely renewal, whichever was later.

*Section 15.* A public employer shall bargain collectively with the representatives of its employees as defined in section 11 and is authorized to make and enter into collective bargaining agreements with such representatives. For the purposes of this section, to bargain collectively is the performance of the mutual obligation of the employer and the representative of the employees to meet at reasonable times and confer in good faith with respect to wages, hours, and other terms and conditions of employment, or the negotiation of an agreement, or any question arising thereunder, and the execution of a written contract, ordinance or resolution incorporating any agreement reached if requested by either party, but such obligation does not compel either party to agree to a proposal or require the making of a concession.

*Section 16.* Violations of the provisions of section 10 shall be deemed to be unfair labor practices remediable by the labor mediation board in the following manner:

(a) Whenever it is charged that any person has engaged in or is engaging in any such unfair labor practice, the board, or any agent designated by the board for such purposes, may issue and cause to be served upon the person a complaint stating the charges in that respect, and containing a notice of hearing before the board or a member thereof, or before a designated agent, at a place therein fixed, not less than 5 days after the serving of the complaint. No complaint shall be issued based upon any unfair labor practice occurring more than 6 months prior to the filing of the charge with the board and the service of a copy thereof upon the person against whom the charge is made, unless the person aggrieved thereby was prevented from filing the charge by reason of service in the armed forces, in which event the 6 month period shall be computed from the day of his discharge. Any complaint may be amended by the member or agent conducting the hearing or the board, at any time prior to the issuance of an order based thereon. The person upon whom the complaint is served may file an answer to the original or amended complaint and to appear in person or otherwise and give testimony at the place and time fixed in the complaint. In the discretion of the member or agent conducting the hearing or the board, any other person may be allowed to intervene in the proceeding and to present testimony. Any proceeding shall be conducted in accordance with the provisions of section 5 of Act No. 197 of the Public Acts of 1952, as amended, being section 24.105 of the Compiled Laws of 1948.

(b) The testimony taken by the member, agent or the board shall be reduced to writing and filed with the board. Thereafter the board upon notice may take further testimony or hear argument. If upon the preponderance of the testimony taken the board is of the opinion that any person named in the complaint has engaged in or is engaging in the unfair labor practice, then it shall state its findings of fact and shall issue and cause to be served on the person an order requiring him to cease and desist from the unfair labor practice, and to take such affirmative action including reinstatement of employees with or without back pay, as will effectuate the policies of this act. The order may further require the person to make reports from time to time showing the extent to which he has complied with the order. If upon the preponderance of the testimony taken the board is not of the opinion that the person named in the complaint has engaged in or is engaging in the unfair labor practice, then the board shall state its findings of fact and shall issue an order dismissing the complaint. No order of the board shall require the reinstatement of any individual as an employee who has been suspended or discharged, or the payment to him of any back pay, if the individual was suspended or discharged for cause. If the evidence is presented before a member of the board, or before examiners thereof, the member, or examiners shall issue and cause to be served on the parties to the proceeding a proposed report, together with a recommended order, which shall be filed with the board, and if no exceptions are filed within 20 days after service thereof upon the parties, or within such further period as the board may authorize, the recommended order shall become the order of the board and become effective as prescribed in the order.

(c) Until the record in a case has been filed in a court, the board at any time, upon reasonable notice and in such manner as it deems proper, may modify or set aside, in whole or in part, any finding or order made or issued by it.

(d) The board may petition for the enforcement of the order and for appropriate temporary relief or restraining order, and shall file in the court the record in the proceedings. Upon the filing of the petition, the court shall cause notice thereof to be served upon the person, and thereupon shall have jurisdiction of the proceeding and shall grant such temporary or permanent relief or restraining order as it deems just and proper, enforcing, modifying, enforcing as so modified, or setting aside in whole or in part the order of the board. No objection that has not been urged before the board, its member or agent, shall be considered by the court, unless the failure or neglect to urge the objection is excused because of extraordinary circumstances. The findings of the board with respect to questions of fact if supported by competent, material and substantial evidence on the record considered as a whole shall be conclusive. If either party applies to the court for leave to present additional evidence and shows to the satisfaction of the court that the additional evidence is material and that there were reasonable grounds for the failure to present it in the hearing before the board, its member or agent, the court may order the additional evidence to be taken before the board, its member or agent, and to be made a part of the record.

The board may modify its findings as to the facts or make new findings, by reasons of additional evidence so taken and filed, and it shall file the modifying or new findings, which findings with respect to questions of fact if supported by competent, material and substantial evidence on the record considered as a whole shall be conclusive, and shall file its recommendations, if any, for the modification or setting aside of its original order. Upon the filing of the record with it the jurisdiction of the court shall be exclusive and its judgment and decree shall be final, except that the same shall be subject to review by the supreme court in accordance with the general court rules.

(e) Any person aggrieved by a final order of the board granting or denying in whole or in part the relief sought may obtain a review of such order in the court of appeals by filing in the court a complaint praying that the order of the board be modified or set aside, with copy of the complaint filed on the board, and thereupon the aggrieved party shall file in the court the record in the proceeding, certified by the board. Upon the filing of the complaint, the court shall proceed in the same manner as in the case of an application by the board under subsection (e), and shall grant to the board such temporary relief or restraining order as it deems just and proper, enforcing, modifying, enforcing as so modified, or setting aside in whole or in part the order of the board. The findings of the board with respect to questions of fact if supported by competent, material and substantial evidence on the record considered as a whole shall be conclusive.

(f) The commencement of proceedings under subsections (e) or (f) shall not, unless specifically ordered by the court, operate as a stay of the board's order.

(g) Complaints filed under this act shall be heard expeditiously by the court to which presented, and for good cause shown shall take precedence over all other civil matters except earlier matters of the same character.

(h) The board shall have power, upon issuance of a complaint as provided in subsection (b) charging that any person has engaged in or is engaging in an unfair labor practice, to petition any circuit court within any circuit where the unfair labor practice in question is alleged to have occurred or where such person resides or exercises or may exercise its govenmental authority, for appropirate temporary relief or restraining order, in accordance with the general court rules, and the court shall have jurisdiction to grant to the board such temporary relief or restraining order as it deems just and proper.

(i) For the purpose of all hearings and investigations, which, in the opinion of the board, are necessary and proper for the exercise of the powers vested in it under this section, the provisions of section 11 shall be applicable, except that subpoenas may be issued as provided in section 11 without regard to whether mediation shall have been undertaken.

(j) The labor relations and mediation functions of this act shall be separately administered by the board.

*Section 2.* Sections 4, 5, and 8 of Act No. 336 of the Public Acts of 1947, being sections 423.204, 423.205 and 423.208 of the Compiled Laws of 1948, are repealed.

This act is ordered to take immediate effect.

## New Hampshire

*Section 31:3 in general.* Towns . . . may recognize unions of employees and make and enter into collective bargaining contracts with such unions; . . . .

## Wisconsin

111.70. MUNICIPAL EMPLOYMENT

1. *Definitions.* When used in this section:

(a) "Municipal employer" means any city, county, village, town, metropolitan sewerage district, school district or any other political subdivision of the state.

(b) "Municipal employe" means any employe of a municipal employer except city and village policemen, sheriff's deputies, and county traffic officers.

(c) "Board" means the Wisconsin employment relations board.

2. *Rights of municipal employes.* Municipal employes shall have the right of self-organization, to affiliate with labor organizations of their own choosing and the right to be represented by labor organizations of their own choice in conferences and negotiations with their municipal employers or their representatives on questions of wages, hours and conditions of employment, and such employes shall have the right to refrain from any and all such activities.

3. *Prohibited practices.*

(a) Municipal employers, their officers and agents are prohibited from:

(1) Interfering with, restraining or coercing any municipal employe in the exercise of the rights provided in sub. (2).

(2) Encouraging or discouraging membership in any labor

organization, employe agency, committee, association or representation plan by discrimination in regard to hiring, tenure or other terms or conditions of employment.

(b) Municipal employes individually or in concert with others are prohibited from:

(1) Coercing, intimidating or interfering with a municipal employe in the enjoyment of his legal rights including those set forth in sub. (2).

(c) It is a prohibited practice for any person to do or cause to be done, on behalf or in the interest of any municipal employer or employe, or in connection with or to influence the outcome of any controversy, as to employment relations, any act prohibited by pars. (a) and (b).

4. *Powers of the Board.* The board shall be governed by the following provisions relating to bargaining in municipal employment:

(a) Prevention of prohibited practices. Section 111.07 shall govern procedure in all cases involving prohibited practices under this subchapter.

(b) Mediation. The board may function as a mediator in disputes between municipal employes and their employers upon the request of both parties.

(d)[1] Collective bargaining units. Whenever a question arises between a municipal employer and a labor union as to whether the union represents the employes of the employer, either the union or the municipality may petition the board to conduct an election among said employes to determine whether they desire to be represented by a labor organization. Proceedings in representation cases shall be in accordance with Ss. 111.02 (6) and 11.05 insofar as applicable, except that where the board finds that a proposed unit includes a craft the board shall exclude such craft from the unit. The board shall not order an election among employes in a craft unit except on separate petition initiating representation proceedings in such craft unit.

(e) Fact finding. Fact finding may be initiated in the following circumstances:

(1) If after a reasonable period of negotiation the parties are deadlocked, either party or the parties jointly may initiate fact finding;

(2) Where an employer or union fails or refuses to meet and negotiate in good faith at reasonable times in a bona fide effort to arrive at a settlement.

[1] No section (c) was shown in the statute.

(f) Same. Upon receipt of a petition to initiate fact finding, the board shall make an investigation and determine whether or not the condition set forth in par. (e) 1 or 2 has been met and shall certify the results of said investigation. If the certification requires that fact finding be initiated, the board shall appoint from a list established by the board a qualified disinterested person, or three-member panel when jointly requested by the parties, to function as a fact finder.

(g) Same. The fact finder may establish dates and place of hearings which shall be where feasible in the jurisdiction of the municipality involved and shall conduct said hearings pursuant to rules established by the board. Upon request, the board shall issue subpoenas for hearings conducted by the fact finder. The fact finder may administer oaths. Upon completion of the hearings, the fact finder shall make written findings of facts and recommendations for solution of the dispute and shall cause the same to be served on the municipal employer and the union.

(h) Parties.

(1) Proceedings to prevent prohibitive practices. Any labor organization or any individual affected by prohibited practices herein is a proper party to proceedings by the board to prevent such practice under this subchapter.

(2) Fact-finding cases. Only labor unions which have been certified as representative of the employes in the collective bargaining unit or which the employer has recognized as the representative of said employes shall be proper parties in initiating fact finding proceedings. Coct of fact-finding proceedings shall be divided equally between said labor organization and the employer.

(i) Agreements. Upon the completion of negotiations with a labor organization representing a majority of the employes in a collective bargaining unit, if a settlement is reached, the employer shall reduce the same to writing either in the form of an ordinance, resolution or agreement. Such agreement may include a term for which it shall remain in effect not to exceed one year. Such agreements shall be binding on the parties only if express language to that effect is contained therein.

(j) Personnel relations in law enforcement. In any case in which a majority of the members of a police or sheriff or county traffic officer department shall petition the governing body for changes or improvements in the wages, hours or working conditions and designates a representative which may be one of the petitioners or otherwise, the procedures in pars. (e) to (g) shall apply. Such representative may be required by the board to post a cash bond in an amount determined by the board to guarantee payment of one half of the costs of fact finding.

(k) Paragraphs (e) to (g) shall not apply to discipline or discharge cases under civil service provisions of a state statute or local ordinance.

(l) Nothing contained in this subchapter shall constitute a grant of the right to strike by any county or municipal employe and such strikes are hereby expressly prohibited.

(m) The board shall not initiate fact-finding proceedings in any case when the municipal employer through ordinance or otherwise has established fact-finding procedures substantially in compliance with this subchapter.

# *Appendix G.* Resolutions of National Organizations on Staff Relations

## American Association of School Administrators

*The Role of the Superintendent* (Adopted February 1965)

The superintendent of schools is the educational leader of the community. His role is that of the statesman. He works with and through many individuals and groups in the development of the educational program and all related matters which impinge on education.

The superintendent of schools is the chief executive officer of the board of education. He is the professional leader of the board, the leader of the staff, and the focal point of educational responsibility within the district.

The superintendent occupies a unique position. He assists the board of education, the staff (singly and in groups), and the citizens of the community as they work through educational problems. He is the chief professional advisor to the board in policy development. He is responsible for developing appropriate educational opportunities to meet the needs of all children. He is a professional educator and a professional school administrator. That which strengthens his effectiveness in any of these roles automatically strengthens the schools.

We strongly urge that boards of education and professional groups insist upon the recognition of the role and responsibility of the superintendent. The Association pledges to resist any effort to displace the superintendent and his authority in matters affecting the interest and welfare of school personnel.

The superintendent has responsibility to give educational leadership in the state and nation wherever curriculum, personnel, finance, and

**269**

other elements of public education are the subject of proposal, debate, or decision.

Finally, the superintendent must recognize the responsibility which these roles place upon him: a responsibility for his own professional development and that of his fellow administrators; a commitment to the basic values of the society and his profession; and the sharing of his responsibility in such manner that teachers, board, and community become an effective team for the advancement of public education.

### Staff Relations (Adopted February 1965)

We believe that teachers, school boards, and administrators are all committed to the advancement of public education and that the goals and interests of these groups are highly interrelated. We believe strongly that the development of school policies and programs and the solution of school problems can best be accomplished by these groups working in harmony and with respect for the roles of each. We believe that effective policy development involves important contributions by each group.

We believe that evaluation in staff relations is to be welcomed. We commend careful study and the development of principles that should govern these relations and define the responsibilities of the various groups while maintaining the integrity of each. We believe that shared responsibility for policy and program development is a professional concept requiring a unique professional approach. We maintain that the superintendent of schools has a unique responsibility to provide leadership in these matters.

## Department of Classroom Teachers

### Professional Negotiation (Adopted June 1965)

The Department believes that local professional associations have the professional right and should have the mandatory legal right, through appropriate professional channels and democratically selected representatives including classroom teachers, to negotiate with boards of education in the determination of policies affecting professional services of teachers, including improvement of instruction, curriculum planning, salaries, and other conditions of work.

The Department therefore urges local associations to strive for adoption of agreements with local boards of education that would (a) provide an orderly method of involving local classroom teacher representatives, administrators, and school board members in the cooperative development of mutually satisfactory policies; (b) define the obligations of the superintendent in his dual role as member of the profession and adviser to the school board; and (c) authorize a means of appeal through designated educational channels when agreement cannot be reached. The Department further urges local associations to join with state associations in seeking state legislation to establish professional negotiations as a legal and mandatory right of local professional associations.

## National School Boards Association

*Informational Service* (Adopted April 1964)

The National School Boards Association should undertake a greatly strengthened program of informational service to state school board associations on the subject of teacher, superintendent, board relationships. To assist state school board associations in development of suggested guidelines, policies and procedures, the National School Boards Association should develop and distribute to state school board associations materials such as NSBA policy statements, national and state trends and legislation, samples of state association actions, sample policies and procedures of local boards of education and information that may result from conferences with other education organizations.

*State Studies* (Adopted April 1964)

The National School Boards Association recommends that each state school board association develop an informational program including a state legal status study of the area of teacher, superintendent, board relationships. The National School Boards Association further recommends that each state school board association develop suggested guidelines and policies to assist local boards of education in developing local policies and procedures for teacher, superintendent, board relationships.

*Teacher-Superintendent-Board Relations* (Adopted April 1963)

The efforts of teacher unions to obtain collective bargaining rights and the activities and programs of professional teacher organizations calling for professional negotiations and sanctions will have significant effect upon the operation of our public schools in the years ahead. The National School Boards Association is opposed to sanctions, boycotts, strikes, or mandated mediation against school districts and does not consider them to be proper remedies for use in problem situations. The authority of the board of education is established by law and this authority may not be delegated to others.

The National School Boards Association, therefore, reaffirms and endorses its policy on teacher relations. In order that the course of action necessary to implement this policy may be planned deliberately and purposely, NSBA urges each local board to review its policies, procedures, and activities and to give careful consideration to incorporating the following items if they are not included:

(a) Procedures which will actively involve school boards, administrative staff and teachers in discussing total budget needs with particular emphasis on the determination of salaries and the handling of grievances.

(b) Written policies concerning the above procedures that are widely disseminated, and presented in such a way that they are clearly understood by all parties concerned—the teachers, administrative staff, the board of education and the general public.

(c) Policies whereby the superintendent, as administrative officer of the board, can function as a channel and interpreter of teacher concerns to the board and the board responsibilities and concerns to the teacher. Direct hearings with the board should be arranged through the superintendent if this proves adequate. In addition, local boards should support their state school boards associations in opposing legislation which condones sanctions, boycotts, strikes, or mandated mediation against school districts. In the event such legislation or judicial decisions exist, state school boards associations are urged to seek appropriate legal means to repeal or overrule them.

# Appendix H. Roles, Responsibilities, Relationships of the School Board, Superintendent, and Staff[1]

## THE PROBLEM

What is the superintendent of schools to do when teacher groups seek to negotiate directly with the board of education on salary and welfare matters? When rival groups seek the right to exclusive representation? When a minority of teachers, or the specialists and supervisory and administrative personnel, are without representation in dominant groups? In some districts these are real and pressing problems that call urgently for solution. Even though exceptional, special, and unrepresentative, they call dramatic attention to the over-all problem, to which mutually satisfactory solutions must be found. The over-all problem is this:

What is the appropriate role of the superintendent in the process and procedures through which his professional colleagues may share in policy making, particularly, though not solely, when their salary, benefits, and working conditions are involved?

## SOME CAUSES

The problems arise because of changing conditions, many but not all of which are signs of health and growth in the profession we serve.

1. As school enrollments have grown, the number of teachers has increased. Consequently, the average number of years of service has declined. At the same time, the number of teachers who are men and heads of families has grown both relatively and absolutely.

2. The teaching profession has matured greatly in professional preparation and competence and in professional independence and dignity.

[1] Published by American Association of School Administrators, 1201 Sixteenth Street, N. W., Washington, D. C. 20036.

3. The educational profession has organized more universally, as have most American career groups.

4. New and reorganized districts have little or no local traditions to guide professional welfare procedures and relationships.

5. In fast-growing districts, with a flood of teachers new to the staff, existing personnel policies and procedures oecome outmoded and need revision at the very time that board and administration are swamped with piled-up problems of rapid expansion.

6. Professional associations, like all social institutions, respond slowly to new pressures.

7. Social change throughout our society accelerates. The surge of unionism in the thirties has been followed by a growing exercise of group powers in the sixties. An increasingly complex and interrelated society has stimulated increasing group pressures. Some press solely for what the group feels to be the general welfare. Some nakedly seek advantage for the group and its individuals. Most are mixtures, seeking special advantage in a context of social betterment.

8. In school districts, in cities, in states, and in the national capital there is a fierce competition for the tax dollar for worthy public purposes and causes. Local school boards, as they seek to provide adequate financial support, are increasingly subject to pressures from legally established finance boards, from self-constituted tax watchdogs, and from growing public resistance to the costs of providing better education with all that it calls for in better staffing, better instructional materials, and more and better school buildings. In short, money is harder to get at a time when much more of it is needed.

9. The state and national governments, and to a minor extent nongovernmental agencies, are providing a growing portion of the money used by local school districts, and their influence on expenditures is increasing. Local school boards have tended to focus attention primarily on local problems including problems of local finance. Other groups with special interests have too often had the field to themselves in presenting educational and financial needs or programs before state legislatures and other state and national agencies. The result has been a steady diminishing of local control over important budgetary and the consequent educational decisions.

10. Teachers, by the very nature of their work, live intimately with problems of the classroom. Superintendents, in their daily duties, deal with problems of over-all policy and procedure. Their concerns are necessarily broader and do diverge from those of teachers to some extent. As school staffs have grown in size and communication has become more difficult, the divergence is occasionally exploited by

ideologists who seek to split the staff and, indeed, the whole profession, with teachers on the one hand and administrators on the other. Such division violates the long tradition of professional unity and of a cooperative approach to all educational matters, including matters directly related to teacher welfare.

11. In districts where there is a long tradition of mutual understanding and cooperative study and a conviction that the character of American education is and ought to be largely determined within the local districts, the increasing inability of the locality to finance an adequate educational program often makes a travesty of hard-won local decisions and policies.

12. Finally, it is increasingly difficult to distinguish educational goals and processes from teacher-welfare goals. The threefold problem is to make the wisest allocation of existing resources, to demonstrate simultaneously the real need and added value of greater resources, and to try everlastingly to muster effective support for the provision of added resources. This is no simple task. Growing professional competence and growing concern for better education for all press for additional expenditures. The ability and willingness in the district and state to provide the needed money have not kept pace with demands.

### A PERSPECTIVE

Creating and sustaining a professional climate and operational procedures that call forth and use the full creative capacities of all employees in the attainment of educational goals is a prime responsibility of school administration. By its very nature this calls for common understanding, mutual respect, and a full measure of confidence among all who work in the schools and all who serve on the school board, the agency to which the people have delegated so large a measure of responsibility for their children's education. There is no place in this mutual responsibility for authoritarian methods of selfish advantage-seeking.

If democracy, with its fundamental emphasis on the worth, dignity, and importance of each individual, has taught the people of this country anything, it is that on the whole the capacities of people are used more fruitfully, results are more rewarding, and the job is better done when the individuals who are directly involved in any common endeavor participate freely in setting goals, developing operational procedures, and establishing general working conditions. To make this principle effective in mobilizing and directing the energies of all employees in the school system is the challenge that at the present time confronts school districts—school boards, administrators, and teachers. This is the kind of school personnel administration that thoughtful people seek.

Personnel administration has felt the impact of cultural change. Like administrative organization, curriculum content, instructional methods, and nearly every other aspect of school organization and operation, it has been evolving steadily over a period of many years. As it has matured, it has sought to give every member of the staff— administrators, supervisors, and teachers—a feeling of responsibility for the total school system that goes beyond immediate personal concerns. It aims to harmonize varying interests and to utilize varying viewpoints, wide ranges of information, and the special capabilities of many people. It seeks to give people who are directly affected by broad policy and operational procedures opportunities to share in developing them, while maintaining vigorously the principles of support and control that characterize public education in our free, self-governing society.

Ever since the third decade of the nineteenth century, the superintendent of schools has been a key person in the educational process. The broad outlines of the community's educational program emerge as he marshals resources, supplies information, stimulates discussion and research, resolutely faces critical problems, and judiciously weighs alternative courses of action; as he extends opportunities for staff members to acquire new insights; and as he evaluates, recommends, and initiates action.

Today, the superintendent of schools occupies a complex and demanding position. He is often torn between diverse alternatives, obligations, and responsibilities.

Yet, it seems clear that the professional superintendent has one allegiance that transcends all other commitments. Although he is a devoted member of his professional group and deeply concerned with the success of his associates, his allegiance to the learner supersedes all other loyalties. This commitment need not and should not place him in conflict with his colleagues. Its very nature makes him seek assiduously and vigorously to maintain environmental circumstances which his associates desire, need, and must have to work to best advantage. One of the major concerns of the superintendent always has been and always should be to help provide those conditions which enable teachers and all other staff members to achieve their professional goals.

Neither does this freedom of operation by the superintendent suggest disloyalty to the school board. It is his professional judgment, wisdom, and leadership that make him valuable to the board. School trustees should never seek nor achieve subservience from the school administrator. In fact, when controversy rages most violently, his role is one of independent, judicious statesmanship governed largely by his depth of professional insights and his primary commitment to improved educational service to pupils and to basic human values.

Old, established traditions and processes may no longer suffice. New processes and new insights into the nature and means of policy formation are needed to upgrade the professional status of teachers and to improve the conditions under which they work. During this period of flux and transition, as personnel policies and administrative processes are revised and improved, much will depend on the wisdom, care, patience, forbearance, and sound judgment of the individuals and groups of individuals in this evolution.

## THE ROLE OF THE SUPERINTENDENT

From the experiences of many successful superintendents and the judgments recorded in professional literature, the following composite has been drawn to represent professional effectiveness in personnel practices:

1. The effective superintendent of schools is sensitive to the growing professional maturity of the teaching profession.

2. He is always concerned for the total welfare and for the just financial compensation of the entire staff.

3. He seeks assiduously to exercise professional leadership, but at the same time he encourages his associates—administrators, supervisors, specialists, and teachers alike—to engage in the development of forward-looking proposals for study and adoption by the board in matters of professional growth and personal welfare, including salaries and working conditions.

4. He knows that welfare gains take on much more value if they have been worked out cooperatively with all concerned.

5. He works with board and staff to the end that a mutually satisfactory plan is adopted and practiced under which working conditions and compensations are continuously studied, and improved contractual and professional programs are presented at intervals to the board of education.

6. He participates, wherever possible and acceptable, with groups of his associates as they gather data, make comparative studies, and develop new and sounder proposals for salary schedules and other

benefits. He enables individuals and groups within the staff to get the information they want and keeps them informed of board actions, both prospective and completed.

7. He works out with his associates, within the framework of board policy and staff organization, appropriate ways and means through which grievances can be appealed to the board when such an appeal is sought by the aggrieved and through which the grievances can be satisfactorily adjudicated with no fear or form of retaliation.

8. He provides the board with a continual flow of information about work loads, working conditions, professional growth activities, evidences of professional and personal competence, and the complexity of the tasks of all of his professional colleagues, together with comparative figures from comparable school districts.

9. He maintains conditions in which teachers and other staff members can readily come before the board in open board meetings without fear of retribution to discuss issues and to present their points of view on school matters under the same rules and procedures established to give any interested party a hearing before the board.

10. He brings staff associates to meet with the school board to explain or demonstrate many aspects of curriculum, of instructional methods and materials, and of relevant professional activities, as well as to present hoped-for gains in improved working conditions and compensation.

11. With the help of the school staff and school board, he keeps the community informed not only of good features of the school program but of system-wide weaknesses and needs, including the need for salaries to attract and hold the best teachers and other staff members, for continuous professional growth of all personnel, for relief from overcrowded and educationally inadequate rooms and buildings, for improvement in the kind and amount of instructional supplies and equipment, and for the other improvements to help the schools serve better all the children and the community. He knows that only a well-informed public will insist that school boards, city councils, boards of finance, and other responsible public agencies secure the funds to remedy deficiencies.

12. He takes leadership to assure equitable representation of all and each of the entire staff on all matters affecting their professional and personal welfare. He knows there is no one pattern—no single process—which is suitable for all the diverse school districts in the nation. He knows that the methods of choosing representatives, and the representation itself, must be the staff's own choice and that no

teacher, supervisor, principal, or administrator should feel under-represented or left out.

13. He constantly exerts leadership to assure that board and staff have a well-founded mutual respect; that mutually satisfactory policies and procedures are established and used for presentation, study, and adoption; and that steps by which differences can be resolved are acceptable to all. Above all, he strives to see that matters are presented fairly, studied objectively, and supported by valid data. He seeks to establish an atmosphere in which differences of opinion are to be expected and respected and in which a community of goals and interests is stressed.

14. He shares his leadership with principals, supervisors, and specialists, as well as with teachers, in helping assure sound policies and acceptable practices.

15. He plays a major role in helping staff members, the school board, and the public know where responsibilities for decision rest. The responsibilities of the board should be made clear to all concerned.

16. He seeks to develop, through cooperation with the staff and the board and with a maximum of satisfaction to all involved, a clear definition of the role of the superintendent himself as well as of the roles of teachers, principals, supervisors, and professional organizations in all personnel matters. Where regional, state, or national association, other agencies of local and state government, or the people at large have roles, they should be known. He knows that clarification and agreement are more easily obtained before pressures or grievances arise.

17. He keeps the board informed about discussions and actions which may affect local policy, whether they are taking place in state and national capitals or in agencies and associations outside the district. He encourages the board to make its voice heard wherever matters affecting the district's budget and program are under consideration, lest the freedom and strength of local action be lost.

18. The effective, professional superintendent of schools confidently and courageously serves as advisor to the board, as chief administrator of the schools, as devoted leader of his professional associates, and as staunch defender of the overriding rights of children to the best education possible.

### THIS WE BELIEVE

• We believe that teachers, school administrators, and school boards must together seek pathways yet uncharted in the area of personnel policies and practices.

- We believe that the superintendent has a responsibility to see that opportunities are provided for staff members—teachers, supervisors, principals, and specialists—to play appropriate roles in developing personnel policies and in maintaining professional working conditions.

- We believe that the superintendent has a responsibility to assist staff members—in ways satisfactory to them—in studying welfare problems, in developing proposals pertaining to staff welfare, and in presenting them to the school board for consideration and action.

- We believe that shared responsibility in policy development is a professional concept. It assumes a commonality of goals and interests among teachers, school boards, and administrators; and it assumes that service to children is the paramount consideration and that welfare provisions for teachers are means to that end.

- We believe that the right to discuss pros and cons and to participate in developing a program does not imply the right to make decisions. Although consensus should always be patiently sought and will often prevail between staff and school board, the board must retain its responsibility and legal right to make decisions.

- We believe that no matter how generous and benevolent arbitrary decisions may be, they have a debilitating effect. When people are involved, they not only assume responsibility for making decisions work, but each performs at a higher level of productivity.

- We believe that failure to find appropriate and acceptable means of involving staff members—teachers, principals, and supervisors—in developing policy that directly affects them will lead to divisiveness, tension, and conflict that will impair the schools and adversely affect the education of children.

- We believe that there is no one best procedure for sharing responsibility for policy development. School board members, administrators, and classroom teachers must develop policies and practices appropriate to local conditions, rather than adopt those established elsewhere.

- We believe that if boards of education fail to make reasonable welfare provisions for all staff members and fail to provide machinery through which grievances can be given appropriate consideration, their respective state legislatures are likely to establish appeal procedures.

- We believe that there is an intrinsic value in local decision making which is worth preserving to the maximum extent consistent with the obligations of citizenship in the state and nation.

- We believe that in those exceedingly rare situations where the professional staff believes that the school board or some other legal fiscal control body has denied reasonable requests for conferences, for study, and for presentation of welfare proposals, or has demonstrated flagrant unwillingness to provide reasonable salary contracts or other welfare provisions, the professional staff has the right to present all the facts to the public and to their professional associates in other school districts. On the other hand, where the staff obstinately holds to an unreasonable position which disrupts or seriously impairs the operation of the schools, the school board has comparable rights and obligations.

- We believe that both the board and the professional staff—teachers, principals, and other administrators—should, at a time that is free from tension and controversy, develop together a plan to be used in case of persistent disagreement. In those few, highly unusual instances where major controversy threatens to disrupt the schools, an appeal to an unbiased body should be available to either the board or the teachers, or both. The function of this third party should be limited to fact finding and to advisory assistance. Its identity might vary from state to state, but it should always be an agency which has responsibility for some segment of public education in the state. Included among such organizations might be a state board of education, a state department of education, a state university, or a state public college. It should be made clear that such a study would be conducted without disruption of the schools. A report should be made to both the board of education and the staff. Alternatives to such an appeal procedure which have been tried include:

  strikes, demagogic appeals, threats, withheld services, and sanctions or threatened sanctions by teachers;

  withholding of contracts, blacklisting, failure of promotion, and other punitive action by school boards; and

  yielding to undue influence of vested interests on the part of both school boards and teachers.

- We believe that such arbitrary action by either staff or school board is not likely to lead to lasting and satisfying resolution of disagreements.

IN CONCLUSION

Responsibility for the orderly and fruitful conduct of public education is shared by the local district and the state. Therefore, a fair and reasonable plan of appeal, which is acceptable to school board and staff and is consistent with policies for the settlement of disagreements in other educational matters, should be worked out in each state and district.

The principle of local and delegated control has served America well. The board of education, as the agency designated by the district and state, is charged not only with the responsibility for serving the interests of the people of the school district and state, but also with the responsibility for the welfare of the teachers and other staff members whose lives are dedicated to education of children and youth. The superintendent shares that charge and that dedication.

Finally, we call attention again to the unique role of the superintendent of schools. He is in a strategic, if trying, position to help both boards of education and teachers, singly or in groups, as they work through their common problems. He is the professional advisor to whom the board looks for recommendations on policy, the chief administrator of the schools, the leader of the professional staff, and the protector and defender of the rights of children to the best and most appropriate educational opportunity. He is a professional educator and a professional school administrator. Anything which weakens his effectiveness in any of these roles will ultimately weaken the schools. And in the long run, what happens in and to the public schools of America happens to America.

# *Appendix I.* Executive Order 10988[1]

*Employee-Management Cooperation in the Federal Service*

WHEREAS participation of employees in the formulation and implementation of personnel policies affecting them contributes to effective conduct of public business; and

WHEREAS the efficient administration of the Government and the well-being of employees require that orderly and constructive relationships be maintained between employee organizations and management officials; and

WHEREAS subject to law and the paramount requirements of the public service, employee-management relations within the Federal service should be improved by providing employees an opportunity for greater participation in the formulation and implementation of policies and procedures affecting the conditions of their employment; and

WHEREAS effective employee-management cooperation in the public service requires a clear statement of the respective rights and obligations of employee organizations and agency management:

Now, THEREFORE, by virtue of the authority vested in me by the Constitution of the United States, by section 1753 of the Revised Statutes (5 U.S.C. 631), and as President of the United States, I hereby direct that the following policies shall govern officers and agencies of the executive branch of the Government in all dealings with Federal employees and organizations representing such employees.

*Section 1.* (a) Employees of the Federal Government shall have, and shall be protected in the exercise of, the right, freely and without fear of penalty or reprisal, to form, join and assist any employee organization or to refrain from any such activity. Except as hereinafter

[1] 27 Fed. Reg. 551 (1962).

expressly provided, the freedom of such employees to assist any employee organization shall be recognized as extending to participation in the management of the organization and acting for the organization in the capacity of an organization representative, including presentation of its views to officials of the executive branch, the Congress or other appropriate authority. The head of each executive department and agency (hereinafter referred to as "agency") shall take such action, consistent with law, as may be required in order to assure that employees in the agency are apprised of the rights described in this section, and that no interference, restraint, coercion or discrimination is practiced within such agency to encourage or discourage membership in any employee organization.

(b) The rights described in this section do not extend to participation in the management of an employee organization, or acting as a representative of any such organization, where such participation or activity would result in a conflict of interest or otherwise be incompatible with law or with the official duties of an employee.

*Section 2.* When used in this order, the term "employee organization" means any lawful association, labor organization, federation, council, or brotherhood having as a primary purpose the improvement of working conditions among Federal employees, or any craft, trade or industrial union whose membership includes both Federal employees and employees of private organizations; but such term shall not include any organization (1) which asserts the right to strike against the Government of the United States or any agency thereof, or to assist or participate in any such strike, or which imposes a duty or obligation to conduct, assist or participate in any such strike, or (2) which advocates the overthrow of the constitutional form of Government in the United States, or (3) which discriminates with regard to the terms or conditions of membership because of race, color, creed or national origin.

*Section 3.* (a) Agencies shall accord informal, formal or exclusive recognition to employee organizations which request such recognition in conformity with the requirements specified in sections 4, 5, and 6 of this order, except that no recognition shall be accorded to any employee organization which the head of the agency considers to be so subject to corrupt influences or influences opposed to basic democratic principles that recognition would be inconsistent with the objectives of this order.

(b) Recognition of an employee organization shall continue so long as such organization satisfies the criteria of this order applicable to such recognition; but nothing in this section shall require any agency to determine whether an organization should become or continue to be recognized as exclusive representative of the employees in any unit within 12 months after a prior determination of exclusive status with respect to such unit has been made pursuant to the provisions of this order.

(c) Recognition, in whatever form accorded, shall not—

(1) preclude any employee, regardless of employee organization membership, from bringing matters of personal concern to the attention of appropriate officials in accordance with applicable law, rule, regulation, or established agency policy, or from choosing his own representative in a grievance or appellate action; or

(2) preclude or restrict consultations and dealings between an agency and any veterans organization with respect to matters of particular interest to employees with veterans preference; or

(3) preclude an agency from consulting or dealing with any religious, social, fraternal or other lawful association, not qualified as an employee organization, with respect to matters or policies which involve individual members of the association or are of particular applicability to it or its members, when such consultations or dealings are duly limited so as not to assume the character of formal consultation on matters of general employee-management policy or to extend to areas where recognition of the interests of one employee group may result in discrimination against or injury to the interests of other employees.

*Section 4.* (a) An agency shall accord an employee organization, which does not qualify for exclusive or formal recognition, informal recognition as representative of its member employees without regard to whether any other employee organization has been accorded formal or exclusive recognition as representative of some or all employees in any unit.

(b) When an employee organization has been informally recognized, it shall, to the extent consistent with the efficient and orderly conduct of the public business, be permitted to present to appropriate officials its views on matters of concern to its members. The agency need not, however, consult with an employee organization so recognized in the formulation of personnel or other policies with respect to such matters.

*Section 5.* (a) An agency shall accord an employee organization formal recognition as the representative of its members in a unit as defined by the agency when (1) no other employee organization is qualified for exclusive recognition as representative of employees in the unit, (2) it is determined by the agency that the employee organization has a substantial and stable membership of no less than 10 per centum of the employees in the unit, and (3) the employee organization has submitted to the agency a roster of its officers and representatives, a copy of its constitution and bylaws, and a statement of objectives. When, in the opinion of the head of an agency, an employee organization has a sufficient number of local organizations or a sufficient total membership within such agency, such organization may be accorded formal recognition at the national level, but such recognition shall not preclude the agency from dealing at the national level with any other employee organization on matters affecting its members.

(b) When an employee organization has been formally recognized, the agency, through appropriate officials, shall consult with such organization from time to time in the formulation and implementation of personnel policies and practices, and matters affecting working conditions that are of concern to its members. Any such organization shall be entitled from time to time to raise such matters for discussion with appropriate officials and at all times to present its views thereon in writing. In no case, however, shall an agency be required to consult with an employee organization which has been formally recognized with respect to any matter which, if the employee organization were one entitled to exclusive recognition, would not be included within the obligation to meet and confer, as described in section 6(b) of this order.

*Section 6.* (a) An agency shall recognize an employee organization as the exclusive representative of the employees, in an appropriate unit when such organization is eligible for formal recognition pursuant to section 5 of this order, and has been designated or selected by a majority of the employees of such unit as the representative of such employees in such unit. Units may be established on any plant or installation, craft, functional or other basis which will ensure a clear and identifiable community of interest among the employees concerned, but no unit shall be established solely on the basis of the extent to which employees in the proposed unit have organized. Except where otherwise required by established practice, prior agreement, or special circumstances, no unit shall be established for purposes of exclusive recognition which includes (1) any managerial executive, (2) any employee engaged in Federal personnel work in other than a purely clerical capacity, (3) both supervisors who officially evaluate the performance of employees and the employees and nonprofessional employees unless a majority of such professional employees vote for inclusion in such unit.

(b) When an employee organization has been recognized as the exclusive representative of employees of an appropiate unit it shall be entitled to act for and to negotiate agreements covering all employees in the unit and shall be responsible for representing the interests of all such employees without discrimination and without regard to employee organization membership. Such employee organization shall be given the opportunity to be represented at discussions between management and employees or employee representatives concerning grievances, personnel policies and practices, or other matters affecting general working conditions of employees in the unit. The agency and such employee organization, through appropriate officials and representatives, shall meet at reasonable times and confer with respect to personnel policy and practices and matters affecting working conditions, so far as may be appropriate subject to law and policy requirements. This extends to the negotiation of an agreement, or any question arising thereunder, the determination of appropriate techniques, consistent with the terms and purposes of this order, to assist in such negotiation, and the execution of a written memorandum of agreement or understanding incorporating any agreement reached by the parties. In exercising authority to make rules and regulations relating to personnel policies and practices and working conditions, agencies shall have due regard for the obligation imposed by this section, but such obligation shall not be construed to extend to such areas of discretion and policy as the mission of an agency, its budget, its organization and the assignment of its personnel, or the technology of performing its work.

*Section 7.* Any basic or initial agreement entered into with an employee organization as the exclusive representative of employees in a unit must be approved by the head of the agency or an official designated by him. All agreements with such employee organizations shall also be subject to the following requirements, which shall be expressly stated in the initial or basic agreement and shall be applicable to all supplemental, implementing, subsidiary or informal agreements between the agency and the organization;

(1) In the administration of all matters covered by the agreement officials and employees are governed by the provisions of any existing or future laws and regulations, including policies set forth in the Federal Personnel Manual and agency regulations, which may be applicable, and the agreement shall at all times be applied subject to such laws, regulations and policies;

(2) Management officials of the agency retain the right, in accordance with applicable laws and regulations, (a) to direct employees of the agency, (b) to hire, promote, transfer, assign, and retain employees in positions within the agency, and to suspend, demote, discharge, or take other disciplinary action against employees, (c) to relieve employees from duties because of lack of work or for other legitimate reasons, (d) to maintain the efficiency of the Government operations

entrusted to them, (e) to determine the methods, means and personnel by which such operations are to be conducted; and (f) to take whatever actions may be necessary to carry out the mission of the agency in situations of emergency.

*Section 8.* (a) Agreements entered into or negotiated in accordance with this order with an employee organization which is the exclusive representative of employees in an appropriate unit may contain provisions, applicable only to employees in the unit, concerning procedures for consideration of grievances. Such procedures (1) shall conform to standards issued by the Civil Service Commission, and (2) may not in any manner diminish or impair any rights which would otherwise be available to any employee in the absence of an agreement providing for such procedures.

(b) Procedures established by an agreement which are otherwise in conformity with this section may include provisions for the arbitration of grievances. Such arbitration (1) shall be advisory in nature with any decisions or recommendations subject to the approval of the agency head; (2) shall extend only to the interpretation or application of agreements or agency policy and not to changes in or proposed changes in agreements or agency policy; and (3) shall be invoked only with the approval of the individual employee or employees concerned.

*Section 9.* Solicitation of memberships, dues, or other internal employee organization business shall be conducted during the nonduty hours of the employees concerned. Officially requested or approved consultations and meetings between management officials and representatives of recognized employee organizations shall, whenever practicable, be conducted on official time, but any agency may require that negotiations with an employee organization which has been accorded exclusive recognition be conducted during the nonduty hours of the employee organization representatives involved in such negotiations.

*Section 10.* No later than July 1, 1962, the head of each agency shall issue appropriate policies, rules and regulations for the implementation of this order, including: A clear statement of the rights of its employees under the order; policies and procedures with respect to recognition of employee organizations; procedures for determining appropriate employee units; policies and practices regarding consultation with representatives of employee organizations, other organizations and individual employees; and policies with respect to the use of agency facilities by employee organizations. Insofar as may be practicable and appropriate, agencies shall consult with representatives of employee organizations in the formulation of these policies, rules and regulations.

*Section 11.* Each agency shall be responsible for determining in accordance with this order whether a unit is appropriate for purposes of exclusive recognition and, by an election or other appropriate means, whether an employee organization represents a majority of the employees in such a unit so as to be entitled to such recognition. Upon the request of any agency, or of any employee organization which is seeking exclusive recognition and which qualifies for or has been accorded formal recognition, the Secretary of Labor, subject to such necessary rules as he may prescribe, shall nominate from the National Panel of Arbitrators maintained by the Federal Mediation and Conciliation Service one or more qualified arbitrators who will be available for employment by the agency concerned for either or both of the following purposes, as may be required: (1) to investigate the facts and issue an advisory decision as to the appropriateness of a unit for purposes of exclusive recognition and as to related issues submitted for consideration; (2) to conduct or supervise an election or otherwise determine by such means as may be appropriate, and on an advisory basis, whether an employee organization represents the majority of the employees in a unit. Consonant with law, the Secretary of Labor shall render such assistance as may be appropriate in connection with advisory decisions or determinations under this section, but the necessary costs of such assistance shall be paid by the agency to which it relates. In the event questions as to the appropriateness of a unit or the majority status of an employee organization shall arise in the Department of Labor, the duties described in this section which would otherwise be the responsibility of the Secretary of Labor shall be performed by the Civil Service Commission.

*Section 12.* The Civil Service Commission shall establish and maintain a program to assist in carrying out the objectives of this order. The Commission shall develop a program for the guidance of agencies in employee-management relations in the Federal service; provide technical advice to the agencies on employee-management programs; assist in the development of programs for training agency personnel in the principles and procedures of consultation, negotiation and the settlement of disputes in the Federal service, and for the training of management officials in the discharge of their employee-management relations responsibilities in the public interest; provide for continuous study and review of the Federal employee-management relations program and, from time to time, make recommendations to the President for its improvement.

*Section 13.* (a) The Civil Service Commission and the Department of Labor shall jointly prepare (1) proposed standards of conduct for employee organizations and (2) a proposed code of fair labor practices in employee-management relations in the Federal service appropriate to assist in securing the uniform and effective implementation of the policies, rights and responsibilities described in this order.

(b) There is hereby established the President's Temporary Committee on the Implementation of the Federal Employee-Management Relations Program. The Committee shall consist of the Secretary of Labor, who shall be chairman of the Committee, the Secretary of Defense, the Postmaster General, and the Chairman of the Civil Service Commission. In addition to such other matters relating to the implementation of this order as may be referred to it by the President, the Committee shall advise the President with respect to any problems arising out of completion of agreements pursuant to section 6 and 7, and shall receive the proposed standards of conduct for employee organizations and proposed code of fair labor practices in the Federal service, as described in this section, and report thereon to the President with such recommendations or amendments as it may deem appropriate. Consonant with law, the departments and agencies represented on the Committee shall, as may be necessary for the effectuation of this section, furnish assistance to the Committee in accordance with section 214 of the Act of May 3, 1945, 59 Stat. 134 (31 U.S.C. 691). Unless otherwise directed by the President, the Committee shall cease to exist 30 days after the date on which it submits its report to the President pursuant to this section.

*Section 14.* The head of each agency, in accordance with the provisions of this order and regulations prescribed by the Civil Service Commission, shall extend to all employees in the competitive civil service rights identical in adverse action cases to those provided preference eligibles under section 14 of the Veterans' Preference Act of 1944, as amended. Each employee in the competitive service shall have the right to appeal to the Civil Service Commission from an adverse decision of the administrative officer so acting, such appeal to be processed in an identical manner to that provided for appeals under section 14 of the Veterans' Preference Act. Any recommendation by the Civil Service Commission submitted to the head of an agency on the basis of an appeal by an employee in the competitive service shall be complied with by the head of the agency. This section shall become effective as to all adverse actions commenced by issuance of a notification of proposed action on or after July 1, 1962.

*Section 15.* Nothing in this order shall be construed to annul or modify, or to preclude the renewal or continuation of, any lawful agreement heretofore entered into between any agency and any representative of its employees. Nor shall this order preclude any agency from continuing to consult or deal with any representative of its employees or other organization prior to the time that the status and representation rights of such representative or organization are determined in conformity with this order.

*Section 16.* This order (except section 14) shall not apply to the Federal Bureau of Investigation, the Central Intelligence Agency, or any other agency, or to any office, bureau or entity within an agency, primarily performing intelligence, investigative, or security functions if the head of the agency determines that the provisions of this order cannot be applied in a manner consistent with national security requirements and considerations. When he deems it necessary in the national interest, and subject to such conditions as he may prescribe, the head of any agency may suspend any provision of this order (except section 14) with respect to any agency installation or activity which is located outside of the United States.

Approved—January 17th, 1962
*John F. Kennedy*

# Bibliography

## Books

American Bar Association, Section of Labor Relations Law. "Report of the Committee on Law of Labor Relations of Governmental Employees." *Proceedings*. Chicago: The Association, 1964. Pp. 355–83.

———, "Report of the Committee on Law of Labor Relations of Governmental Employees." *Proceedings*. Chicago: The Association, 1963. Pp. 126–62.

American Federation of Teachers, Commission on Educational Reconstruction. *Organizing the Teaching Profession*. New York: The Free Press of Glencoe, 1955. 320 pp.

Carr, William G. "The Breakthrough." *Addresses and Proceedings, 1965*. Washington, D.C.: National Education Association, 1965. Pp. 19–29.

———. "The Turning Point." *Addresses and Proceedings, 1962*. Washington, D.C.: National Education Association, 1962. Pp. 18–28.

———. "The Year of Decision." *Addresses and Proceedings, 1964*. Washington, D.C.: National Education Association, 1964. Pp. 16–29.

Chamberlain, Neil W. *Collective Bargaining*. New York: McGraw-Hill Book Co., 1951. 534 pp.

Garber, Lee O., and Newton Edwards. *The Law Governing School Board Members and School Board Meetings*. Danville, Ill.: Interstate Printers and Publishers, 1963. 96 pp.

Hamilton, Robert R., and E. Edmund Reutter, Jr. *Legal Aspects of School Board Operations*. New York: Columbia University Press, 1958. 199 pp.

Hart, Wilson R. *Collective Bargaining in the Federal Civil Service.* New York: Harper and Brothers, 1961. 302 pp.

Lieberman, Myron. *Education as a Profession.* Englewood Cliffs, N.J.: Prentice Hall, 1956. 540 pp.

————. *The Future of Public Education.* Chicago: University of Chicago Press, 1960. 294 pp.

National School Boards Association. *School Boards Shape a Free Nation's Future.* Proceedings of the 1964 Convention. Evanston, Ill.: The Association, 1964. 435 pp.

Nolte, M. Chester, and John Phillip Linn. *School Law for Teachers.* Danville, Ill.: Interstate Printers and Publishers, 1963. 643 pp.

Reeves, Charles E. *School Boards.* Englewood Cliffs, N.J.: Prentice Hall, 1954. 368 pp.

Remmlein, Madaline K. *School Law.* Second· edition. Danville, Ill.: Interstate Printers and Publishers, 1962. 346 pp.

Reutter, E. Edmund, Jr. *Schools and the Law,* 2nd rev. ed. New York: Oceana Publications, 1964. 112 pp.

Rhyne, Charles S. *Municipal Law.* Washington, D.C.: National Institute of Municipal Law Officers, 1957. 1,125 pp.

Shister, Joseph, Benjamin Aaron, and Clyde W. Summers. *Public Policy and Collective Bargaining.* New York: Harper & Row, 1962. 248 pp.

Taft, Philip. *Organized Labor in American History.* New York: Harper & Row, 1964. 818 pp.

Warner, Kenneth O. (ed.). *Management Relations with Organized Public Employees.* Chicago: Public Personnel Association, 1963. 239 pp.

Wilson, Wesley M. *Labor Law Handbook.* Indianapolis: Bobbs-Merrill Co., 1963. 518 pp.

Winters, Glenn R. *Bar Association Organization and Activities.* Ann Arbor, Mich.: American Judicature Society, 1954. 243 pp.

## Pamphlets

American Association of School Administrators. *Roles, Responsibilities, Relationships of the School Board, Superintendent, and Staff.* Washington, D.C.: The Association, a department of the National Education Association, 1963. 15 pp.

Bowman, Thomas R. "Participation of Superintendents in School Board Decision-Making." *Administrator's Notebook,* Vol. 11, No.

5. Chicago: Midwest Administration Center, University of Chicago, January 1963. 4 pp.

Kratzmann, Arthur. "The Alberta Teachers' Association: A Prototype for the American Scene?" *Administrator's Notebook*, Vol. 12, No. 2. Chicago: Midwest Administration Center, University of Chicago, October 1963. 4 pp.

McNamara, E. J. *The Superintendent's Role in Professional Negotiation*. Bulletin 1964–65:13. Seattle, Wash.: School Information and Research Service, May 19, 1965 (mimeographed).

National Association of Secondary School Principals. *The Principal's Role in Collective Negotiations Between Teachers and School Boards*. Washington, D.C.: The Association, a department of the National Education Association, 1965. 12 pp.

National Education Association, Commission on Professional Rights and Responsibilities. *Guidelines for Professional Sanctions*. Washington, D.C.: The Commission, 1963. 13 pp.

————, ————. *Implementing the Code of Ethics of the Education Profession and Strengthening Professional Rights*. Washington, D.C.: The Commission, June 1964. 61 pp.

————, Department of Classroom Teachers. *Classroom Teachers Speak on Professional Negotiations*. Washington, D.C.: The Department, 1963. 16 pp.

————, Office of Professional Development and Welfare. *Guidelines for Professional Negotiation*. Washington, D.C.: The Association, 1963. 45 pp.

————. *Guidelines for Professional Negotiation*, Rev. ed. Washington, D.C.: The Association, 1965. 54 pp.

————. *Professional Negotiation: Selected Statements of School Board, Administrator, Teacher Relationships*. Rev. ed. Washington, D.C.: The Association, 1965. 63 pp.

————, Research Division. *Professional Negotiation with School Boards: A Legal Analysis*. Research Report 1965-R3. Washington, D.C.: The Association, March 1965. 41 pp.

————. *Public School Teachers and Collective Bargaining*. Special Memo. Washington, D.C.: The Association, March 1958. 20 pp.

———— and American Association of School Administrators, Educational Policies Commission. *The Public Interest in How Teachers Organize*. Washington, D.C.: The Commission, 1964. 6 pp.

————. *The Structure and Administration of Education in American Democracy.* Washington, D.C.: The Commission, 1938. 128 pp.

————. *The Unique Role of the Superintendent of Schools.* Washington, D.C.: The Commission, 1965. 25 pp.

President's Task Force on Employee-Management Relations in the Federal Service. *A Policy for Employee-Management Cooperation in the Federal Service.* Washington, D.C.: The Task Force, November 30, 1961. 54 pp.

Shelton, Donald K. *Qualifications of Present and Future Oregon School Administrators for Dealing with Organized Employee Groups.* Bulletin of the Oregon School Study Council, Vol. 8, No. 10. Eugene: School of Education, University of Oregon, April 1965. 26 pp.

Steffensen, James P. *Teachers Negotiate with Their School Boards.* U.S. Department of Health, Education, and Welfare, Office of Education, Bulletin 1964, No. 40. Washingtton, D.C.: Government Printing Office, 1964. 84 pp.

White, Alpheus L. *Local School Boards: Organization and Practices.* U.S. Department of Health, Education, and Welfare, Office of Education, Bulletin 1962, No. 8. Washington, D.C.: Government Printing Office, 1962. 103 pp.

Wildman, Wesley A. "Collective Action by Public School Teachers." *Administrator's Notebook,* Vol. 11, No. 6. Chicago: Midwest Administration Center, University of Chicago, February 1963. 4 pp.

————. *Collective Action by Public School Teachers.* Reprint Series No. 119. Chicago: Industrial Relations Center, University of Chicago, October 1964. 19 pp.

### Periodicals

Aalzaard, R. "Ten Commandments for Negotiation." *School Activities,* 35:174; February 1964.

Anderson, Arvid. "Labor Relations in the Public Service." *Wisconsin Law Review,* 22:601; 1961.

Barstow, Robbins. "The Right To Negotiate." *Connecticut Teacher,* 32:16–17; March 1965.

————. "Teachers and Boards of Education Need to Work Jointly to Determine Policies of Common Concern." *NEA Journal,* 50:61–64; October 1961.

Becker, Harry A. "The Role of School Administrators in Professional

Negotiations." *American School Board Journal,* 50:9–10; May 1965.

Betchkal, James. "NEA and Teachers Unions Bicker and Battle for Recognition." *Nation's Schools,* 74:35–41; August 1964.

Blanke, Virgil E. "Teachers in Search of Power." *The American School Board Journal,* 151:7–9; November 1965.

Bloom, Arnold M. "More Militant Profession." *American School and University,* 37:17; October 1964.

Brooks, George. "A Case for Teachers' Unions." *Monthly Labor Review,* 87:292; March 1964.

Bruce, W. C. "Teachers versus School Boards." *American School Board Journal,* 149:29; November 1964.

Caliguri, J. "Teacher Bargaining, Ready or Not?" *California Journal of Educational Research,* 16:46–48; January 1965.

Campbell, Dave. "School Boards versus Teacher Organizations—Let's Start by Being Honest with Ourselves!" *American School Board Journal,* 149:65–66; October 1964.

Carr, William G. "Assault on Professional Independence." *Phi Delta Kappan,* 46:17–19; September 1964.

Cherry, H. L. "Negotiations Between Boards and Teacher Organizations." *American School Board Journal,* 146:7–9; March 1963.

Colorado School Journal. "Professional Negotiation." *Colorado School Journal,* 80:14–15; April 1965.

Cron, Theodore O. "Inside the Teachers Union." *American School and University,* 36:42–49; November 1963.

Denemark, George W. "Schools Are Not Factories." *NEA Journal,* 53:25–27; March 1964.

Doyle, Roy P. "Negotiations and Sanctions in Public Education." *Arizona Teacher,* 52:12–14; September 1963.

Elam, Stanley. "Collective Bargaining and Strikes or Professional Negotiation and Sanctions?" *Phi Delta Kappan,* 44:1–11; October 1962.

———. "Who's Ahead and Why: The NEA-AFT Rivalry." *Phi Delta Kappan,* 46:12–16; September 1964.

Epstein, Benjamin. "What Status and Voice for Principals and Administrators in Collective Bargaining and Professional Negotiation by Teacher Organizations?" *Bulletin of the National Association of Secondary-School Principals,* 49:226–259; March 1965.

Exton, Elaine. "NEA Blueprint for Professional Negotiation." *American School Board Journal,* 147:35–37; September 1963.

————. "NSBA at the Crossroads." *American School Board Journal,* 147:31–33; December 1963.

————. "NSBA Opposes Teachers' Strikes and Sanctions." *American School Board Journal,* 146:41–46; June 1963.

————. "Pros and Cons of Sanctions Invoked by Utah's Public School Teachers." *American School Board Journal,* 147:35–37, 41; July 1963.

————. "Teachers' Groups Challenge Lay School Board Control." *American School Board Journal,* 147:28–29, 32; August 1963.

Gillie, Paul. "Professional Negotiations—The Other Side." *Washington Education,* 76:12; April 1965.

Gross, Calvin. "Ways to Deal with the New Teacher Militancy." *Phi Delta Kappan,* 46:147–152; December 1964.

Guba, Egen G., and Shirley L. Borcover (eds.). "Negotiations in Education." *Theory into Practice,* 4:49–80; April 1965. (Bureau of Educational Research and Service, College of Education, Ohio State University.)

Hardbeck, George W. "Unionism at the Crossroads." *Labor Law Journal,* 16:100; 1965.

Harvard Law Review. "Labor Relations in the Public Service." *Harvard Law Review,* 75:391; 1961.

Hipp, Frederick L. "Advancing the Welfare of Members: Urban Associations." *NEA Journal,* 53:19–20; January 1964.

Jones, Arthur. "Professional Negotiations: A Proper Procedure, A Potential Boon." *Washington Education,* 76:10; January 1965.

Jordan, K. F. "Who Shall Be the Effective Voice for American Teachers?" *American School Board Journal,* 147:38; July 1963.

Lieberman, Myron. "Power and Policy in Education." *Power and Professionalism in Teaching.* Bulletin of the School of Education, Vol. 40, No. 5, pp. 21–29. Bloomington: Indiana University, September 1964.

————. "Teachers' Strikes: Acceptable Strategy?" *Phi Delta Kappan,* 46:237–241; January 1965.

————. "Teachers' Strikes: An Analysis of the Issues." *Harvard Educational Review,* 26:39–70; Winter 1956.

McCann, Lloyd E. "The Right to Talk or the Right to Be Heard." *American School Board Journal,* 147:11–12; June 1963.

Michigan Education Association. "Basis of Professional Negotiation." *Michigan Education Journal,* 41:6–7; November 1963.

————. "Procedure for Negotiation." *Michigan Education Journal,* 41:9–10; November 1963.

————. "Professional Negotiation Guide to Help Local MEA Units Develop Professional Negotiations." *Michigan Education Journal,* 42:17–19; May 1965.

————. "Tenure Professional Negotiation." *Michigan Education Journal,* 41:5; November 1963.

————. "Why of Professional Negotiation." *Michigan Education Journal,* 41:35–36; October 1963.

Moskow, Michael H. "Collective Bargaining for Public School Teachers." *Labor Law Journal,* 15:787; 1964.

————. "Recent Legislation Affecting Collective Negotiations for Teachers." *Phi Delta Kappan,* 47:136–141; November 1965.

————. "Teacher Organization: An Analysis of the Issues." *Teachers College Record,* 66:453–463; February 1965.

Nation's Schools. "Collective Bargaining for Teachers?" *Nation's Schools,* 68:41–42; July 1961.

————. "Role of New York Teachers in Forming School Policy Starts Controversy." *Nation's Schools,* 72:80; November 1963.

Newton, R., and B. J. Lee. "Denver Achieves Professional Negotiations." *NEA Journal,* 52:14–16; February 1963.

Phi Delta Kappan. "A Series on Teacher Organizations," *Phi Delta Kappan,* 45:270–296; March 1964.

Phillips, Isaac E. "Professional Negotiations in Jefferson County." *Colorado School Journal,* 78:13–14; December 1963.

Radke, Mrs. Fred A. "Real Significance of Collective Bargaining for Teachers." *Labor Law Journal,* 15:795; 1964.

Rice, Arthur. "Why Teachers Do Not Accept Superintendent as Spokesman." *Nation's Schools,* 75:36; April 1965.

Rutgers Law Review. "State Antistrike Legislation and Seizure Provisions." *Rutgers Law Review,* 18:647; Winter 1964.

Scanlon, John. "Strikes, Sanctions, and the Schools." *Saturday Review,* 46:51–55, 70–74; October 19, 1963.

Schaub, D. W. "Focus on Professional Negotiations." *Ohio Schools,* 41:12–13; March 1963.

School Management. "The American Federation of Teachers." *School Management,* 8:56–62, 102; February 1964.

————. "Negotiating with Teachers." *School Management,* 9:81–87; May 1965.

Smith, F. M. "Teachers Union vs. the Professional Association." *School and Society,* 90:439–440; December 15, 1962.

Stinnett, T. M. "A New Era, A New Breed." *Kansas Teacher,* 73:23; April 1965.

———. "Professional Negotiation, Collective Bargaining, Sanctions, and Strikes." *Bulletin of the National Association of Secondary-School Principals,* 48:93–105; April 1964.

———. "Professional Negotiations: Representation for Administrators and Supervisors." *School Administrator,* 22:2; May 1965.

———. "Improving School Board-Superintendent-Teacher Relationships." *Bulletin of Education,* Vol. 20 (Fall Issue), November 1965. Lawrence, Kansas: The University of Kansas. Pp. 5–11.

Stutz, Robert L. "Collective Bargaining by City Employees." *Labor Law Journal,* 15:696; 1964.

Ware, Martha L. "Professional Negotiation." *NEA Journal,* 51:28–30; November 1962.

———. "Professional Negotiation." *New Mexico School Review,* 43:24–25; December 1963.

Washington Education. "The Whys, Whats, and Hows of Professional Negotiation" (symposium). *Washington Education,* 75:11–17, 20–22; January 1964.

West, Allan M. "Local Associations Move Toward Professional Negotiation." *NEA Journal,* 53:18–20; February 1964.

———. "Professional Negotiations or Collective Bargaining?" *National Elementary Principal,* 42:20–25; February 1963.

Wildman, Wesley A. "Implications of Teacher Bargaining for School Administration." *Phi Delta Kappan,* 46:152–158; December 1964.

———. "Group Conflict and School Organization." *Phi Delta Kappan,* 47:244–251; January 1966.

Wollett, Donald H. "The Public Employee at the Bargaining Table: Promise or Illusion." *Labor Law Journal,* 15:8; 1964.

Wortman, Max S., Jr. "Collective Bargaining Strategies and Tactics in the Federal Civil Service." *Labor Law Journal,* 15:482; 1964.

Wyatt, Robert H. "Professional Negotiations Require Fair Dealings from All Concerned." *Indiana Teacher,* 109:273; May–June, 1965.

# Index